Act One Wales

seren drama

Act One Wales

Thirteen One Act Plays

EDITED BY PHIL CLARK
Series Editor Brian Mitchell

seren

seren
is the book imprint of
Poetry Wales Press Ltd
First Floor, 2 Wyndham Street
Bridgend, Wales

© The Authors as Acknowledged
Selection & Introduction © Phil Clark, 1997
Preface © Sian Phillips, 1997

Cataloguing In Publication Data for this title
is available from the British Library

ISBN 1-85411-152-3

The publisher works with the financial support of the
Arts Council of Wales

Cover: Andy Dark

Printed by Creative Print & Design Wales, Ebbw Vale

Contents

Preface

As we reach the Millennium it is exciting to reflect on the recent work of Welsh Playwrights. The last fifty years have been an important time for English language playwrights in Wales. We Welsh are world famous for our love of language, stretching right back to the ancient traditions of *cynghanedd* and although our poets thrive, our playwrights, working in English, are rarely celebrated.

English language theatre in Wales is still a new and young industry, but it is important that the writers' recent achievements are recorded.

Many of the actors of Wales will have begun their careers performing in one act plays at an amateur level. This practice still remains a thriving activity throughout Wales. The emergence of the half hour TV play and the skill of the radio dramatist have played an important role in the development of our one act plays.

This snap-shot view of the one act play in Wales is an important and exciting record of a young and flourishing culture that needs to be celebrated internationally. *Act One Wales* ensures that the work is recorded and made accessible across the globe, and as the industries expand and the writers of tomorrow are encouraged, I'm sure that *Act Two Wales* will be on our bookshelves sooner than we expected.

Siân Phillips

Introduction

Writing for the theatre in English is still in its infancy in Wales. In the last fifty years we have seen a substantial change from plays written only for amateur use to a growing professional theatre movement. One key to this change has been the emergence of radio and television and their regular commissioning of new drama. Another important element in the growth of new writing has been the young people's theatre and community theatre movements. Stemming from a thriving amateur tradition in Wales whereby one-act plays were written for young farmers' clubs, womens' institutes and youth clubs, they have helped to foster new talent and establish a base upon which the professional movement can develop. Also notable in recent years is the rise of innovative small theatre companies in Wales such as Moving Being, Theatr Y Byd, Y Cwmni, Made in Wales and others.

In the last five years HTV has collaborated with the Sherman Theatre Company to commission new half-hour dramas that have been staged and filmed. Also involved have been the Drama Association of Wales who, with the financial assistance of the Arts Council of Wales and HTV, have published the twenty new commissions. As a result of the partnership, the new plays have. been performed to packed houses, helped the theatre profession to identify new audiences, had strong viewing figures for the televised production and been distributed world-wide in print. It is encouraging to note that many of these new plays have had second and third publications internationally. Some have been translated into Welsh and performed at the National Eisteddfod of Wales. Alongside these developments, the Seren Drama series, devoted to publishing the best plays in English from Wales, helps to promote and ensure the status of drama from Wales.

INTRODUCTION

As the short story is to the novel, so the one act play is to the full play. The craft of the single act play is distinctly different and arguably more challenging than any other piece of dramatic writing. The play must entice, entertain and satisfy an audience, all within thirty minutes. A common technique is to place an inciting incident before the action begins, the play is then concerned with taking the audience on a journey of explanation, or through the consequence of an incident they did not witness. A number of different uses of the inciting incident are to be found in the plays that follow.

Another crucial technique for the brief play is a sharp focus on character. The one act play often features just two characters who question and confront each another. When they are family members, an automatic intimacy and intensity is implied; when they are strangers, the drama can consist of each character discovering the other, their initial revelations and confrontations. Or the plot can centre on a single character who becomes the protagonist within the play. The audience will then see the world through this character's eyes, enabling the writer to set events in context.

Complementing the author's choice of character is the physical space in which the action takes place. Often, this is a single, carefully chosen setting. It is interesting to note the peculiar hold the landscape of Wales has upon the psyches of its playwrights. While Dylan Thomas presents a nostalgic map of a vànished Swansea in *Return Journey*, Tim Rhys offers us a deranged heritage park in *The Old Petrol Station*. The imposing edifice of culture is literally implied by Lisa Hunt with her use of the National Museum as the setting for *A Night Under Canvas*.

Time also plays an important role in the one act play. Because of the length of the piece writers usually work in continuous time, drawing their audience into a single web of intrigue. There is only so much a writer can do in half and hour and only so much an audience can absorb. It is important that the audience experience a range of emotions that are accessible and rooted in the dilemma of the drama. Occasionally, such as in Charles Way's *Looking Out to See*, the episodic nature of a piece allows events to take place over the course of a day.

The type and texture of the language used is also relevant.

Accent and slang are indicators of social milieu and many of the playwrights here are quick to stress that their characters are "average" or working class though the studied realism of Duncan Bush and Helen Griffin contrasts with the lush rhetoric of Dylan Thomas and Ian Rowlands. Edward Thomas and Alan Osborne adopt a harsh colloquialism and add deliberately surreal touches.

The choice of plays for this volume is personal and I know there are more plays out there that demand publication. Those selected are placed in a rough chronological order from 1950 to date, starting with Dylan Thomas' *Return Journey*.

There has always been controversy about Thomas' plays for voices when it comes to staging them, but with imagination and invention *Return Journey* and his full-length play, *Under Milk Wood*, can work as stage plays. The main theme in *Return Journey* of "the exile's return" resonates throughout the recent history of Welsh writing. *Return Journey* is a fine example of poetic language intertwined in a contemporary modern setting of domesticity that celebrates the richness of language.

T. C. Thomas' *The Sound of Stillness* was written in 1959. The story is based upon real events on the Epynt Mountains in mid Wales when the army occupied the range for manoeuvres. The play is essentially about who owns the land and who has the rights to the land. It raises important and passionate issues concerning displacement and the plight of rural communities at a time of war. Thomas gives his characters beautiful poetic language which contrasts with the brutal act of eviction that is the main action of the play. The same situation still exists on the Epynt Mountains some forty years later.

In contrast, Gwyn Thomas transports us into the close-knit mining communities of the Rhondda valleys in *Gazooka*. Set in the summer of the General Strike of 1926, it follows the colourful adventures of a group of enthusiasts trying to find suitable costumes for the local gazooka band. Often extremely funny, and at times bizarre, the play reflects a passionate and vocal community tradition that still survives in the post-industrial valleys of south Wales.

Dannie Abse, one of Wales' most distinguished poets, is also the author of a number of plays. Written in the late 50s and roughly contemporary with the rise of "kitchen sink" dramas such as

Osborne's *Look Back in Anger*, the protagonist of *The Eccentric* is the non-conforming tobacco shop owner Goldstein who resists the sale of his shop to corporate interests. Goldstein's sly individualism alternately piques, amuses and inspires the young man who arrives looking for a job.

Sailing to America, also in an urban setting, is by another prominent poet, Duncan Bush. Two women in the terminal ward of a hospital discuss their situation, reminisce about the past and speculate upon the future. The revealed details of their lives reflect the social changes and economic fluctuations of the post-war decades.

The rapid changes of the late 1970s: the erosion of communities caused by the closure of the coal mines in many valleys of the old industrial heartlands of Wales, and the rise of a centralised London Conservatism as the ruling politic heavily influenced a new generation of playwrights in Wales. Characterised by stylistic innovation and often peopled by angry young men caught in a vicious circle of unemployment, drug abuse and family disintegration, these disturbing and powerful plays reflect the rage of a new underclass.

Alan Osborne's *Redemption Song* is the archetypal play from this period. Two young "entrepreneurs" beset by hoods and stymied by their own reliance on drugs fail to organise a business deal. Osborne's innovative techniques, his freedom with language and structure, inspire succeeding writers of the 80s and 90s who recognise the limitations of conventional methods for conveying the outrage and frustration of their characters.

Sexual politics dominates Frank Vickery's play *The Drag Factor*. Loyalty and "family values" are tested to the limit when a happily married middle-age couple discover their son is not only gay, but the very visible star attraction of a touring drag act. One of Wales' most popular playwrights, Vickery's many plays often present themes of subversion and delight in exposing the darker secrets of their protagonists.

Looking Out to See is one of the several plays that the established playwright Charles Way has written for young people. A school trip to a beautiful island off the coast of Wales provides the setting where these students are forced to make decisions and come to terms with with their futures. Way has captured the volatile nature of adolescence, the optimism and uncertainty of these young people, in a way that never condescends to his youthful audience.

Edward Thomas is foremost among the younger writers who began to make their names in the 1980's. In his most famous work, *House of America*, now a major feature film, a family unravels against a backdrop of the son's fantasy for a better life based on Jack Kerouac's Beat bible *On the Road*. In *Hiraeth*, two heads without bodies, trapped in a weird limbo, discuss their "hopeless" or "un-bastard-bearable" situation. Characters in Thomas's work are often caught in time and seem unable to move on. Their wit and resilience helps them survive and hope.

The re-invention of self and country necessary in post-industrial Wales often involves the humorous pillorying of cultural clichés. Tim Rhys in his alternately hilarious and frightening *The Old Petrol Station*, written in 1994, takes this tendency to its extreme. He shoots us into the future where the Welsh nation only exists as a heritage theme park. No re-invention of the self here, just the perpetual image of what we were. This play coincides with the spectacle of redundant miners drafted in to play "pretend" miners in theme parks in the 1990s.

Swansea born actress and playwright Helen Griffin is one of the few women playwrights in Wales in the 1990s. *The Ark* is a beautifully constructed drama where a mother and two adult daughters grieve for the loss of the husband/father. She reveals how a major crisis can be the catalyst for raising all sorts of previously unexplored needs and concerns.

The women characters in Lisa Hunt's *A Night Under Canvas* also defy stereotype. Working class neighbours Brenda and Valmai struggle with personal concerns (and an unwieldy modern sculpture) after having been accidentally locked in the National Museum of Wales Art Gallery overnight. Notably less angry than their male counterparts, the women characters in these two plays find more solace and enlightenment in friendship and family.

In the final play, Ian Rowland's powerful *Ogpu Men*, the two protagonists await their appointments in a DHSS office. The elder man is racked with colourful bitterness about his predicament while the younger man is hopeful, though far from optimistic. Influenced by the artful rhetoric of Dylan Thomas, Rowland's fascination for the sound of words and the rhythm of language is apparent throughout this piece.

The playwrights of the last fifty years in Wales have been unusually reactive and reflective of the tenor of their times. Their achievements can take a place alongside the noted novelists and poets of the period in Wales. This book is as much a history book as it is a recording of achievement in literature. The writers are the inventors and engineers to steer our imaginations and perceptions using dramatic form, to observe and comment upon the Wales we have inherited.

Phil Clark

DYLAN THOMAS
Return Journey

Dylan Thomas (1914-1953) was born in Swansea. Though best known for his poetry, Thomas was also a fine playwright, short-story writer and broadcaster. Written in the early 1950s, *Return Journey*, like the more famous *Under Milk Wood*, is a play for voices. The narrator returns to his home town of Swansea and revisits scenes from his lively youth. *Return Journey*, though written for voices, can be staged with invention. It is interesting to note how Thomas' unique style influenced so many writers in Wales during the next forty years.

CHARACTERS
Narrator
Barmaid
Customers
Five Voices
Two Reporters
Girls
Park-Keeper
Schoolmaster
Promenade Man

NARRATOR: It was a cold white day in High Street, and nothing to stop the wind slicing up from the docks, for where the squat and tall ships had shielded the town from the sea lay their blitzed flat graves marbled with snow and headstoned with fences. Dogs, delicate as cats on water, as though they had gloves on their paws, padded over the vanished buildings. Boys romped, calling high and clear, on top of a levelled chemist's and a shoe-shop, and a little girl, wearing a man's cap, threw a snowball in a chill deserted garden that had once been the Jug and Bottle of the Prince of Wales. The wind cut up the street with a soft sea-noise hanging on its arm, like a hooter in a muffler. I could see the swathed hill stepping up out of the town, which you never could see properly before, and the powdered fields of the roofs of Milton Terrace and Watkin Street and Fullers Row. Fish-frailed, netbagged, umbrella'd, pixie-capped, fur-shoed, blue-nosed, puce-lipped, blinkered like drayhorses, scarved, mittened, galoshed, wearing everything but the cat's blanket, crushes of shopping-women crunched in the little Lapland of the once grey drab street, blew and queued and yearned for hot tea, as I began my search through Swansea town cold and early on that wicked February morning. I went into the hotel. "Good Morning."

The hall-porter did not answer. I was just another snowman to him. He did not know that I was looking for someone after fourteen years, and he did not care. He stood and shuddered, staring through the glass of the hotel door at the snowflakes sailing down the sky, like Siberian confetti. The bar was just opening, but already one customer puffed and shook at the counter with a full pint of half-frozen Tawe water in his wrapped-up hand. I said "Good Morning", and the barmaid, polishing the counter vigorously as though it were a rare and valuable piece of Swansea china, said to her first customer:

BARMAID: Seen the film at the Elysium Mr Griffiths there's snow isn't it did you come up on your bicycle our pipes burst Monday...

NARRATOR: A pint of bitter, please.

BARMAID: Proper little lake in the kitchen got to wear your Wellingtons when you boil an egg one and four please...

CUSTOMER: The cold gets me just here...

BARMAID: ...and eightpence change that's your liver Mr Griffiths you been on the cocoa again...

NARRATOR: I wonder whether you remember a friend of mine?

He always used to come to this bar, some years ago. Every morning, about this time.

CUSTOMER: Just by here it gets me. I don't know what'd happen if I didn't wear a band...

BARMAID: What's his name?

NARRATOR: Young Thomas.

BARMAID: Lots of Thomases come here it's a kind of home from home for Thomases isn't it Mr Griffiths what's he look like?

NARRATOR: He'd be about seventeen or eighteen... (*slowly*)

BARMAID: ...I was seventeen once...

NARRATOR: ...and above medium height. Above medium height for Wales, I mean, he's five foot six and a half. Thick blubber lips; snub nose; curly mousebrown hair; one front tooth broken after playing a game called Cats and Dogs, in the Mermaid, Mumbles; speaks rather fancy; truculent; plausible; a bit of a show-er-off; plus-fours and no breakfast, you know; used to have poems printed in the *Herald of Wales*; there was one about an open-air performance of *Electra* in Mrs Bertie Perkins's garden in Sketty; lived up the Uplands; a bombastic adolescent provincial Bohemian with a thick-knotted artist's tie made out of his sister's scarf, she never knew where it had gone, and a cricket-shirt dyed bottle-green; a gabbing, ambitious, mock-tough, pretentious young man; and moley, too.

BARMAID: There's words what d'you want to find *him* for I wouldn't touch him with a barge-pole... would you, Mr Griffiths? Mind, you can never tell. I remember a man came here with a monkey. Called for 'alf for himself and a pint for the monkey. And he wasn't Italian at all. Spoke Welsh like a preacher.

NARRATOR: The bar was filling up. Snowy business bellies pressed their watch-chains against the counter; black business bowlers, damp and white now as Christmas puddings in their cloths, bobbed in front of the misty mirrors. The voice of commerce rang sternly through the lounge.

1st VOICE: Cold enough for you?

17

2nd VOICE: How's your pipes, Mr Lewis?

3rd VOICE: Another winter like this'll put paid to me, Mr Evans.

4th VOICE: I got the 'flu...

1st VOICE: Make it a double...

2nd VOICE: Similar...

BARMAID: Okay, baby...

CUSTOMER: I seem to remember a chap like you described. There couldn't be two like him let's hope. He used to work as a reporter. Down the Three Lamps I used to see him. Lifting his ikkle elbow. (*confidentially*)

NARRATOR: What's the Three Lamps like now?

CUSTOMER: It isn't like anything. It isn't there. It's nothing mun. You remember Ben Evans's stores? It's right next door to that. Ben Evans isn't there either...

NARRATOR: I went out of the hotel into the snow and walked down High Street, past the flat white wastes where all the shops had been. Eddershaw Furnishers, Curry's Bicycles, Donegal Clothing Company, Doctor Scholl's, Burton Tailors, W.H. Smith, Boots Cash Chemists, Leslie's Stores, Upson's Shoes, Prince of Wales, Tucker's Fish, Stead & Simpson — all the shops bombed and vanished. Past the hole in space where Hodges & Clothiers had been, down Castle Street, past the remembered, invisible shops, Price's Fifty Shilling, and Crouch the Jeweller, Potter Gilmore Gowns, Evans Jeweller, Master's Outfitters, Style and Mantle, Lennard's Boots, True Form, Kardomah, R.E. Jones, Dean's Tailor, David Evans, Gregory Confectioners, Bovega, Burton's, Lloyd's Bank, and nothing. And into Temple Street. There the Three Lamps had stood, old Mac magisterial in his corner. And there the Young Thomas whom I was searching for used to stand at the counter on Friday paynights with Freddie Farr Half Hook, Bill Latham, Cliff Williams, Gareth Hughes, Eric Hughes, Glyn Lowry, a man among men, his hat at a rakish angle, in that snug, smug, select Edwardian holy of best-bitter holies... (*bar noises in background*)

OLD
REPORTER: Remember when I took you down the mortuary for the first time, Young Thomas? He'd never seen a

18

corpse before, boys, except old Ron on a Saturday night. "If you want to be a proper newspaperman," I said, "you got to be well known in the right circles. You got to be *persona grata* in the mortuary, see." He went pale green, mun.

1st YOUNG
REPORTER: Look, he's blushing now...

OLD
REPORTER: And when we got there what d'you think? The decorators were in at the mortuary, giving the old home a bit of a re-do like. Up on ladders having a slap at the roof. Young Thomas didn't see 'em, he had his pop eyes glued on the slab, and when one of the painters up the ladder said "Good morning, gents" in a deep voice he upped in the air and out of the place like a ferret. Laugh!

BARMAID: (*off*) You've had enough, Mr Roberts. (*noise of a gentle scuffle*) You heard what I said.

2nd YOUNG
REPORTER: (*casually*) There goes Mr Roberts.

OLD
REPORTER: Well fair do's they throw you out very genteel in this pub...

1st YOUNG
REPORTER: Ever seen Young Thomas covering a soccer match down the Vetch and working it out in tries?

2nd YOUNG
REPORTER: And up the Mannesman Hall shouting "Good footwork, sir," and a couple of punch-drunk colliers galumphing about like jumbos.

1st YOUNG
REPORTER: What you been reporting to-day, Young Thomas?

2nd YOUNG
REPORTER: Two typewriter Thomas the ace news-dick...

OLD
REPORTER: Let's have a dekko at your note-book. "Called at British Legion: Nothing. Called at Hospital: One broken leg. Auction at the Metropole. Ring Mr Beynon *re* Gymanfa Ganu. Lunch: Pint and pasty at the Singleton with Mrs Giles. Bazaar at Bethesda Chapel. Chimney on fire at Tontine Street. Walters

Road Sunday School Outing. Rehearsal of the *Mikado* at Skewen" — all front page stuff... (*fade*)

NARRATOR: The voices of fourteen years ago hung silent in the snow and ruin, and in the falling winter morning I walked on through the white havoc'd centre where once a very young man I knew had mucked about as chirpy as a sparrow after the sips and titbits and small change of the town. Near the *Evening Post* building and the fragment of the Castle I stopped a man whose face I thought I recognized from a long time ago. I said: I wonder if you can tell me...

PASSER-BY: Yes?

NARRATOR: He peered out of his blanketing scarves and from under his snowballed Balaclava like an Eskimo with a bad conscience. I said: If you can tell me whether you used to know a chap called Young Thomas. He worked on the *Post* and used to wear an overcoat sometimes with the check lining inside out so that you could play giant draughts on him. He wore a conscious woodbine, too...

PASSER-BY: What d'you mean, conscious woodbine?

NARRATOR: ...and a perched pork pie with a peacock feather and he tried to slouch like a newshawk even when he was attending a meeting of the Gorseinon Buffalos...

PASSER-BY: Oh, him! He owes me half a crown. I haven't seen him since the old Kardomah days. He wasn't a reporter then, he'd just left the grammar school. Him and Charlie Fisher — Charlie's got whiskers now — and Tom Warner and Fred Janes, drinking coffee-dashes and arguing the toss.

NARRATOR: What about?

PASSER-BY: Music and poetry and painting and politics. Einstein and Epstein, Stravinsky and Greta Garbo, Death and religion, Picasso and girls...

NARRATOR: And then?

PASSER-BY: Communism, symbolism, Bradman, Braque, the Watch Committee, free love, free beer, murder, Michelangelo, ping-pong, ambition, Sibelius, and girls...

NARRATOR: Is that all?

PASSER-BY: How Dan Jones was going to compose the most prodigious symphony, Fred Janes paint the most miraculously meticulous picture, Charlie Fisher catch the poshest trout, Vernon Watkins and Young Thomas write the most boiling poems, how they could ring the bells of London and paint it like a tart...

NARRATOR: And after that?

PASSER-BY: Oh the hissing of the butt-ends in the drains of the coffee-dashes and the tinkle and the gibble-gabble of the morning young lounge lizards as they talked about Augustus John, Emil Jannings, Carnera, Dracula, Amy Johnson, trial marriage, pocket-money, the Welsh sea, the London stars, King Kong, anarchy, darts, T.S. Eliot, and girls.... Duw, it's cold!

NARRATOR: And he hurried on, into the dervish snow, without a good morning or good-bye, swaddled in his winter woollens like a man in the island of his deafness, and I felt that perhaps he had never stopped at all to tell me of one more departed stage in the progress of the boy I was pursuing. The Kardomah Café was razed to the snow, the voices of the coffee-drinkers — poets, painters, and musicians in their beginnings — lost in the willynilly flying of the years and the flakes.

    Down College Street I walked then, past the re-membered invisible shops, Langley's, Castle Cigar Co., T.B. Brown, Pullar's, Aubrey Jeremiah, Goddard Jones, Richards, Hornes, Marles, Pleasance & Harper, Star Supply, Sidney Heath, Wesley Chapel, and nothing.... My search was leading me back, through pub and job and café, to the School. (*fade, school bell*)

SCHOOL-
MASTER: Oh yes, yes, I remember him well,
though I do not know if I would recognize him now:
nobody grows any younger, or better,
and boys grow into much the sort of men one would
                              suppose
though sometimes the moustaches bewilder
and one finds it hard to reconcile one's memory of a
                              small
none-too-clean urchin lying his way unsuccessfully

21

out of his homework
with a fierce and many-medalled sergeant-major
with three children or a divorced chartered
accountant;
and it is hard to realize
that some little tousled rebellious youth whose only
claim
to fame among his contemporaries was his
undisputed right
to the championship of the spitting contest
is now perhaps one's own bank manager.
Oh yes, I remember him well, the boy you are
searching for:
he looked like most boys, no better, brighter, or more
respectful;
he cribbed, mitched, spilt ink, rattled his desk and
garbled his lessons with the worst of them;
he could smudge, hedge, smirk, wriggle, wince,
whimper, blarney, badger, blush, deceive, be
devious, stammer, improvise, assume
offended dignity or righteous indignation as though
to the manner born;
sullenly and reluctantly he drilled, for some small
crime, under Sergeant Bird, so wittily nicknamed
Oiseau, on Wednesday half-holidays,
appeared regularly in detention classes,
hid in the cloakroom during algebra,
was, when a newcomer, thrown into the bushes of
the Lower Playground by bigger boys,
and threw newcomers into the bushes of the Lower
Playground when *he* was a bigger boy;
he scuffled at prayers,
he interpolated, smugly, the time-honoured wrong
irreverent words into the morning hymns,
he helped to damage the headmaster's rhubarb,
was thirty-third in trigonometry,
and, as might be expected, edited the School
Magazine. (*fade*)

NARRATOR: The Hall is shattered, the echoing corridors charred
where he scribbled and smudged and yawned in the
long green days, waiting for the bell and the scamper
into the Yard: the School on Mount Pleasant Hill has
changed its face and its ways. Soon, they say, it may

be no longer the School at all he knew and loved when he was a boy up to no good but the beat of his blood: the names are havoc'd from the Hall and the carved initials burned from the broken wood. But the names remain. What names did he know of the dead? Who of the honoured dead did he know such a long time ago? The names of the dead in the living heart and head remain for ever. Of all the dead whom did he know? (*funeral bell*)

VOICE: Evans, K.J.
Haines, G.C.
Roberts, I.L.
Moxham, J.
Thomas, H.
Baines, W.
Bazzard, F.H.
Beer, L.J.
Bucknell, R.
Tywford, G.
Vagg, E.A.
Wright, G. (*fade*)

NARRATOR: Then I tacked down the snowblind hill, a cat-o'-nine-gales whipping from the sea, and, white and eider-downed in the smothering flurry, people padded past me up and down like prowling featherbeds. And I plodded through the ankle-high one cloud that foamed the town, into flat Gower Street, its buildings melted, and along long Helen's Road. Now my search was leading me back to the seashore. (*noise of sea, softly*)

NARRATOR: Only two living creatures stood on the promenade, near the cenotaph, facing the tossed crystal sea: a man in a chewed muffler and a ratting cap, and an angry dog of a mixed make. The man dithered in the cold, beat his bare blue hands together, waited for some sign from sea or snow; the dog shouted at the weather, and fixed his bloodshot eyes on Mumbles Head. But when the man and I talked together, the dog piped down and fixed his eyes on me, blaming me for the snow. The man spoke towards the sea. Year in, year out, whatever the weather, once in the daytime, once in the dark, he always came to look at

23

the sea. He knew all the dogs and boys and old men who came to see the sea, who ran or gambolled on the sand or stooped at the edge of the waves as though over a wild, wide, rolling ash-can. He knew the lovers who went to lie in the sandhills, the striding masculine women who roared at their terriers like tiger tamers, the loafing men whose work it was in the world to observe the great employment of the sea. He said:

PROMENADE-
MAN: Oh yes, yes, I remember him well, but I didn't know what was his name. I don't know the names of none of the sandboys. They don't know mine. About fourteen or fifteen years old, you said, with a little red cap. And he used to play by Vivian's Stream. He used to dawdle in the arches, you said, and lark about on the railway-lines and holler at the old sea. He'd mooch about the dunes and watch the tankers and the tugs and the banana boats come out of the docks. He was going to run away to sea, he said. I know. On Saturday afternoon he'd go down to the sea when it was a long way out, and hear the foghorns though he couldn't see the ships. And on Sunday nights, after chapel, he'd be swaggering with his pals along the prom, whistling after the girls. (*titter*)

GIRL: Does your mother know you're out? Go away now. Stop following us. (*another girl titters*)

GIRL: Don't you say nothing, Hetty, you're only encouraging. No thank *you*, Mr Cheeky, with your cut-glass accent and your father's trilby! I don't want *no* walk on *no* sands. What d'you say? Ooh listen to him, Het, he's swallowed a dictionary. No, I don't want to go with nobody up no lane in the moonlight, see, and I'm not a baby-snatcher neither. I seen you going to school along Terrace Road, Mr Glad-Eye, with your little satchel and wearing your red cap and all. You seen me wearing my... no you never. Hetty, mind your glasses! Hetty Harris, you're as bad as them. Oh go away and do your homework, you. No I'm not then. I'm nobody's homework, see. Cheek! Hetty Harris, don't you let him! Oooh, there's brazen! Well, just to the end of the prom, if you like. No further, mind...

PROMENADE-
MAN: Oh yes, I knew him well. I've known him by the thousands...

NARRATOR: Even now, on the frozen foreshore, a high, far cry of boys, all like the boy I sought, slid on the glass of the streams and snowballed each other and the sky. Then I went on my way from the sea, up Brynmill Terrace and into Glanbrydan Avenue where Bert Trick had kept a grocer's shop and, in the kitchen, threatened the annihilation of the ruling classes over sandwiches and jelly and blancmange. And I came to the shops and houses of the Uplands. Here and around here it was that the journey had begun of the one I was pursuing through his past. (*old piano cinema-music in the background*)

1st VOICE: Here was once the flea-pit picture-house where he whooped for the scalping Indians with Jack Basset and banged for the rustlers' guns.

NARRATOR: Jackie Basset, killed.

3rd VOICE: Here once was Mrs Ferguson's, who sold the best gob-stoppers and penny packets full of surprises and a sweet kind of glue.

1st VOICE: In the fields behind Cwmdonkin Drive, the Murrays chased him and all cats.

2nd VOICE: No fires now where the outlaws' fires burned and the paradisiacal potatoes roasted in the embers.

3rd VOICE: In the Graig beneath Town Hill he was a lonely killer hunting the wolves (or rabbits) and the red Sioux tribe (or Mitchell brothers). (*fade cinema-music into background of children's voices reciting, in unison, the names of the counties of Wales*)

1st VOICE: In Mirador School he learned to read and count. Who made the worst raffia doilies? Who put water in Joyce's galoshes, every morning prompt as prompt? In the afternoons, when the children were good, they read aloud from Struwelpeter. And when they were bad, they sat alone in the empty classroom, hearing, from above them, the distant, terrible, sad music of the late piano lesson. (*The children's voices fade. The piano lesson continues in the background.*)

NARRATOR: And I went up, through the white Grove, into Cwmdonkin Park, the snow still sailing and the childish, lonely, remembered music fingering on in the suddenly gentle wind. Dusk was folding the Park around, like another, darker snow. Soon the bell would ring for the closing of the gates, though the Park was empty. The park-keeper walked by the reservoir, where swans had glided, on his white rounds. I walked by his side and asked him my questions, up the swathed drives past buried beds and loaded utterly still furred and birdless trees towards the last gate. He said:

PARK-
KEEPER: Oh yes, yes, I knew him well. He used to climb the reservoir railings and pelt the old swans. Run like a billygoat over the grass you should keep off of. Cut branches off the trees. Carve words on the benches. Pull up moss in the rockery, go snip through the dahlias. Fight in the bandstand. Climb the elms and moon up the top like a owl. Light fires in the bushes. Play on the green bank. Oh yes, I knew him well. I think he was happy all the time. I've known him by the thousands.

NARRATOR: We had reached the last gate. Dusk drew around us and the town. I said: What has become of him now?

PARK-
KEEPER: Dead.

NARRATOR: The Park-keeper said: (*the park bell rings*)

PARK-
KEEPER: Dead... Dead... Dead... Dead... Dead... Dead.

T.C. THOMAS
The Sound of Stillness

Trevor C. Thomas (1896-1989) was a teacher by profession and retired as headmaster after thirty years to take up horticulture. He wrote numerous one act plays for his drama company, the Llynsafadden Players, based in Brecon. Many of his actors, such as Gerald James and Jack Walters, became professionals working at the Royal Shakespeare Company, The National Theatre and in television. He wrote the comedy series *Davy Jones' Locker* for the BBC in the 1960s. *The Sound of Stillness*, written in 1959, won the British Drama League Festival Award. The story was taken from real events that occurred on the Epynt Mountains in mid Wales when the army occupied the range for manoeuvres. It is interesting to note that the same situation still exists on the Epynt Mountains some forty years later.

Author's Note

Since that bitter winter when weary remnants of the shattered armies of Charles I struggled across the Epynt, peace has reigned on those windswept slopes. Throughout the intervening centuries, sheep have grazed on the hillsides, undisturbed, and the hill farmers, sturdy, independent folk, content in their isolation, have gone quietly about their work, waging a constant struggle against nature.

War came again to the Epynt. In 1940, when broken armies were concentrating at Dunkirk, another evacuation was taking place. Men whose ancestors had farmed the Epynt for centuries were compelled to leave their homes, to make way for the guns that thunder across the mountain.

Visit the Epynt and see for yourself. In the hollow called Cwm, you will find the little chapel of Babell. Without windows or doors, it lies at the mercy of the winds. Hill ponies shelter behind its crumbling walls; sheep wander over the graves of men who once farmed the slopes.

On the breast above is the heap of stones "That once was Ffynnon".

CHARACTERS

Rhys y Ffynnon
Wil y Ffynnon (his brother)
Dewi
The Private
The Sergeant
The Lieutenant

(*Scene: The one-time living-room of Ffynnon; a lonely farm high on the slopes of the Epynt, before dawn in August, 1941. A door, upstage left, opens to a mountain track. There is a window downstage left and the remains of a fireplace downstage right. Old, blind Rhys sits on a rusty oil-drum near the small fire burning in the grate. His slightly younger brother, Wil, enters through the door, carrying some pieces of wood. He walks to the fire.*)

RHYS: What are you burning?

WIL: The barn door.

RHYS: It's down then?

WIL: Aye. The wind, most like.

RHYS: Couldn't you have found something else?

WIL: Might as well burn it as let it rot. (*He examines one of the pieces of wood.*) Do you remember this, Rhys?

RHYS: (*running his fingertips over the wood*) Our names. It's a long time since we carved those. We might as well have carved them on the wind.

WIL: (*taking the wood and throwing it on the fire*) Ashes to ashes. (*He walks to the doorway. A cock grouse gives its metallic call.*) Rhys.

RHYS: What is it?

WIL: Are you sure that what we are doing is right?

RHYS: Why ask a thing like that? Could you stand by and

	see Ffynnon destroyed without lifting a hand to save it? Is it afraid you are?
WIL:	Afraid! You know me better than that.
RHYS:	What is it, then?
WIL:	This waiting — that's what I don't like. An hour ago I felt like a young man with the blood running strong in my veins. Why don't they come, damn them, before this quiet turns me into an old man again?
RHYS:	They will come soon enough. Have patience now, and fix your mind on what you have to do.
WIL:	It's easy for you to talk.
RHYS:	You won't draw back?
WIL:	I know what I have to do without you reminding me — and I will do it. But this waiting, it weakens a man's purpose. What's the point of putting up one's fists when it's useless to fight? You know as well as I do that Ffynnon must go.
RHYS:	Ffynnon may go, but if we make those who destroy it see the madness of what they are doing, then other places like Ffynnon may be left untouched.
WIL:	No. We missed our chance. Why pretend? We should have made a stand a year ago. It's too late now. (*He looks through the window and becomes tense.*) Rhys!
RHYS:	They are coming?
WIL:	Something moved behind the barn. (*He looks again.*) No, it's only shadows playing tricks.
RHYS:	You are sure?
WIL:	Aye. Things are deceiving in this light. (*He moves to the door.*) There's beautiful it is now. The moon has come through the clouds and is lighting up the Cwm.
RHYS:	Do you hear anything?
WIL:	Only the whisper of the hill grass.
RHYS:	I heard voices... singing.
WIL:	Where?
RHYS:	Down in the hollow — in Babell. (*They listen.*)
WIL:	There is nothing.
RHYS:	I heard men singing hymns; I heard it plainly.
WIL:	There's nothing, I tell you.

RHYS:	Maybe sounds don't die, only drift away to come back on the winds like an echo, even after a long time. So quietly do they come, that only the mind can hear.

WIL:	It was real singing that Powell, Cilienni, heard in Babell last week.

RHYS:	Soldiers?

WIL:	Aye. They had made a fire in the shelter of the chapel and were singing songs not fit to hear.

RHYS:	Why didn't Powell order them out? Why didn't he tell them that Babell is the House of God?

WIL:	What would be the use? Besides, Powell is only half a man at the best of times.

RHYS:	Small wonder that homes are being lost with men like Powell about.

WIL:	(*sigh*) Aye. (*He pauses to listen.*) There's quiet it's gone.

RHYS:	Trwst tawelwch.

WIL:	The sound of stillness.

RHYS:	Aye. The sound of stillness. That's what the preacher called it — in the last sermon he preached before they closed the chapel.

WIL:	Fine words indeed, but they meant nothing. Like one of the prophets he should have spoken out, rousing us to fight, but it was a home in the world to come, a home that no-one can take away, that's what he promised us. And like sheep we let ourselves be driven from the mountain.

RHYS:	(*as if to himself*) "A great and strong wind rent the mountain, but the Lord was not in the wind; and after the wind an earthquake, but the Lord was not in the earthquake; and after the earthquake a fire, but the Lord was not in the fire; and after the fire a still, small voice —" .

WIL:	God's voice.

RHYS:	Aye. A pity it is that only a few can hear.

WIL:	Aye.

RHYS:	The noise of the guns, that is the devil's voice. Now in this quiet God is speaking. Loud enough the guns may be to shake the hills, but never will they silence the stillness.

WIL: It was the stillness I missed down in the village. What fools we were to have listened to those people in the first place. They should have given us a new home on the lower slopes, out of the reach of the guns, where we could have been happy.

RHYS: No! Like old trees on the hillside we were, driving our roots down. When the roots are ripped up, the end comes slowly, but surely. I have seen big trees, thrown down by the storm, fighting to live, until the wind strips off the last leaf. That is how we would have been, struggling to draw life through the slender roots of memory. Better it is to be dead than to live like that.

WIL: They will have missed us by now. They will have guessed where we have gone and come to take us back.

RHYS: Suppose we don't go back?

WIL: Not go back? Talk sense, Rhys. In the end we will have to go, whether we like it or not. We'll make our protest and then return to the village. We are only two old men; the odds against us are too great.

RHYS: (*after a pause*) Is the dawn showing yet?

WIL: (*going to window*) It's a job to tell; there's so much moonlight. It can't be far away.

RHYS: Then the guns will start.

WIL: Aye. Yesterday the target was Ynys Hir. It is a heap of stones.

RHYS: Yesterday Ynys Hir, today Ffynnon. Already shells have fallen near here. They leave great gashes in the red earth and the soil pours out like blood. Is that how it looks?

WIL: Aye. Great holes have they torn in the hillside.

RHYS: When the guns have gone the hill grass will grow again, and sheep will shelter in the hollows the guns have made. But Ynys Hir, Babell and Ffynnon will be gone forever. Shepherds will cross the slopes and point to heaps of stones. "That was Ynys Hir," they will say. "That was Babell; that was Ffynnon."

WIL: Until clumps of nettles hide the stones for ever.

31

RHYS: What if the soldiers do not come? Have you thought of that?

WIL: They will come.

RHYS: We came by the sheep walks, and not a soul did we meet. No one knows that we are here.

WIL: If they do not come soon, then what we are doing will be in vain.

RHYS: No!

WIL: What shall we do then? Shall we shout our protests to the winds of the Epynt and return to the village like a pair of old fools that we are?

RHYS: How much do you care for Ffynnon?

WIL: As much as you do.

RHYS: Not by the way you talk.

WIL: What do you mean?

RHYS: You talk about going back to the village.

WIL: So we will, as soon as our protest is made.

RHYS: You had better know now, Wil, that, whatever happens, I am not going back.

WIL: What are you saying?

RHYS: We could stay.

WIL: Stay! Stay to be killed?

RHYS: What is there to go back to? We could sleep in peace under the ruins they will make of Ffynnon.

WIL: No! Never! You mustn't even think like that. It's true that down in the village there are times when I am unhappy, when my heart feels like a lump of lead in my breast. But never have I felt that life was finished for me. Life is too precious to be thrown away, Rhys. Far better to go on lifting our voices against the wrong that has been done to us.

RHYS: There are times when the tongues of dead men speak louder than those of the living.

(*There is a sound offstage. WIL moves to the window.*)

WIL: Rhys!

RHYS: What is it?

WIL: I heard somebody in the fern.

RHYS: Is the gun loaded?

WIL: (*picking up gun from corner near window*) Aye. (*pause*) Shoot over their heads, is it?

RHYS: You know what to do.

WIL: (*loudly*) Don't come any nearer or it will be the worse for you.

VOICE: (*off*) It's me, Wil!

RHYS: Dewi! (*The young lad, DEWI, enters. He crosses to RHYS.*) What are you doing here?

DEWI: I knew you'd be here. When they said, down in the village, that you had gone, I knew that this is where I'd find you. Why didn't you tell me you were coming here?

RHYS: Because we didn't want you to know.

DEWI: It was wicked of you, stealing away in the dark.

RHYS: Does anyone else know that we are here?

DEWI: No, they never thought you'd come back here. But I knew. It was silly of me to have told you about Ffynnon — that it was going to be used as a target. That's why you came, isn't it? To take a last look at the old place. Well, you've had your look, and no doubt you feel better for it. I've come to take you back. (*pause*) You can't stay here; you know you can't. You've got to come back. (*pause, then persuasively*) Of course it was nice to visit the old house again, to feel the mist wet on your faces and to smell the mountain. We were happy here, the three of us. But that's all over. Come on, now, let's go.

RHYS: You shouldn't have come, Dewi.

DEWI: *You* shouldn't have come, you mean. Your eyes — anything might have happened.

RHYS: I don't need eyes for this mountain. I know every stone, every tree....

DEWI: But the mountain is changing, Rhys; you know that. Beside, you've got to come back. Now — and you know why. You know as well as I do. You saw it as you were coming up the Cwm, didn't you, Wil?

WIL: The flag.

DEWI: (*pointing out of window*) Yes. There it is — plain

33

	enough in the moonlight. You know what that means as well as I do.

RHYS/DEWI dialogue:

WIL: Danger.

DEWI: Yes. Soon the guns will start firing. It's not safe here; you know it isn't. I told you yesterday about Ynys Hir, what the guns had made of it. It will be the same with Ffynnon. Nothing can stop that. So, come, now; let's go.

RHYS: Dewi.

DEWI: What?

RHYS: Come here. (*DEWI moves towards RHYS.*) Nearer, so that I can touch you. (*DEWI kneels by RHYS.*) I want to tell you about something that happened a long time ago. Only a boy I was at the time and, like a boy, thoughtless. I did a wicked thing. But when I found out how cruel it was, it was too late to put things right.

DEWI: This is not the time for talking. You can tell me later.

RHYS: Listen, Dewi. The summer had gone and the corn had come in — good ripe corn, for the weather was kind. Around the headland only withered knapweed and seeded docks were left. Then they came, finches by the hundred, like red clouds, settling on the docks. Beautiful they were, and I wanted one, to carry the beauty of the autumn through the bleakness of the winter. I made nooses of horse-hair, tied them to the docks — and waited. Presently, the cloud drifted away, but one, its leg caught in the noose, was left. Warm and beautiful it was, and I carried it into the house and put it in a cage. Before the snow came, it was dead. It was dead because, far away from the things it loved, it didn't want to live.

DEWI: I won't listen to you. It is time to go.

RHYS: You wouldn't do a cruel thing like that, would you? You wouldn't take a creature away from what it loves — to pine and die.

DEWI: I know what you are trying to say — that, away from the mountain you will die, like that bird in the cage. It isn't true. I have grown up on the mountain, too, and I love it. I belong to the mountain as much as you do, but I know I can live away from it — not so happy, perhaps, but content.

RHYS: If you can take a young bird straight from its nest, then it may live in a cage.

DEWI: I won't listen to you. You've got to come back before the guns blow this place to bits. You'll have to; the soldiers are on their way. I saw a truck on the new road; I saw the headlights as I was coming up the Cwm.

WIL: (*taking up gun*) We have been waiting for them long enough.

DEWI: Wil! You wouldn't use the gun?

WIL: Not if they keep their distance. But they had better not set one foot inside Ffynnon.

DEWI: You musn't do it! Rhys, tell him not to be a fool. Only evil will come of it. Those soldiers know nothing about Ffynnon; they'd never even heard about it, till now. They know nothing about you. Can't you see that it would be murder? You couldn't do it, Wil.

RHYS: Let them keep away, then.

DEWI: They won't keep away. You know very well that they'll come. That's why you've got the fire going, isn't it? You're inviting them to come.

RHYS: If it's God's will that brings them here....

DEWI: Don't be such a hypocrite, Rhys. God's will, indeed! You know they'll see the light. I could see it a mile off.

RHYS: Wil, stamp out the fire.

(*WIL puts down the gun and crosses to the fire. DEWI snatches the gun and runs out of the door.*)

WIL: Dewi! Come back!

RHYS: What's happening?

WIL: He's taken the gun. (*WIL rushes to the window.*) No, Dewi; don't! (*A splash is heard.*) He's thrown it down the well. Dewi! (*DEWI enters.*) Why did you do that?

DEWI: Because it is mad you are, with anger in your hearts. The gun is safer down the well. I couldn't let you do a thing that later you would regret.

RHYS: It makes no difference.

DEWI: What do you mean?

RHYS: Whatever happens, I am not going back.

WIL: Come on, Rhys, the boy is right. I couldn't have used that gun. It's time we stopped pretending. Let's go now.

RHYS: Go you, if you want to; I shall stay.

DEWI: The soldiers won't let you. You know they won't.

RHYS: If they force us to go, we will — but not for long.

WIL: What do you mean — not for long?

RHYS: If they turn us out, Dewi, you must pretend to take us back to the village. You shall take Wil down the Cwm — and I shall come back, alone.

WIL: Rhys! No!

DEWI: Come back to be killed? Is that what you are saying? You must be mad. You know I'd never let you do a thing like that!

PRIVATE: (*off*) It's a light, right enough.

SERGEANT: (*off*) Who the hell can it be?

(*PRIVATE enters*)

PRIVATE: Blimey! A couple of tramps. Sarge! Tramps!

DEWI: Tramps, indeed!

PRIVATE: And a boy.

(*Sergeant enters*)

SERGEANT: What's all this? Who the hell are you?

DEWI: They are Rhys and Will, y Ffynnon.

SERGEANT: They can be Moses and Elias for all I care. Out you go, the lot of you! And no loitering on your blasted mountain-top, either. Are you blind? Or daft? Didn't you see the flag? What the hell do you think a red flag is for? Come on, jump to it! (*The old men do not move.*) Hey! What's the matter with you? Are you deaf?

WIL: We hear you; now you hear me. This is Ffynnon, our home. A year ago we were fools enough to leave it. We have been cheated once, but never again. So stop your shouting. No man, not even the King himself, has the right to turn us out.

SERGEANT: No right? Who do you think you are?

36

DEWI:	Not Moses and Elias.
SERGEANT:	That's enough from you. (*looks around*) Home, they call it. Must be crackers! (*to RHYS*) Come on, Methuselah, it ain't healthy here. Up you come.
DEWI:	Take your hands off him!
PRIVATE:	Easy now, lad.
DEWI:	Then you tell him to keep his hands off.
SERGEANT:	This is getting us nowhere. Calm down and we'll try and sort things out. Right. (*to WIL*) Who are you?
WIL:	Wil y Ffynnon.
SERGEANT:	And him?
WIL:	My brother — Rhys y Ffynnon.
SERGEANT:	(*to DEWI*) And you?
DEWI:	My name is Dewi. I used to work for Wil and Rhys. Like a son they treated me, and like a son I will stand by them. So you keep your hands off them, or...
SERGEANT:	That's enough of that. So, this is Ffynnon?
DEWI:	It is.
SERGEANT:	How long has it been empty?
DEWI:	About a year.
WIL:	More shame to them who turned us out.
SERGEANT:	What are you doing here?
DEWI:	Have you never been homesick?
SERGEANT:	Homesick? Oh, yes, I've been homesick. I'm homesick now. We're all homesick, all the bloody time. What are you getting at — that the old 'uns are homesick? That they deserve special treatment? You want me to cry my eyes out?
DEWI:	You couldn't if you tried.
SERGEANT:	Home be blowed! It's a ruin.
DEWI:	Not to them.
SERGEANT:	They must be round the bend. (*to PRIVATE*) That's it; they're round the bend.
PRIVATE:	Crackers!
SERGEANT:	Well, whether you like it or not, out you must go. It beats me, this does. Here you are shouting about leaving a mouldy old ruin, when the whole blasted

world is crashing about our ears. Come on, you ruddy old fools.

RHYS: Here we are — and here we'll stay.

SERGEANT: There's nothing for it; we'll have to pitch them out.

WIL: You won't have it all your own way.

SERGEANT: Talk sense, you old fool. You haven't the strength to swat a fly! Look, we don't want to use force, but if...

WIL: (*squaring up to him*) You get back! You've no right...

PRIVATE: Now, now, Grandpa; this ain't a matter of what's right and what's wrong. Once the balloon goes up there's no such thing as right in the whole bloomin' world. Only one thing counts at a time like this — and that's orders. Somebody gives them — and we mugs obey them. Ain't that right, Sarge? That's the way it is, when there's a war on. Obey and don't ask questions. Now, the order is that this range has to be cleared, so that our boys can get in a bit of practice. (*to RHYS*) So, ups-a-daisy, Grandad. (*DEWI and WIL move to protect RHYS.*) Now what, Sarge?

SERGEANT: Ask me another. I don't like manhandling them without orders.

PRIVATE: Use tact. That's what the Captain said.

SERGEANT: He ought to be here himself, using bloody tact. They're an awkward lot, the Welsh. I should know. I'm one myself.

WIL: Ydych chi'n siarad Cymraeg? (*you speak Welsh?*)

RHYS: Pam na fasech chi'n dweud? (*why didn't you say so?*)

SERGEANT: Hold it! I can't manage that. "Iechyd da. Shwd mae?" That's about my limit. Now, look, let's be reasonable. I can't stay here all day arguing. It'll get us nowhere. For the last time, will you go? (*There is no reaction.*) Keep an eye on them, George. I'll go down for the Lieutenant. Perhaps he'll know what to do. I'm damned if I do! (*exits*)

PRIVATE: (*removing helmet*) Might as well be comfortable. A bad job, this, Moses and Elias.

DEWI: Can't you leave them alone?

PRIVATE: I'm only trying to put a bit of sense into their heads. There's a packet of trouble coming to you for this.

It's bad enough obstructing the police, but when it comes to obstructing the military — I wouldn't be in your shoes for all the tea in China! They're a bit old for jail, if you ask me.

DEWI: Jail? For what? You're trying to frighten us, aren't you? What will I get — six months?

PRIVATE: No. Shot at dawn, that's what you'll be!

DEWI: I'm glad you can find something to laugh at.

PRIVATE: Look here, lad, take a bit of advice. The old 'uns may be living in the past, but you aren't. Pack this in before the Sarge returns. It beats me why anyone should want to hang on to a ruin like this. You've heard it's going up — is that it? Well, between you and me, that's all it's good for now — a target. It couldn't last out much longer. In a couple of years it would have been a goner. Once the old 'uns had gone, who would live here then?

DEWI: You don't know what you're talking about!

PRIVATE: Don't you make that mistake. I'm talking sense, and you know it. Of course, it's hard for them to stand by and see the old place blown up. I can understand that. After spending nearly all your life in one place, you're bound to get attached to it. I'm not much of a home bird, myself, but I can understand that.

RHYS: You wouldn't understand if you were to live for a thousand years.

PRIVATE: So you were listening, were you? P'raps I understand more than you think. This is the second war I've been in, and, believe me, everyone likes to have a place to slink to when the going gets tough.

RHYS: Your home — fond of it, were you?

PRIVATE: Home? Funny, I never thought about it. I suppose I was, in a way. It was in a big town.

RHYS: Streets of houses close together?

PRIVATE: That's it. So close that the sun didn't have much of a chance, and there was always smoke hanging about. A slum some people would call it, as if it were our fault. No wonder we were a tough lot! At the end of the row, that's where I lived. It wasn't much of a house.

RHYS: You wouldn't call it home?

PRIVATE: No, never used the word. But I was fond of it just the same.

RHYS: You will go back happy to a place like that?

PRIVATE: No. No, I'll never go back. There's nothing to go back to. Bombers came over, and when they had gone, it was a heap of stones.

RHYS: Like Ffynnon will be.

PRIVATE: Like Ffynnon will be. What do you think of that, Moses and Elias? What the hell have you got to moan about? It's not enemy bombers that are going to send this ruin sky-high, but our own guns. And the men firing them will soon be over there, fighting to save your skins. Can't you get it into your heads what war means? Don't you know that there's a bloody great world out there, where men haven't feelings any more?

RHYS: That heap of stones — when you saw it, did it hurt to look?

PRIVATE: Hurt? Oh, no! I laughed my fool head off, like you'll be laughing tomorrow when you see what's left of Ffynnon! For Christ's sake, stop asking me questions! Where the hell has the Sarge got to? (*pause*) Sorry, Grandad, I didn't mean to fly off the handle. You see, that heap of stones... my missus was under it... that's all.

SERGEANT: (*off*) Stubborn as hell, Sir. You'll see for yourself...

(*SERGEANT and LIEUTENANT enter. PRIVATE salutes.*)

LIEUT.: (*to PRIVATE*) At ease. These are the men, Sergeant?

SERGEANT: Sir!

LIEUT.: They don't look capable of much resistance. Why fetch me?

SERGEANT: You'll soon find out, Sir.

LIEUT.: The lad?

SERGEANT: As awkward as they are, Sir.

LIEUT.: Now, look here. The Sergeant has explained the situation, and the sooner you accept it, the better it will be for all of us.

WIL: That's what they said a year ago — "Accept it". And that's what we did, without having time to think. Don't you understand, this is our home — and you are trying to destroy it.

LIEUT.: It's not much good my saying how sorry I am, is it? There's a war on, don't forget, and all sorts of unpleasant things have to be done. It's no use arguing; nothing will alter the position. You must get out — and quickly at that. You can't blame me for that. This is a gunnery range. You must have seen the flag, and you know what that means. Nobody — nobody — must be left in the target area when the guns open up. So, come now, be reasonable.

RHYS: Couldn't you pretend that you hadn't seen us?

LIEUT.: What! Are you out of your senses? You wouldn't stay here to be killed, would you? Or would you? (*to SERGEANT*) I think I understand what they have in mind. Imagine the newspaper headlines: WELSH HILL-FARMERS DIE AS A GESTURE AGAINST LOSING THEIR HOMES!

SERGEANT: Bloody martyrs!

LIEUT.: There will be no martyrs. We've wasted enough time. Pack them into the truck and take them back to the village. Tell the police to keep them under observation. We don't want any — accidents.

WIL: Beth nawr, Rhys? (*What now, Rhys?*)

RHYS: Oes gennym ni ddewis? (*Do we have any choice?*)

WIL: Dim. Mae'n rhaid iddyn nhw wneud yn ôl y gorchmynion. Paid â'u beio nhw, Rhys. Fe siarada i â'r gwr ifanc. (*No. They have to obey orders. Don't blame them, Rhys. I'll talk to the young man.*)

RHYS: Na, fe wna i. (*No. I'll do it.*)

WIL: Mae'n ddrwg gen i. (*I am sorry.*)

LIEUT.: Well, now that you seem to have talked things over, what have you decided.

RHYS: We will go.

LIEUT.: Good! (*to SERGEANT*) I've missed my vocation; I should have been a diplomat!

41

WIL: (*pointing to PRIVATE*) We will go because of him.

SERGEANT: What the...?

RHYS: That heap of stones — and what was under it.

PRIVATE: Thank you, Grandad. I'm glad you understand.

SERGEANT: Understand what?

PRIVATE: Nothing that matters — now, Sir.

SERGEANT: Time, Sir?

LIEUT.:   Yes. Come along, down to the truck.

WIL: We will walk.

SERGEANT: You bloody well won't! I'm not letting you out of my sight. You'll come with us — in the truck.

RHYS: If we can't walk, we will stay.

LIEUT.:   For goodness sake, humour them.

SERGEANT: All right, then, walk. Garrison marches out with full honours!

LIEUT.:   Can you look after them, lad?

DEWI: You bet! We'll take the sheep-walk through the fern — and get to the village before you!

LIEUT.:   Good. (*to RHYS*) I'm sorry about this. Perhaps you'd let me call and see you, the next time I'm in the village.

RHYS: Thank you, Sir.

WIL: Come on, Rhys.

                (*WIL and DEWI help RHYS out.*)

LIEUT.:   It's strange what home means to some people.

SERGEANT: The time, Sir. Hadn't we better be going?

LIEUT.:   Give them a moment or two, so that they may keep the only thing they have left.

SERGEANT: Sir?

LIEUT.:   Their dignity, Sergeant. (*He looks out of the window.*) They've gone. Thank the Lord for that.

SERGEANT: You think you can trust them, Sir? Not to come back?

LIEUT.:   That's a risk I'll have to take. (*looks at watch*) My God! We're cutting it fine. If we don't get out of here, we'll be the martyrs!

                (*He goes out followed by the SERGEANT. The PRIVATE*

follows them to the doorway, then turns to look around.)

PRIVATE: Goodbye, Ffynnon.

(*He goes out. There is silence. Then comes the sound of distant gunfire and flashes of light as shells scream overhead, their target — Ffynnon.*)

(*slow curtain*)

GWYN THOMAS
Gazooka
A Rhondda Reminiscence

Gwyn Thomas (1913-1981) was born in Cymmer in the Rhondda Valley, educated at Oxford and worked for some years as a teacher. Author of novels, short-stories, memoirs and plays, he also enjoyed a thirty-year career in radio and television. One of the most widely admired Welshman of his era, he was once called "The greatest talker in the world". His best known drama, *The Keep*, was first staged at the Royal Court Theatre in London in 1960. *Gazooka* is a typical subject of Thomas's — set in the Rhondda Valley in the summer of the general strike in 1926, it follows the colourful exploits of a group of friends trying to find costumes for the local gazooka band.

CHARACTERS

Narrator
Gomer Gough
Edwin Pugh
Cynlais Coleman
Milton Nicholas
Willie Silcox
Uriah Smayle
Mathew Sewell
Tasso
Mrs Hallam
Moira Hallam
Mrs Ephraim Humphries
Ephraim Humphries
Jedediah Judge

Kitchener Caney
Teilo Dew
Scout; Voice

(Faintly, drums and gazookas playing "Swanee". The sound approaches, grows louder, then fades away again.)

NARRATOR: And to my ears, whenever that tune is played, the brave ghosts march again and my eyes are full of the wonder they knew in the months of that long, idle, sunlit summer of 1926. By the beginning of June the hills were bulging with a clearer loveliness than they had ever had before. No smoke rose from the great chimneys to write messages on the sky that saddened and puzzled the minds of the young. The endless journeys of coal-trams on the inclines, loaded on the upward run and empty on the down, ceased to rattle through the night and mark our dreams. The parade of nailed boots on the pavements at dawn fell silent, and day after glorious day the sun came up over hills that had been restored by a quirk of social conflict to the calm they lost a hundred years before. When the school holidays came we took to the mountain tops, joining the liberated pit ponies among the ferns on the broad plateaus. That was the picture for us who were young. For our fathers and mothers, there was the inclosing fence of hinted fears, fear of hunger, fear of defeat. And then, out of the quietness and the golden light, partly to ease their fret, a new excitement was born. The carnivals and the jazz bands.

Rapture can sprout in the oddest places and it certainly sprouted then and there. We formed bands by the dozen, great lumps of beauty and precision, a hundred men and more in each, blowing out their songs as they marched up and down the valleys, amazing and deafening us all. Their instruments were gazookas, with an occasional drum. Gazookas; small tin zeppelins through which you hummed the tune as loudly as possible. Each band was done up in the uniform of some remote character never before seen in Meadow Prospect; Foreign Legionnaires, Chinamen, Carabinieri, Grenadiers, Gauchos, or what we thought these performers looked like. There was even one group of lads living up on the cold slopes of Mynydd Coch who did themselves up as Eskimos, but they were liquidated because even Mathew Sewell the Sotto, our leading maestro and musical adviser, couldn't think up a suitable theme song for boys dressed as delegates from the Arctic.

And with the bands came the fierce disputes inseparable from any attempt to promote a little beauty on this planet, the too-hasty crowding of chilled men around its small precious flame. The thinkers of Meadow Prospect, a small and anxious fringe, gathered in the Discussion Group at the Library and Institute to consider this new marvel. I can see the room now and hear their voices. Gomer Gough, the chairman, broad, wise, enduring and tolerant as our own scarred hillsides, sitting at his table beneath two pictures: a photograph of Keir Hardie and an impression, done in charcoal and a brooding spirit, of the betrayal and death of Llewelyn the Last. Then there was my uncle, Edwin Pugh, called Pugh the Pang for his way of wincing at every mention of the bruises sustained by our species in the cause of being so special. Then there was Milton Nicholas...

It was on a Tuesday evening that Milton took my Uncle Edwin and me down to an emergency meeting of the Discussion Group.

(A rustle of bodies and a slough of voices is heard. Courtroom scene .)

MILTON: Here, Edwin, and you, Iolo, here in the second row.

EDWIN: Stop pulling at me, Milton. Why so far down?

MILTON: This is the place to catch Gomer Gough's eye for a quick question.

EDWIN: What is this crisis, anyway? Show me the agenda, boy. I don't want to be mixed up in anything frivolous.

MILTON: You know me, Edwin. Always earnest. Uriah Smayle has prepared a very bitter report on the carnivals and bands. Uriah reckons the bands are spreading a mood of pagan laxity among the people and he's out to stop it. I've heard you put up some

	very good lines of argument against Uriah in the past, so just tell your mind to gird up its loins and prepare for its sternest fight.
EDWIN:	He's a very restrictive element, that Smayle. Any stirring on the face of life and he faints.
MILTON:	He's dead against delight.
EDWIN:	All right, boy. I'll do what I can. Oh, this is a fine gathering, a room full of people, keen, with their minds out like swords to carve their names on the truth.
MILTON:	If that article ever gets as far as this on its travels.
EDWIN:	Hullo, Uriah.
URIAH:	Good evening.
EDWIN:	You're looking very grey and tense tonight, boy. What new terror is gnawing at you now? If life's a rat, you're the cheese, boy.
MILTON:	Well put. I've always said that if anybody's got the gift of laying words on like a poultice, it's Edwin Pugh.
URIAH:	Mock on, Edwin. But some of my statements tonight are going to shake you rodneys.
EDWIN:	Good. Set the wind among our branches, and we'll make you a bonus of all the acorns that fall.
URIAH:	Who's the chairman here? I've got a meeting of the Young Men's Guild at eight o'clock and it'll be a real relief to have a headful of their quiet piety after the clatter of this unbelieving brood.
GOMER:	I'm in the chair, Mr Smayle, and I don't rush things. This Discussion Group is out to examine the nature of mankind and the destination of this clinker the earth; big themes, Mr Smayle, and we favour a cautious approach. We try not to be hysterical about them, and the best thing you can do is set a dish of leek soup in front of your paler fears.
URIAH:	Stop putting yourself to sleep, Gomer, and get on with it.
GOMER:	(*testily*) All right. Brothers, at this extraordinary meeting of the Discussion Group we are to hear a special statement from Brother Smayle. He thinks the

47

epidemic of carnivals is a menace and likely to put morals through the mincer. And he says that we, as serious thinkers, ought to do something about it.

EDWIN: Mr Chairman, ask Smayle to tighten his washers and define this mincer. Tell him, too, that there has never been any period when the morals of mankind, through fear, poverty and ignorance, have not been well minced and ready for the pastry-case.

GOMER: Begging your pardon, Edwin, just keep it simmering on the hob, if you don't mind, until Uriah has had his canter. Carry on, Mr Smayle.

URIAH: Mr Chairman. Since these bands came, decency has gone to the dogs. There is something about the sound of a drum that makes the average voter as brazen as a gong. The girls go up in droves to the hillsides where the bands practise; and there is some quality about these gazookas that makes the bandsmen so daring and thoughtless you've got to dig if you want to find modesty any more. And as for the costumes worn by some of these turn-outs they make me blink. I am thinking particularly of the band led by that Powderhall runner there, Cynlais Coleman the Comet, who is sitting in the third row looking very blank and innocent but no doubt full of mischief.

CYNLAIS: Who, me?

URIAH: Yes, you. I've always known Cynlais to be as dull as a bat. How does he come to be playing the cuckoo in this nest of thinkers, Gomer? What sinister new alliance is this, boy?

GOMER: Keep personalities out of this, Mr Smayle.

URIAH: Do you mind if I ask Cynlais a few questions about his band? Mr Ephraim Humphries, the ironmonger, has been requested by some of us to serve as moral adviser at large to all the carnival committees of the area, and he wants me to prepare a special case-book on Cynlais.

GOMER: Do you mind being questioned, Cyn?

CYNLAIS: Oh no. You know me, Gomer. Very frank, and always keen to help voters like Mr Smayle who are out to keep life scoured and fresh to the smell.

URIAH: Tell me, Cynlais, my boy. I have now watched you in

three carnivals and each time you've put me down for the count with worry and shock. Let me explain why, Mr Chairman. He marches at the head of a hundred young elements, all of them half-naked, with little more than the legal minimum covered over with bits of old sheet, and Cynlais himself working up a colossal gleam of frenzy in his eye. He does a short sprint at the Powderhall speed and then returns to the head of his retinue looking as if he'd just gone off the hinge that very morning. Cynlais is no better dressed than his followers. His bits of sheet are thicker and whiter but they hang even looser about the body. He also has a way, when on the march, of giving his body a violent jerk which makes him look even more demented. This is popular among the thoughtless, and I have heard terrible shrieks of approval from some who are always present at these morally loose-limbed events. But I warn Cynlais that one day he will grossly overdo these pagan leaps and find his feet a good yard to the north of his loincloth and a frost on his torso that will finish him for such events as the Powderhall Dash. His band also plays "Colonel Bogey", an ominous tune even when played by the Meadow Prospect Silver Jubilee Band in full regalia. But Coleman's boys play it at slow march tempo as if to squeeze the last drop of significance out of it. Now tell me, Coleman, what's the meaning of all this? What lies behind these antics? What are you supposed to be?

CYNLAIS: Dervishes.

URIAH: Dervishes? What are they?

CYNLAIS: A kind of fanatic. We got the idea from Edwin Pugh the Pang here. When we told him that we were very short of fabric for our costumes and that we'd got no objection to going round looking shameless, out he came with this suggestion that we should put on a crazed, bare, prophetic look, as if we had just come in from the desert with an old sunstroke and a fresh revelation.

URIAH: (*horrified*) You've been the tool of some terrible plotters, Cynlais. And is that leap to show that you

49

are shaking the sand out of your sash?

CYNLAIS: Oh no. I'm supposed to be the leader of these Dervishes, the Mad Mahdi. I got a lot of information about him from Jedediah Knight the Light.

JEDEDIAH: True, but I told him that the Mahdi would never have advanced against the Empire playing so daring a tune with so little on.

GOMER: What do you say to these charges, Cynlais?

CYNLAIS: Fair enough, Gomer. When we get some money for new costumes we'll come out of the Middle East at a quick trot.

GOMER: Any more, Brother Smayle?

URIAH: A lot more. I have a pint of gall on my mind about that band organised by Georgie Young, but that will have to wait. Good night.

ALL: Good night, Mr Smayle.

MILTON: Come on, Edwin. Let's go and have some tea and beef extract at Paolo's.

(sounds fade)

NARRATOR: Later that night, at Paolo Tasso's Coffee Tavern, my Uncle Edwin looked sad and fretful. Over a glass of scalding burdock he admitted that he'd been thinking a lot about what Uriah had said. He made it clear to us that he was in no way siding with Uriah Smayle. The pageantry of life had long passed us by in Meadow Prospect and he was glad of the colour and variety brought into our streets by the costumes worn by some of the boys. It would help us, he said to recover from the sharp clip behind the ear dealt us by the Industrial Revolution. But all the same he claimed that he and his friends had been holding the sponge for thought and uplift for years and it had been cold, lonely work. Now with all these drum beats and marching songs the place could well become a mental boneyard overnight.

But for most of us a tide of delight flowed in with the carnivals. At first we had two bands in Meadow Prospect: Cynlais Coleman's and the Boys from Dixie. The Boys from Dixie wore black suits and we never got to know where voters who had so little surplus to buy bottles ever got the cork from to make themselves look so dark. They were good marchers, though, and it was impressive to see these 120 jet black pillars moving down the street in perfect formation playing "Swanee".

There were some who said it was typical of a gloomy place like Meadow Prospect that it should have one band walking about in no tint save sable and looking like an instalment of eternal night, while another, Cynlais Coleman's, left you wondering whether to give it a good clap or a strong strait-jacket. At marching, the Boys from Dixie could not be beaten. Their driller was a cantankerous and aged imperialist called George Young the Further Flung, a solitary and chronic dissenter from Meadow Prospect's general radicalism. He had fought in several of our African wars and Uncle Edwin said it gave Georgie his youth back to have this phalanx of darkened elements wheeling and turning every whipstitch at his shout of command.

Most bands went in for vivid colours, though there was often far too little coloured fabric to go around. If any voter had any showy stuff at home he was well advised to sit tight on the box, or the envoy of some band would soon be trundling off with every stitch of it to succour some colleague who had been losing points by turning out a few inches short in the leg or deficient in one sleeve. We urged Georgie that the Boys from Dixie should brighten themselves up a little, with a yellow sash or even a scarlet fez, a tight fitting and easily made article which gave a very dashing look to the Tredomen Janissaries, a Turkish body. But Georgie was obdurate. His phobias were down in a lush meadow and grazing hard. It was black from tip to toe, or nothing, he said. However, he relented somewhat when he formed the first women's band. These were a broad-bodied, vigorous crew, strong on charabanc outings that finished on a note of blazing revelry with these elements drinking direct from the petrol tank. Their band had uniforms made roughly of the colour and pattern of the national flag, and their tune was "Rule Britannia". They began well every time they turned out, but they were invariably driven off key by their shyer members, who couldn't keep their minds on the score of "Rule Britannia" while their Union Jacks kept slipping with the convulsive movements of the march. They had even called in Mathew Sewell the Sotto as musical adviser and Mathew had given them a grounding in solfa and self-confidence. But they went as out of tune as ever. Nevertheless, both Georgie Young's Bands had a smartness that completely eclipsed Cynlais Coleman's bedraggled covey in their flapping sheets. So it was decided by the group which met at Tasso's that the time had come to arrange a new deal for the Dervishes. We left it to Mathew Sewell to put the matter to Cynlais.

(*Fade in the hissing of a tea-urn and a rattle of cups. Tasso's Coffee House.*)

MATHEW: So you see, Cynlais, there are no two twos about it, you've got to put a stop to this business of going about half-nude. It's out of place in such a division as this. I speak as an artist and without malice, but it's about time you and the boys dressed in something a bit more tasteful. Something soft and sensuous, that's what we want.

CYNLAIS: I say to you, Mathew, what I said to Smayle. Get us the costumes and we'll be as soft and sensuous as whipped cream.

MATHEW: That's the spirit. Think it over now, and when you're fitted out consult me about the music and I'll prescribe some tune with a lullaby flavour that you can march to. I've got to go now. Bona notte, Signor Tasso.

ALL: So long, Mathew.

CYNLAIS: (*admiringly*) Did you hear that? Oh, he's so smooth and operatic, that Mathew Sewell the Sotto. A treat. Don't you like to have Sewell come out with these little bits of Italian, Tasso?

TASSO: It is true, Cynlais. More than once Signor Sewell the Sotto has eased the burden of my old longing for Lugano.

GOMER: Now, let's get down to this. We've got to fit Cynlais up with a band that will make a contribution to

52

beauty and keep Uriah Smayle out of the Cottage Hospital. We can't leave the field undisputed to Georgie Young and his Boer War fancies. Have you got any money Cynlais?

CYNLAIS: (*bemused*) Money? Money?

GOMER: Forget that I asked. But I think it's a shame that a boy like you who made so much at the coalface and at professional running should now be whittled down to a loincloth for the summer and a double-breasted waistcoat for the winter. Come over here, Milton Nicholas. You're looking very nimble-witted since you got that job in the gas works. How do you think Cynlais Coleman could get hold of some money to deck his band out in something very special? I mean some way that won't have Cynlais playing his last tune through the bars of the County Gaol.

MILTON: Well, he's known as Coleman the Comet, isn't he? Let him find somebody who wants to hire a fast runner.

GOMER: In this area at the moment, Milton, even an antelope would have to make Welsh cakes and mint toffee on the side to make both ends meet. Be practical, boy.

MILTON: I heard today that a group of sporting elements in Trecelyn with a definite bias against serious thought are going to stage a professional sprint with big cash prizes. Comes off in three weeks.

TEILO DEW: Don't forget that Cynlais is getting on a bit, for this high-class running, anyway. I've heard him wheeze a bit on the sharper slopes.

CYNLAIS: Trust Teilo Dew the Doom to chip in with an item like that. Whenever Teilo talks to you he's peering at you from between his two old friends, Change and Decay. In three weeks I could be at my best and if you boys could take up a few collections to lay bets on me we'd have a treasury.

EDWIN: That's a very backward habit, gambling.

GOMER: Remind me to hire a small grave for the scruples of Edwin Pugh. Right. That's how we'll raise the cash. Off to bed with you now, Cynlais. You've got to be as fit as a fiddle for the supreme test. No more staying up till twelve and drinking hot cordial in Tasso's.

(*sounds fade*)

NARRATOR: We all joined in the task of helping Cynlais regain his old tremendous speed. We got him training every night up on the waun. Sometimes he was like a stag and our only trouble was to keep up with him to give him tips and instructions, and fit his neck back on when he went flying over molehills. At first he was a bit stiff around the edges owing to a touch of rheumatism from standing in too many High Street breezes in the role of dervish. Milton Nicholas got some dabs of wheel-grease from the gasworks, and my uncle Edwin Pugh, whose sympathy of soul made his fingers just the right thing for slow massage, rubbed this stuff into Cynlais until both he and Edwin got so supple they had to be held upright for minutes on end. We looked after Cynlais' nourishment too, for his diet had been scraggy for the last few months. Teilo Dew approached that very sullen farmer Nathan Wilkins up on the top of the hill we called Merlin's Brow, and asked him for some goat milk, but Nathan said not on your life, so Teilo bypassed Nathan and approached the goat direct, and in no time we had Cynlais growing stronger daily. But there was still something jerky and unpredictable about some of his movements. So Gomer Gough and Uncle Edwin decided to consult their friend Willie Silcox. Now Willie was often called Silcox the Psyche because he had read every book on psychology in the Library and Institute and was the greatest tracker in our Valley of those nameless beasts that roam the inward jungles. A week before the race at Trecelyn we met Willie Silcox at Tasso's.

TASSO: One coffee, Mr Gough.

GOMER: Thanks Tasso. Oh there you are, Willie. Glad you were able to come, boy.

WILLIE: Hullo, Gomer. What mental stoppage have you got for me to disperse now?

GOMER: I'm all right. My pipes were never more open. It's Cynlais Coleman I'm worried about.

WILLIE: Look, Gomer. To prescribe a pill for the mentally ill, the patient must have a mind. That's in the rule book. Coleman mentally is still unborn. What makings of a mind he might still have had he dropped into a bin years ago by outrunning the wind, and setting up as a great lover in the area that favours a slow humility in the affairs of the heart.

GOMER: Don't quibble, Willie. Cynlais isn't running as well as he should and we want the cure.

WILLIE: All right. Take me to where I can see him, and if Sigmund Freud can possibly crawl into Cynlais' furthest cranny I'll give you a report.

(Sounds fade down and then fade up. We hear cries of "Come on, Cynlais", "Let's have you, Coleman", "Don't look around, boy". Then sounds of Cynlais gasping painfully as he finishes his sprint.)

EDWIN: Well run, Cynlais.

MILTON: Put your head between your legs and squeeze hard, Cynlais boy. That'll cool you off.

GOMER: Well, Willie? What's your diagnosis?

WILLIE: Easy. D'you notice the way he seems to pause sometimes in his running and look back? That's a habit he got into while acting as the Mad Mahdi. All fanatics are persecution maniacs and Cynlais has now got into the way of looking over his shoulder even in the middle of the waun where his shoulder is about the only thing in sight. And again, that band of Cynlais' contains some torpid boys, and Cynlais is so fleet he has to keep turning around to make sure that he and they are still in the same town. But Coleman's real trouble is love.

GOMER: Love?

WILLIE: Love.

GOMER: But Cynlais told me he was no longer worried about this impulse.

WILLIE: I've only got to look at a man and I can sniff the urge to love and be loved as a lion does water, however deep and quiet it flows. For months Cynlais has been hopelessly in love with Moira Hallam.

GOMER: Moira Hallam? That dark, blazing-eyed girl from Sebastopol Street?

WILLIE: That's the one. The thoughts that girl inspires in a single day would fill a whole shelf in the Institute and you'd need a strong binding to keep them in the case.

GOMER: And she's turned Cynlais down?

WILLIE: She looks at him with disgust and treats him with contempt.

GOMER: But wouldn't this make Cynlais run even better, to show off?

WILLIE: You don't know, Gomer, what a cantankerous article the mind is. Even as he runs Cynlais looks down at the fine big chest beneath his singlet and becomes aware of his frustrated passions. It's a wall, a cruel blank wall. His heart breaks its nose against it. His limbs wince and they lose pace.

GOMER: Willie, I can never listen to you without feeling that you put a new and terrible complexion on this planet.

WILLIE: Anything to oblige.

GOMER: Well, thank you, Willie, for your report.

(Lights fade. Fade up again to street. Street noises.)

EDWIN: *(fading in)* Where to now, Gomer?

GOMER: Moira Hallam's.

EDWIN: What for?

GOMER: To talk her out of this nonsense of frustrating and slowing down Cynlais Coleman the Comet. According to Willie Silcox, between being a dervish and a disappointed lover it's a wonder Cynlais can walk, let alone run.

EDWIN: But why bring me? I'm not interested in Cynlais and I don't know this Miss Hallam.

GOMER: I'm bringing you along for the same reason that you're called Edwin Pugh the Pang. You are so full of pity the sight and sound of you would bring tears to the eyes of Nathan Wilkins' goat. You can play on the feelings of this Moira. Don't be surprised if I pass you off as Cynlais Coleman's father and explain that you took up thinking instead of sprinting. Here we are.

(He knocks and door opens.)

GOMER: Oh, good evening to you, Mrs Hallam.

MRS H.:   What do you two want? If you are after my husband to join the Discussion Group again, save your wind. The last time he went the topic was hanging and he had the migraine for a week.

GOMER: No. It's about your daughter Moira.

MRS H.:   All day long there's a knock at the door and it's the same old tale. Moira, Moira, Moira. But you are the two oldest performers to turn up so far. Why don't you two boys stick to debating?

EDWIN: Here am I, my senses in this field out for the count since 1913, and I have to stand here and listen to this prattle.

GOMER: Wait, Edwin. We are here, Mrs Hallam, on behalf of that fine runner, Cynlais Coleman.

MRS H.:   What's he running for? Whenever my husband runs he gets the migraine.

GOMER: Cynlais loves your daughter. *(a slight groan from Edwin)* He's losing sleep and health over her. We were wondering if you...

MRS H.:   Not a hope. Moira was in the Trecelyn Amateur Operatics last winter. They did Carmen and now she's daft about that young baritone, Moelwyn Cox, who took the part of the toreador. You ought to see his velvet coat and his satin breeches. So tight, so shiny. A picture.

EDWIN: *(softly)* Gomer, could I make a short statement here that will cover both love and bullfighting?

GOMER: *(quietly)* No. Sebastopol Street is no place to be discussing ethics. You know that, boy. *(louder and in the most bedside of manners)* Mrs Hallam, how is your husband's migraine now?

MRS H.:   Twice a week he wears a brown paper turban soaked in vinegar and it's like having chips in the house. A treat.

GOMER: Will you put in a word with Moira for Cynlais Coleman?

MRS H.:   I'll mention it. But only because you asked about the migraine. Sympathy is what matters. But I can tell you now, Moira's daft about Moelwyn Cox.
            (sounds fade)

NARRATOR: On the day of the sports we went as a body to Trecelyn to watch Cynlais run. There was a large crowd and the field was fine, well-flagged and happy. Cynlais was put on edge by having Uncle Edwin sidle up to him on the pavement and try to give him a little supplementary massage, and he broke away from us as we entered the field.

(*some bustling crowd noises*)

EDWIN: How do you think Cynlais is feeling, Gomer?

GOMER: Fine, Edwin. Can't you see he looks fine?

EDWIN: Frankly, I think there is a very lax, bemused look about him. He doesn't seem too solid on his pins to me. Milton Nicholas says he's been overtrained and worn out by dodging those mole-hills up on the waun while travelling faster than light. They've certainly enjoyed full employment, those moles up on the waun.

GOMER: Don't go saying things like that to Cynlais. The race is due in twenty minutes and I don't want to upset him. I told him Mrs Hallam was going to do all she could for him. That'll buck Cynlais up a bit. But I'm taking no chances. You know how upset he was last Monday.

EDWIN: Last Monday?

GOMER: Yes. Cynlais' band and the Boys from Dixie went to the carnival at Tregysgod, and Georgie didn't finish last because Cynlais was there before him. It's enough to drive Mathew Sewell the Sotto off his head-notes. Cynlais' band lost points for obscurity and brazen indecency so the judges said, and Georgie's platoon was denounced as too sombre and austere. It was a terrible day for Meadow Prospect. So I went to Kitchener Caney.

EDWIN: (*astonished*) Caney the Cure, the Herbs?

GOMER: That's him. Compared with Caney, Merlin was a learner. He gave me a herbal concoction for Cynlais called "soul-balm" which makes the heart serene and oblivious.

EDWIN: Cynlais is certainly oblivious. Look at him over there now. He looks as dull as a bat.

GOMER: I got Tasso to slip the balm in Cynlais' last cocoa and for the next few hours his mind will be sunlit. Here he is now. Just look at him, Edwin. I've seen taller men, wiser men, but fitter and faster, never.

CYNLAIS: (*plaintively*) I've just seen Moira over there by that flag pole. Could I nip over and have a chat with her, Gomer?

GOMER: Not before the race. I see some very keen looking athletes about here. You'll have to stay calm as a rock to bring the prize home. Come back here, you jay... Oh, dammo!

(*Background of crowd noises gets slightly louder.*)

CYNLAIS: Hullo, Moira. Oh, it's good to see you again after so long.

MOIRA: (*in wrath*) Don't talk to me, Cynlais Coleman. Sending those two jokers to my front door to get around my mother, indeed. What kind of serpent are you developing into, Cynlais?

CYNLAIS: They didn't tell me they were going, honest. Gomer and Edwin were working off their own bats and you know what a subtle pair they are. Can I see you tonight, Moira?

MOIRA: Not tonight or ever. I'm meeting Moelwyn Cox in front of the Gaiety at seven. Plush seats, back row, one and three, made to measure. Have you ever seen Moelwyn in his bullfighter's uniform? After that you'll always look very colourless to me, Cynlais. Has your heart ever been in the orange groves of Seville?

CYNLAIS: (*humbly*) Never. You know that, Moira. The furthest I've been is that bus trip to Tintern with the Buffs.

(*MOIRA gives a loud contemptuous laugh. Crowd background noises briefly.*)

GOMER: (*fading in*) You hear that? The sight of Moelwyn's satin trousers has even got her laughing like that Carmen. (*calling*) Come on, Cynlais, forget about Seville and get your knicks on.

CYNLAIS: I can't, Gomer, not after that. I haven't got the heart. Not after that.

GOMER: Come on. Think of the prize money.

EDWIN: Aye, and the stinging way those carnival judges spoke to you last Monday. One of them said that as soon as he could arrange the fare to Africa the whole pack of you would be on the boat addressed to the jungle.

GOMER: Look over there. There's that big auctioneer, Erasmus John the Going Gone, wearing a cloth hat and shaking his gun to show he's the starter.

EDWIN: He's a very cunning boy, that Erasmus John, and I hear he's got a favourite of his own competing here today. See that he keeps his auctioneering slogans out of the formula used for starting the race.

CYNLAIS: All right then. For your sake, that's all. That Moira... just one look from her and she scoops the heart right out of me, leaving not even the wish to whistle.

GOMER &
EDWIN: Good luck, Cyn.

           (*Crowd noises up.*)

EDWIN: That soul balm is wearing off.

GOMER: Caney should have doubled the dose but he said it's a tricky mixture.

EDWIN: Isn't that Caney over there now? He's waving at you, Gomer.

           (*Crowd noises.*)

GOMER: What is it, Mr Caney?

CANEY: That stuff I gave you for Coleman. It wasn't the soul balm after all. My wife made a mistake with the gummed labels. She's a fine woman but the taste of gum makes her giddy. That was some very funny stuff that Coleman actually took.

GOMER: (*very soberly*) Cynlais is out there, Mr Caney, faced with the hardest race of his life. His girl has just spurned him and given him a laugh that for sheer contempt and coldness would freeze a seal. And now you tell me, very jocose, that he has some sinister herb under his belt as well. What is it?

CANEY: A stirring draught for lazy kidneys.

GOMER: How will it take him?

CANEY: It varies. Sometimes when it begins its healing work there is a flash of discomfort, even pain, and I have known surprised clients come back to me hopping.

GOMER: What do you mean, hopping? Let's have the truth, Caney.

CANEY: One leg seems to leave the ground as if trying to kick the kidneys into a brighter life.

GOMER & EDWIN: (*very softly*) Duw, Duw, Duw!

(*The starter's gun goes off. Cheers from the crowd. Fade slowly out. Then fade in sounds of Tasso's Coffee Tavern.*)

TASSO: Accept this rum and butter toffee, Mr Gough. It will sweeten your mood... And then, when the race started, what befell Mr Coleman?

GOMER: For five seconds he went so fast everybody thought he had left by way of the starter's gun. Didn't he, Edwin?

EDWIN: Fact. He seemed to be in flight from all the world's heartbreak and shame.

GOMER: Then Caney's Cure struck. Have you, Tasso, ever seen a man trying to finish a hundred and twenty yard dash on one leg?

TASSO: Not on one leg. Always, in Italy, both the legs are used.

GOMER: It's a terrible sight. Cynlais gave some fine hops. On that form I'd enter him any day against a team of storks, but against those other boys he was yards behind, with Erasmus John the Going Gone running alongside him and asking sarcastically if Cynlais would like the stewards to do something about the leg he still had on the ground.

TASSO: Where's Cynlais now?

GOMER: In bed, trying to explain about Caney, his wife and the gum on the labels to his kidneys, which are frankly worried.

EDWIN: It was that Moira Hallam that did it. Compared with this business of love the Goodwin Sands are a meadow. I'd like to make her sorry for the way she flicks acid over the tender hearts of boys like Cynlais.

(*sounds fade*)

NARRATOR: It was Milton Nicholas who held up the torch that showed us and Cynlais the path to cash and new costumes. He attended a meeting at which Ephraim Humphries the ironmonger gave a report of his work as moral adviser to the carnival committees. Ephraim was very comfortably off and had a great weakness for budgerigars of which he had a front room full. His cordial urges had been cooled years since by handling cold metal in a shop full of draughts, and he really didn't see why the average human should want to eat, wander, or love more than the average budgerigar.

(*fade in Tasso's*)

MILTON: Most of what Ephraim said was about his visit last week to the carnival at Tregysgod, and if he ever gets the sight of Cynlais and his boys out of his mind most of his mind will go with it. He's convinced now that Coleman is to morals what Guy Fawkes was to Parliament, a one and fourpenny banger waiting for November. That gave me an idea of how we might get Humphries to help us.

EDWIN: Put a light to Coleman's fuse and shock Humphries out of his wits, you mean?

MILTON: No, no, no!

GOMER: But isn't Humphries dead against the bands?

MILTON: Not altogether. He says that if they take the people's minds off class rancour, agnosticism, and the Sankey Award, he's for them. So why not approach him and explain that Cynlais and his boys wouldn't be nearly as repulsive if they had decent costumes? Then tap him for some cash. He must have a soft side to his nature or he wouldn't keep all those birds in his front room.

GOMER: From what I know of Humphries he probably keeps them to test for gas. When the birds die Humphries changes the potted shrubs. He was the grumpiest boy I ever met behind a counter. He was the one ironmonger who sold paraffin that put out the match. But let's go and see him anyway... (*fading*)

(*A knock from outside the front door.*)

MRS
HUMPHRIES:(*startled*) There are four men at the front door, Ephraim.

EPHRAIM: Who are they?

MRS H.: Can't tell for sure. There's a shady look about them. I told you you should never have accepted that invitation to go to the Carnival as adviser on morals. These are probably some louts you offended with your straight talk. Very likely a group sent here by Cynlais Coleman the leading dervish, to do you some mischief. (*in a strained, schoolmarmy tone*) Do you know that the very word assassin comes from the Middle East where Coleman has his spiritual home? Let's bar the doors.

EPHRAIM: Stop being such a teacher, Harriet, and throw the bolts back.

(*The door is opened.*)

EPHRAIM: What is it?

GOMER: We'd like a word with you, Mr Humphries.

EPHRAIM: Come on into the front room.

(*Front room door is opened and the chirping of many budgerigars is heard.*)

MILTON: Oh, nice birds.

EPHRAIM: Would that man were more like them. So bright, so brief, so harmless, and no sorrow in their singing.

MILTON: You're right, boy. Give us the same seed and the same sure accommodation, and we'd be there.

EPHRAIM: Your business, gentlemen?

GOMER: We want to thank you for the fine stand you made at Tregysgod and the remarks you made about Cynlais Coleman's band. We think the same. We are collecting among ourselves to fit Coleman and his men up in such a way that they will not cause the very hillsides to blush as they do now. Could you help us?

EPHRAIM: As a matter of fact I could and will. I am vice-president of a committee which is gathering funds to supply wholesome entertainments for the valley folk. I will leave it to you men to think out an alternative costume for this buffoon and you may leave the bill, within reason, to me. Nothing too royal or lavish, of course.

GOMER: Of course. By the way, Mr Humphries, have you seen Georgie Young's Women's band, the Britannias?

EPHRAIM: I'm afraid I haven't. They were not competing at Tregysgod.

GOMER: You take a good look at them. First you'll lose what's left of your hair, then you'll start another fund to have Young hung and the bandswomen treated with balsam of missionary. Thank you and goodnight.

EPHRAIM: Goodnight. I'm surprised to find you men so helpful, such watch-dogs in the cause of wholesomeness.

MILTON: Just let us catch a whiff of that unwholesomeness, Mr Humphries, then watch us bark and bite.

(*fade in CYNLAIS' bedroom*)

NARRATOR: Gomer and his companions went straight to the house of Cynlais. Cynlais' mother showed them into the bedroom where Cynlais was reassembling the fragments of himself after the two disasters. Mrs Coleman explained that she had given him a Bible to read the Book of Job and keep his troubles in proportion, but Cynlais kept flicking the pages and referring to Moira Hallam as Delilah.

GOMER: (*fading in*) Hullo Cynlais. Big news. We've got the money for the new costumes. What fancies have you got on this subject and for goodness' sake keep inside Europe this time because we've got enough to cover you all from top to bottom.

EDWIN: Come on, Cynlais. Buck up, boy, and stop looking so shattered. This isn't the end of the world. It's only the first crack.

CYNLAIS: I keep thinking of what Moira told me. She said: "Has your heart ever been in the orange groves of Seville?"

GOMER: You can't possibly have a band of marching oranges, Cynlais. You can be too subtle in these matters. Look what happened to those Eskimos? You remember their manoeuvre of shuddering at the end of every blast from the gazookas to show extreme cold? No one ever understood it.

CYNLAIS: I don't mean oranges. I mean bullfighters, with me dressed up in the front as an even better bullfighter than Moelwyn Cox.

GOMER: Oh, that's a fine idea. Come over to Tasso's tonight and we'll talk it over. Do you think you can manage it?

(fade in hiss of urn, rattle of cups, Tasso's)

WILLIE: What do you say this new band will be called?

CYNLAIS: The Meadow Prospect Toreadors, Willie.

WILLIE: Very nice, very exotic. It will help to show what little is left of our traditional earnestness to the back gate. But good luck to you. It will bring the voters an illusion of the sun and a strong smell of marmalade, both much needed.

GOMER: What would be the best tune for these boys, Mathew?

MATHEW: Something Spanish, of course.

CYNLAIS: Try to make it something operatic. I want to show that Moira that I'm as cultured as Moelwyn Cox. What about the "Toreador" song?

MATHEW: Just sing it over.

(all present give a brisk rendering of the "Toreador" song)

MATHEW: A little bit too complicated to play on the march. We want something a bit witless, something everybody'll know.

GOMER: What about "I'm One of the Nuts from Barcelona"?

EDWIN: What's nutting got to do with bullfighting? Let's lift the tone of these carnivals. I'm for the operatic tune.

GOMER: Don't make difficulties, Edwin.

WILLIE: There's another thing too. Do you still want Cynlais to win the esteem of that Moira Hallam?

GOMER: Oh definitely. That would give Cynlais that extra bit of sparkle. What are you hinting at, Silcox?

WILLIE: This girl has got some sort of Spanish complex. What better than to have her dressed up as Carmen in front of the band?

GOMER: Oh, that's a notion. Paolo, give Silcox another raspberry cordial. He's the Livingstone in our mental

Congo. *(fading)*

(Fade in drum beats and a soft distant gazooking of "I'm One of the Nuts".)

GOMER: Well, tomorrow's the day, the Trecelyn Competitive Carnival.

TASSO: What are the prospects, Mr Gough?

GOMER: Never better. You should see Cynlais. Side-boards down to the chin, little moustache, a black hat like Valentino, his every glance a search for a bull. It took him a bit to remember that he was no longer the Mad Mahdi and to stop looking demented, but he's fine now.

TASSO: And the signorina Hallam?

GOMER: Don't talk! Carmen in the flesh. Red shawl and we've collected so many combs to stick in her hair there isn't a kempt head on our side of Meadow. We've had to keep her dark so far because we don't want Ephraim Humphries to see her and start accusing her of goading the pure to ruin. Ephraim paid for most of the costumes and on questions of decorum he's touchier than a boil.

TASSO: And how, Mr Sewell, are the ladies Britannias?

MATHEW: *(giving a deep groan)* Slip another beef-cube in my cup, Paolo, while I tell you of my troubles with these women. I've got five members of my madrigal group to march on each side of them keeping them to a pitch but I don't know how the judge will take to that tactic. We'll have to have the madrigal singers edging in on them from time to time as if they were members of the public. But my biggest trouble now is that drummer, Olga Rowe. She's been driven hysterical by the new pattern of vibrations set up in her by the drumming and now she gets a laughing fit every time she touches the pig skin. Is Willie Silcox the Psyche here? Oh, ay. Tell me, Silcox, what psychological approach would you recommend for a woman in such a fix as this Olga Rowe?

WILLIE: I don't know. Freud is silent about women being driven mad by their own drumming.

MATHEW: Never mind though. Of one thing we can all be

certain. Tomorrow will be Cynlais Coleman's day. *(fading)*

NARRATOR: But it was not to be. The prize was not to be ours. It was a day of oven heat. We all travelled on foot to Trecelyn. By noon the cork stain on Georgie Young's Boys from Dixie was already streaked into a dramatic leopard pattern. The Britannias were thrown into confusion by Olga Rowe tickling herself into the loudest laughing fit of this century and she was last seen drumming away at forty miles an hour down a side street. By the time we reached Trecelyn the last petal had dropped from the red rose that Moira Hallam held in her mouth but she kept chewing at the bare stem and made up for the lack of petals by making more challenging the fine swing of her body beneath the lovely shawl. But it was a new body, the Aberclydach Sheiks, who did for us in the end. A few furlongs outside Trecelyn one of our scouts ran back to give us a report.

(fade up "Barcelona" and maintain behind speech)

SCOUT: Gomer, Gomer! I've just seen the Sheiks from Aberclydach and you've got a surprise coming.

GOMER: What's up, Onllwyn?

SCOUT: I've just seen them. They're wearing grey veils and dressed like they think Arabs dress in Aberclydach. They're playing some slow dreamy tune about Araby and swaying from side to side with the music, looking and acting as slinky as you please and promoting a mood of sensuous excitement among the voters.

GOMER: Come on, boy. Let's run ahead and see these Sheiks. I don't like the sound of this. Ephraim Humphries is one of the judges. He's going to like the notion of those veils because a wholly concealed humanity would be welcome to Ephraim.

SCOUT: No doubt indeed.

GOMER: And when he takes a look at Moira with that stem in her mouth and the shapes she's making, he'll think she swallowed the petals of that rose herself to keep fresh for some new round of sinning. Come on, boy.

(fade out "Barcelona", fade in crowd)

67

GOMER: Where are the judges?

VOICE: Over there in the open bay window of the Con Club.

GOMER: (*shouting up*) Mr Judges, an appeal, please. I've just seen the Aberclydach Sheiks. They are swaying like pendulums and I'm too well up in the carnival law to let these antics go unchallenged. The rules we drew up at the conference in Meadow Prospect clearly state that bandsmen should keep a military uprightness on the march, and here are these boys from Aberclydach weaving in and out like shuttlecocks in their soft robes. This is the work of perverts and not legal.

JUDGE: Stewards, remove that man. He's out to disrupt the carnival. Meadow Prospect has always been a pit of dissent. Here come the Sheiks now. Oh a fine turn-out, a fine turn-out.

(*"The Sheik of Araby" is heard being played very softly*)

NARRATOR: Gomer took one look at the Sheiks and gave up the ghost. For the Sheiks as they turned the corner in the Con Club Square had played their supreme trump. They slowed down to a crawl and out of a side street, goaded on by a cloud of shouting voters, came the Sheiks' deputy leader, Mog Williams, dressed in Arab style and mounted on an old dignified camel which he had borrowed from a menagerie that had gone bankrupt and bogged down in Aberclydach a week before. It was this animal that Olga Rowe caught a glimpse of as she was being led back into position on the square and it finished her off for good.

(*fade up "Araby" and crowd applause. Then down.*)

NARRATOR: At the carnival's end Gomer and Cynlais said we would go back over the mountain path, for the macadamed roads would be too hard to tread after the disappointments of the day. Up the mountain we went. Everything was plain because the moon was full. The path was narrow and we walked single file, women, children, Toreadors, Boys from Dixie. We reached the mountain top. We found the straight green path that leads past Llancysgod on down to Meadow Prospect. And across the mountain we

walked slowly, like a little army, most of the men
with children hanging on to their arms, the women
walking as best they could in the rear. Then they fell
quiet. We stood still, I and two or three others, and
watched them pass, listening to the curious quietness
that had fallen upon them. Far away we heard a high
crazy laugh from Cynlais Coleman, who was trying
to comfort Moira Hallam in their defeat. Some kind
of sadness seemed to have come down on us. It was
not a miserable sadness, for we could all feel some
kind of contentment enriching its dark root. It may
have been the moon making the mountain seem so
secure and serene. We were like an army that had
nothing left to cheer about or cry about, not sure if it
was advancing or retreating and not caring. We had
lost. As we watched the weird disguises, the strange,
yet utterly familiar faces, of Britannias, Matadors and
Boys from Dixie, shuffle past, we knew that the
bubble of frivolity, blown with such pathetic care,
had burst for ever and that new and colder winds of
danger would come from all the world's corners to
find us on the morrow. But for that moment we were
touched by the moon and the magic of longing. We
sensed some friendliness and forgiveness in the loved
and loving earth we walked on. For minutes the
silence must have gone on. Just the sound of many
feet swishing through the summer grass. Then
somebody started playing a gazooka. The tune he
played was one of those sweet, deep things that form
simply as the dew upon a mood like ours. It must
have been "All Through the Night" scored for a
million talking tears and a basic disbelief in the
dawn. It had all the golden softness of an age-long
hunger to be at rest. The player, distant from us now,
at the head of the long and formless procession,
played it very quietly, as if he were thinking rather
than playing. Thinking about the night, conflict,
beauty, the intricate labour of living and the dark
little dish of thinking self in which they were all
compounded. Then the others joined in and the
children began to sing.

DANNIE ABSE
The Eccentric

Dannie Abse (b.1923) was born and grew up in Cardiff. A prominent poet, he has also written fiction, memoirs and plays. His first full length play, *House of Cowards*, when produced at the Questors Theatre, London in 1960 won the Charles Henry Foyle Award for the best play produced that year outside the West End. It has been collected along with two other of his later plays in *The View from Row G* (Seren). His early one act play, *The Eccentric*, was written in 1959 and was first produced at the Mountview Theatre, London. It is a cheerful, persuasive character study of a non-conforming businessman.

CHARACTERS
Mr John Smith, a potential customer
Daniel Robinson, a student in search of a part-time job
Mr Goldstein, a tobacconist
Also a Man and a Girl and another Customer
Noises Off: It shouldn't happen to a dog. A Telephone.

> (*Scene: A rather shabby tobacconist shop. Behind a decrepit counter, stacks of shelves carry dummy cigarette cartons. In a dusty glass case some unlikely pipes are for sale. Nearby a cash register waits optimistically. There is a customer in the shop, but no one is behind the counter. The customer is a MR JOHN SMITH, whose name, by the way, matches the clothes he wears. When the curtain rises MR SMITH is shouting the name of the proprietor, MR GOLDSTEIN, who, it would seem from the script that follows, is adamantly staying in the backroom of the shop cutting up horse-meat for his dog. However, at present, MR GOLDSTEIN remains invisible.*)

SMITH: (*shouting*) Mr Goldstein! Mr Goldstein! Come out and serve me. Please, Mr Goldstein! (*to himself*) Mad. Stark raving mad. Mr Goldstein, Mr Goldstein. (*to himself*) You go into a shop, you expect to be served. That's current practice, Mr. Goldstein. (*to himself*) If this sort of thing happened all the time, where would we be? Mr Goldstein, I demand you serve me. (*to himself, angrily*) People come into this country, they want everything, they take everything, they do everybody. (*furious, he smashes his umbrella down on the counter*) Lord, now look he's bent my umbrella. Mr Goldstein! I'll take twenty cigarettes. I'll leave the money, that's what I'll do. (*MR SMITH goes behind the counter but just then DANIEL ROBINSON, a young student, enters the shop, making the bell ring as he opens the door.*)

DANIEL: Good afternoon.

SMITH: (*guiltily*) Eh? Oh, good afternoon! (*MR SMITH, as if caught red-handed, comes back in front of the counter, still without cigarettes.*)

DANIEL: From the card in the window, I see you are looking for an assistant.

SMITH: No! No! I mean I'm not Mr Goldstein!

DANIEL: I beg your pardon?

SMITH: Mr Goldstein, he's in the back there. He's the man you wish to interview. Oh, dear no, I'm not Mr Goldstein, fortunately. My name is Smith. I'm a customer. At least I want to be a customer. Mr Goldstein!

DANIEL: I don't follow you, sir. The card in the window...?

SMITH: He won't serve me. Mr Goldstein! Mr Goldstein! (*Alarmed, DANIEL backs towards the door.*) Don't go. I'll go. I don't see why you should suffer on my account. Mr Goldstein!

DANIEL: (*still alarmed*) Not at all. It doesn't really matter. I'll... er... come back another time.

SMITH: No, please. I insist. You stay. He won't see you whilst I'm in the shop. Mr...

TOGETHER: Goldstein!

DANIEL: (*apologetically*) I thought I'd give you a hand.

SMITH: For years I've lived only three doors from this shop.
             But Goldstein won't serve me. I can't think why not.
             It's most inconvenient if you happen to be a heavy
             smoker, as I am.

DANIEL: (*blankly*) Yes. Oh yes, I see.

SMITH: It's a twenty minute walk to O'Reilly's, the next
             tobacconist. But when you live three doors away it's
             patently ridiculous to have to walk twenty minutes
             there and twenty minutes back.

DANIEL: (*sympathetically*) Forty minutes.

SMITH: Exactly. Just to buy cigarettes. The buses are very
             irregular. They come three at a time with long
             intervals between each batch of three. It's very
             aggravating. I usually take a bus. Anyway, I'll go
             now, then he'll creep out and serve you. It's quite
             unjust.

DANIEL: I don't want to be served. I want a job.

SMITH: Oh, yes, I forgot. You really want to work for Mr
             Goldstein?

DANIEL: You make it sound like a prison sentence.

SMITH: I don't want to put you off. In fact, I hope you get the
             job. Then you could serve me.

DANIEL: I suppose so. I mean...

SMITH: Twenty minutes there, twenty minutes back. You
             must get the job. I'd like to help you, though, alas, a
             reference from me would hardly promote your
             interests. Still, knowing Mr Goldstein a little, I can
             give you advice. Mr Goldstein is a bit eccentric.

DANIEL: (*ironically*) Mr Goldstein is a bit eccentric!

SMITH: Quite eccentric, exactly. Why, when I first came into
             the shop his phone was ringing, and he didn't even
             answer it. (*From the back room there is the sound of a
             dog growling.*)

DANIEL: Good Lord, is that Mr Goldstein?

SMITH: No, no. For heaven's sake, that's his dog. What was I
             saying? Ah, yes. I shouldn't go at it like a bull at a
             gate. Study the man first. Humour him. Agree with
             everything he says. If you got the job it would be a
             relief to me. You wouldn't discriminate?

DANIEL: I'll buy some cigarettes, then ask for the job. Do you think that would be a good stroke?

SMITH: Hmmm. Just don't argue with him. That might have been my mistake.

DANIEL: Buying cigarettes might give me a few minutes to size up the man. His eccentricities. Is it a full-time job?

SMITH: I'm not Mr Goldstein. I can hardly tell you what's in his mind. I might add it's a more un-English mind even than O'Reilly's.

DANIEL: No, no, of course you could hardly tell me about the job. But I'm a student. I just need a part-time job to help me out a bit.

SMITH: Good luck! Bon chance, as they say. I wish you well from my heart. If you get the job I'll come in when he's away and you're serving. I hope my kind advice meets with reciprocal consideration. Tit for tat, what? Anyway, jolly good luck. Remember, agree with him. That probably was my downfall. Good-bye! Good-bye, Mr Goldstein! I'm leaving, Mr Goldstein! Oh, look, look, there go three buses. Twenty minutes there, twenty minutes back. Oh, the swine. Well, good-bye. Don't forget. Agree with the blighter. Everything he says, however outrageous, be in accord with. I hope I have the honour to encounter you behind the counter.

DANIEL: Good-bye, sir. (*MR SMITH goes out. DANIEL waits. Nothing happens. He coughs loudly. Goes to the door and opens it, making the bell ring with prolonged insistency. He shuts it and waits. Enter MR GOLDSTEIN, carrying a Flit syringe. MR GOLDSTEIN is a small kyphotic, elderly man. Unaccountably he wears a trilby hat set dead straight over his forehead. One feels he never discards his hat even in his morning bath. GOLDSTEIN pumps Flit into the air all round the shop.*)

GOLDSTEIN: Has he gone?

DANIEL: Yes.

GOLDSTEIN: That man costs me a fortune in Flit. Once a month he comes in here regular. I'll tell you something. For me, he don't exist.

73

DANIEL: You don't like him, Mr Goldstein?

GOLDSTEIN: The man's an official. Who likes an official? Eh? How do you know my name's Goldstein? Are you a spy or something?

DANIEL: Why? ...it's written outside the shop.

GOLDSTEIN: Outside the shop it's written Goldberg, not Goldstein. How come you know my name is really Goldstein? Are you a visionary or from the Government?

DANIEL: I must have made a mistake.

GOLDSTEIN. A mistake, yes. But a correct mistake. That's a very clever thing to do, Mister. With such mistakes ships were launched, wars declared, empires born, women were married, so what you want?

DANIEL: I'm sorry, Mr Gold... I'm so sorry.

GOLDSTEIN: What you want off of me?

DANIEL: Cigarettes.

GOLDSTEIN: You come in here demanding cigarettes.

DANIEL: This is a tobacconist's.

GOLDSTEIN: Does it look like a haberdasher's? That's a bad business. Fifteen years ago I owned a haberdasher's. Twenty years ago I used to deal in minerals. That was better.

DANIEL: How interesting.

GOLDSTEIN: Mmmm.

DANIEL: (*desperately*) What did you deal in? Diamonds? Gold?

GOLDSTEIN: Nah. Nah. Minerals. You know, minerals.

DANIEL: Sapphires, emeralds?

GOLDSTEIN: Minerals, I said. Sarsaparilla. Lemonade. Yes, it was better. We had hot summers then, before the H-bomb. People were thirsty. I used to sell a raspberry lemonade that looked like blood, genuine blood. Ah. So you want cigarettes. What brand? Have you a brand in mind? Capstan, perhaps?

DANIEL: No, Players.

GOLDSTEIN: Players. You want Players. How many?

DANIEL: Twenty, please.

GOLDSTEIN: Twenty? Nah, I don't have Players.

DANIEL: Well, Senior Service. Twenty.

GOLDSTEIN: They don't make 'em in twenties. (*DANIEL is taken aback. GOLDSTEIN stares at his fingernails.*) You want to go to Spain to get twenty Senior Service. They don't make 'em in twenties in this country. Where've you been livin'? You can have a hundred if you like.

DANIEL: I used to buy them regularly in twenties.

GOLDSTEIN: Not round 'ere. No, no. Old wives' tales. Fairy stories. I know my business.

DANIEL: Of course, of course. I'm no expert.

GOLDSTEIN: You're a humble man, Mr, er, ra?

DANIEL: Robinson. Daniel Robinson.

GOLDSTEIN: Robinson. Hmm. At least that's better than Smith.

DANIEL: Smith is an unexciting name. Very unexciting, don't you agree?

GOLDSTEIN: Smith, that one. He's no good. The man who was in here before. The one who wastes my Flit. The one who don't exist.

DANIEL: Oh, him.

GOLDSTEIN: His name is John Smith. Hm. What a name. If my name was Smith, at least, if I had a son, I'd have enough sense to call him Plain.

DANIEL: Plain?

GOLDSTEIN: Sure, Plain Smith. That would be something. But John Smith. Er, two a penny. Mind you, I don't say they're all like that John Smith.

DANIEL: You make him sound like poison, Mr Gold...er.

GOLDSTEIN: Not Mr Golder. Nah. You can call me Goldstein. A humble fellah like you, sure. Now what was you saying?

DANIEL: I said you think Mr Smith, the one you waste Flit on, is poison?

GOLDSTEIN: Poison! Poison! Worse. He's normal. I tell you he's normal. 'ave you seen how he dresses? A bowler. Striped black trousers. Socks the same colour.

DANIEL: Most people wear socks the same colour.

GOLDSTEIN: Nah, nah. Nah, nah. Black socks. The same colour as his trousers. He takes *The Times* every day. I know;

75

he lives three doors away. And on Sunday, what you tink? He takes the *Sunday Times*. I tell you he's a conformist. So why should I insult myself by serving him? He tinks because I've got character I'm crazy.

DANIEL: Oh, you've got character, Mr Goldstein.

GOLDSTEIN: Exactly! Have I ever said different? But the other John Smith, why he's worse. The lowest of the low.

DANIEL: The other John Smith?

GOLDSTEIN: Lower than that even. Sure, the one who keeps ringing me up. For the last week. Obscene, I tell you. He's changin' my life.

DANIEL: You get obscene telephone messages? You should let the police know.

GOLDSTEIN: It's a point of view. To me it's obscene. He don't use dirty words or anything. But he wants to buy my shop. Offers me money. One tousand, eight hundred pounds. I told him I wouldn't sell for two and seven-eighth tousand. Not even cash.

DANIEL: Well, that's not exactly obscene. I mean, you could hardly complain to the police.

GOLDSTEIN: You don't understand. Do you know who this John Smith represents? I'll tell yer. A chain of tobacconists. Uniformity that's what they stand for. Nah. But that ain't all. Every time he rings me up I get excited. I keep on thinking of the money. I could go to America. I could go to Israel. Who wants Niagara Falls?

DANIEL: It's nice to travel. I agree with you. I'd like to go round the world.

GOLDSTEIN: It's a question of integrity. Be to your own self true, says Ben Gurion.

DANIEL: I don't think it was Ben Gurion who said that.

GOLDSTEIN: Who cares who said. A detail.

DANIEL: Quite, quite.

GOLDSTEIN: But the temptation when he rings me. You don't know. I don't answer the phone no more. Hear no evil, as Ben Gurion said. (*The shop bell rings as a MAN enters. GOLDSTEIN stares above the head of the MAN at the bell on top of the door. Both DANIEL and*

76

the MAN who looks over his shoulder gaze towards the door to see what GOLDSTEIN is staring at.)

(at last) A good bell. *(nods his head several times)* A beautiful bell.

MAN: Twenty Capstan, please.

GOLDSTEIN: *(still staring at the bell)* You open the door an' a bell rings. Inventions, I tell you.

MAN: I'm sorry, but I'm in a hurry. Could I have twenty Capstan?

GOLDSTEIN: It's always been my dream to make an invention. Since I've been a little boy, something for the benefit of humankind. I told my father I wanted to be an inventor.

MAN: Twenty Capstan.

GOLDSTEIN: Boychick, he'd say, first make a livin' then you can be an inventor. Was he right, I wonder?

MAN: *(to DANIEL)* Is he deaf? Twenty Capstan!

GOLDSTEIN: Mmm? No Capstan.

MAN: Players, then.

GOLDSTEIN: I've only got them in fifties.

MAN: Only in fifties? *(looks at his watch)* Right, fifty.

GOLDSTEIN: You shouldn't be in a hurry. Heart attacks people get.

MAN: *(taking cigarettes and change).* Thank you. *(He begins to go out. The dog in the back begins to bark.)*

GOLDSTEIN: *(shouting)* Quiet Abraham!

MAN: I beg your pardon?

GOLDSTEIN: I was talking to my dog. Is it permitted? *(MAN goes out banging door hard.)* *(Nodding his head)* Speed! Malcolm Campbell! Schmalz herrings! Well, I too must move with the times.

DANIEL: Mr Goldstein...

GOLDSTEIN: Yes, I must finish cutting up the horse-meat for my dog.

DANIEL: Just a minute, please.

GOLDSTEIN: You want me?

DANIEL: *(desperately)* Gold Flake.

GOLDSTEIN: Goldstein.

DANIEL: Twenty Gold Flake, please.

GOLDSTEIN: Aw. I can only spare you ten.

DANIEL: Thank you. Thank you, very much.

GOLDSTEIN: (*suspiciously*) Is it my fault that I'm a bit low in my stocks of Gold Flake?

DANIEL: No, no. You misunderstand me. I'm very happy to have ten Gold Flake.

GOLDSTEIN: Anyway, a boy like you shouldn't smoke really.

DANIEL: Yes, yes.

GOLDSTEIN: You agree with me all the time. An' you're humble. That's very good.

DANIEL: You're quite right, I shouldn't smoke. It's deleterious to one's health.

GOLDSTEIN: Nah. That's propaganda. But it stops you growing. For why do you want to smoke? Look at me. I'm a small man. I smoked too early. Smoked haddock's all right, smoked kippers, smoked salmon. But smoking, nah. Don' smoke. You could grow as tall as Romeo. Ah, we could talk all day. I must feed my dog.

DANIEL: Of course. Dogs must be fed first.

GOLDSTEIN: A do-og is a man's best friend. You read philoso-phy? Besides, he's all I got. So what more do I want? A nice shop, educated customers, and a dog. Round here, people don't work with their hands. It's an heducated district.

DANIEL: Yes, it is. Some very interesting —

GOLDSTEIN: People die. Wives die. Brothers die, cousins go to America. But dogs. Nah. If a dog gets run over you get yourself a new dog. At my age, a new wife is not so easy to get. I tell you, a living do-og is better than a dead lion.

DANIEL: I like dogs.

GOLDSTEIN: Think of the dogs that have become proverbial. There's Argus. Beautiful Joe. Jip Katmir. Rin Tin Tin. Oi, a breed worth a fortune. So who wants a cat? All right to wear in Brighton. Schmatters. Cats are no good. No good. They stay out all night. Abraham there — (*points to back of shop*) — he sleeps at my feet. Every night at my feet. Would a woman do better? Noch, my Abie doesn't even snore. (*Bell rings. This time a GIRL enters. Incongruously MR GOLDSTEIN raises his hat.*) Miss?

GIRL: Ten Craven A, please.

GOLDSTEIN: Craven A? You want to go to Paraguay to get Craven A. (*to DANIEL*) I gotta relative in Paraguay, in Villarrica. Never writes to me.

DANIEL: (*to GIRL*) He's run out of Craven A.

GIRL: Run out! Dunhill, then.

GOLDSTEIN: Dunhill? A pipe you want? They don't make cigarettes.

GIRL: But they do. You're mistaken.

GOLDSTEIN: Here. Twenty Senior Service. All right?

GIRL: You're sure you haven't Craven A or Dunhill? What about those on your shelf, there?

GOLDSTEIN: Dummies. Hundred years old. You want to buy some dummies? A little dummy eh, eh, eh?

GIRL: I've seen you before.

GOLDSTEIN: You want Senior Service? Yes or no?

GIRL: Some years ago. Yes, I remember. Aren't you Sally Goldstein's father? (*Goldstein seems as if he's been hit*)

GOLDSTEIN: You knew Sally?

GIRL: Yes, I knew her. (*telephone bell rings in the back room*)

DANIEL: There goes your telephone, Mr Goldstein.

GOLDSTEIN: Yes, the telephone. Inventions, I tell you.

DANIEL: Aren't you going to answer it?

GOLDSTEIN: So you were a friend of Sally's?

GIRL: The telephone, Mr Goldstein.

DANIEL: He's not interested. It's probably someone wanting to be obscene.

GIRL: What? Obscene? I beg your pardon!

DANIEL: A take-over bid. I'm beginning to see his point of view.

GIRL: I don't follow you. (*telephone stops*)

DANIEL: Anyway, they've rung off.

GOLDSTEIN: My Sally.

GIRL: How is she?

GOLDSTEIN: She's in Birmingham. She's extinct.

GIRL: How do you mean?

GOLDSTEIN: She got married to a dull mister, a yes man, a success man. I tell you it's not sanitary. I won't have him in the house.

GIRL: Sorry to hear about Sally and you. I was at school with her.

(*MR GOLDSTEIN raises his hat. The GIRL and MR GOLDSTEIN stare at each other a moment before she goes out.*)

DANIEL: You must miss your daughter, Mr Goldstein.

GOLDSTEIN: My Sally had character. Nowadays who's got character? (*pause*) A disgrace, women smoking. In my day no respectable woman smoked, not even in the heducated districts. Soon dogs will be smoking.

DANIEL: I wonder if you'd mind me asking you a question, Mr Goldstein. I mean... Mr Goldstein, why don't you give people the brand of cigarettes they want? (*MR GOLDSTEIN doesn't answer. He looks at the bell. Then he turns to go. He stops half-way, turns and speaks.*)

GOLDSTEIN: Excuse me, please, I must feed my dog.

DANIEL: But I'd like to know, Mr Goldstein. I'd like to understand your method of business. Why don't you give them what they want?

GOLDSTEIN: Give 'em what they want? What you mean? I give everybody what they ask for if I got it. The trouble is.... Do they know? Sometimes a man can't have everything. Things are denied him. Did I want my wife to die? God doesn't say yes to everything. Maybe that's what makes a man. Take Jonah. Did Jonah get straightaway what he asked for? And Job? An' King David? What did he do to get what he wanted? He killed Uriah. (*shouts*) He killed a man. He took away life which is beautiful, unique and holy. Was this right? Nah. It shouldn't be too easy for people. (*pause*) Now I must feed my dog.

DANIEL: Mr Goldstein. Are you looking for an assistant?

GOLDSTEIN: An assistant? For why do I need an assistant? Should I look for somebody to spoil my business? Smoke the cigarettes, steal the money, insult the customers. No, thank you. No, no, thank you.

DANIEL: But the notice? The notice in the window?

GOLDSTEIN: The notice. Propaganda. Helps to bring in customers. It makes people stop outside and read it. Draws attention to the shop. Sometimes I change it to Budgerigar Lost. Five pounds reward. Good business, eh? People look, the schmoks. So gullible. You'd be surprised.

DANIEL: Then there's no job?

GOLDSTEIN: I wouldn't say that. You might do. Yes, I could use a dog-walker. You want to be a dog-walker?

DANIEL: A dog-walker? I don't really think I...

GOLDSTEIN: Abraham needs exercise. Someone to take him every day for a stroll. I'm too old, and short of breath. I take him for a ride on the bus most evenings. But it's not the same thing. A dog needs fresh air, lamp-posts. If you're interested we can draw up a contract. Me, Goldstein, and you, Daniel Robinson. (*takes out a very large cigar, lights it, blows out smoke*)

DANIEL: All right, Mr Goldstein, I'll take Abraham for regular walks.

GOLDSTEIN: I must warn you Abie has personality.

DANIEL: I hope Abraham isn't fierce?

GOLDSTEIN: From Venezuela.

DANIEL: A Venezuelan dog!

GOLDSTEIN: No, no, the cigar. Abraham is as gentle as a lamb. (*smokes cigar again*) Oi, if you want a cigar with smoke in it, go to Venezuela. Now about this dog-walking. How do I know if you can handle dogs? Have you references? Daniel might have been good with lions, but with a do-og. Nah (*flicks ash on floor*) Noah was a different proposition. (*enter JOHN SMITH*) Oi, it's Haman, Hitler.

SMITH: Please, Mr Goldstein, it's Saint Patrick's Day. The other tobacconist is closed. I'm dying for a smoke.

GOLDSTEIN: Where's my Flit? I'm busy. I'm just about to sign a

81

contract.

SMITH: Just ten cigarettes to keep me going. Please. Your assistant can serve me.

GOLDSTEIN: You mean my dog-walker? Nah.

SMITH: What have you got against me? What have I ever done to you?

GOLDSTEIN: Such lack of dignity. And a smoke addict. He's so normal.

DANIEL: He won't serve you, Mr Smith, because you're a conformist.

GOLDSTEIN: You're right. I know your sort, Mr John Smith, esquire. In East Germany you'd be an East German. In West Germany, a West German. In Russia you'd be a Communist, in Cuba, a cubist.

SMITH: I'm an anti-Communist.

GOLDSTEIN: I don't care what sort of Communist you are. I only serve eccentrics.

SMITH: If that was so, you wouldn't have hardly any customers.

GOLDSTEIN: You're wrong, Mr John Smith, esquire. Eccentricities humanize even people. You get me? Show me a man who hasn't one eccentricity and there you'll find an anti-Semite. Have you got one sock inside out?

SMITH: No, certainly not.

GOLDSTEIN: There you are. Nebisch, I bet you even got a wireless licence.

SMITH: Of course I have.

DANIEL: Please, Mr Goldstein, let him have some cigarettes.

GOLDSTEIN: My Flit? Where did I put it?

SMITH: It's illegal not to serve customers. I'll see your licence is taken away. (*telephone rings in back room*)

GOLDSTEIN: Do you hear that? I'm busy, can't you see? (*begins to go towards back room*) Customers, contracts, employees, conferences. Telephone calls, day in and day out. Not even Ben Gurion was so busy. And you worry about an insignificant packet of cigarettes. (*MR GOLDSTEIN goes out.*)

SMITH: Why does he discriminate against me? It's unjust.

DANIEL: He doesn't like people called Smith.

SMITH: Isn't that ridiculous? To generalize about Smiths. There are good Smiths and bad Smiths.

DANIEL: There have been some very great Smiths.

SMITH: Exactly. I'm proud to be a Smith as a matter of fact. Of course there are a few black sheep Smiths. There's bound to be, there are so many of us.

DANIEL: Quite.

SMITH: There are some Smiths, of course, who change their name. Call themselves Smythe. That fools no one. Least of all another Smith. Some damage the name Smith but these are not real Smiths whatever they might write in hotel registers.

DANIEL: Most of the Smiths I've met are very nice, however orthodox they might be. In fact one of my best friends is a Smith. (*pause*) I call him Smudger.

SMITH: You call him Smudger?

DANIEL: Yes, I call him Smudger.

SMITH: Smudger?

DANIEL: Yes. (*pause*)

SMITH: That betrays, I fear, an unconscious prejudice.

DANIEL: Nonsense. I've got nothing against Smudger. I admire him. Of course he's clever, very clever, in fact. Almost sharp. A bit of a lawyer, know what I mean? (*getting worked up*) A real foxy acute bastard come to think of it. A lousy, mean swine who'd double cross his own mother. (*pause*) I've got nothing really against old Smudge.

SMITH: Smudge?

DANIEL: Yes, you know, Smudger.

SMITH: Do you know, I think Lord Nelson was a Smith — on his maternal side, of course. Probably so was Gladstone, and Shakespeare. Yes, Shakespeare was no Bacon. He was definitely a Smith. And so was Clive of India.

DANIEL: Of course, Clive Smith! Anyway, some Smiths might buy this place. Yes, a chain of tobacconists want to take Goldstein's shop on.

SMITH: That would be marvellous.

DANIEL: That's probably what the telephone call is about.

SMITH: I hope they make him a good offer and he accepts. They'd turn this into an efficient place. It would become like any other tobacconist's. Wouldn't that be a relief?

DANIEL: I don't know. Bang goes my job, if that happens, for a start.

SMITH: Meantime, do you think it would be all right if I took twenty cigarettes and left you the money? I'm dying for a smoke.

DANIEL: I don't want any part of it.

SMITH: You'll only have to hand him the money.

DANIEL: No, no. I'd rather not. You deal with him, direct.

SMITH: He'll never sell me half a Woodbine. Prejudice is a terrible thing. (*enter GOLDSTEIN*) I'm still here.

GOLDSTEIN: What you want?

SMITH: Twenty Players.

GOLDSTEIN: Twenty Players, yes. Here.

SMITH: I can have them?

GOLDSTEIN: A penny change. Thank you, sir.

SMITH: You're thanking me? Did you hear that? He thanked me. He called me "sir". Good Lord. Did you see what he did? He gave me, of his own free will, quietly, without fuss or protest, a packet of cigarettes. Why, Mr Goldstein, you've conformed to normal patterns of behaviour. I'm delighted. Well, goodbye. Cheerio, Mr Goldstein. (*at the door to DANIEL*) Did you see that? He raised his hat to me. (*exit*)

GOLDSTEIN: I've conformed, he said. My wife should have heard him. Killed in the war by a bomb dropped by a young German pilot. By a pilot who obeyed orders. Who was a conformist. That she should have lived to hear the day when I was called a conformist.

DANIEL: What's the matter, Mr Goldstein? Oh dear, you haven't accepted the offer? You're not selling your shop?

GOLDSTEIN: That was the other John Smith on the phone.

DANIEL: The obscene one. I guessed.

GOLDSTEIN: I shouldn't have answered. I shouldn't have listened with my big ears. I should have cut the wires mit a pincers. Me, of all people. But he offered three tousand.

DANIEL: You accepted. You sold out. Mr Goldstein!

GOLDSTEIN: Nah. I didn't accept.

DANIEL: You refused. Oh good, I thought...

GOLDSTEIN: Nah, I didn't refuse.

DANIEL: What then?

GOLDSTEIN: I said I'd tink about it. Three tousand, that's a lot of money. Every man has his price, Ben Gurion says.

DANIEL: Ah, but not you. That's all right. You haven't sold the shop. And you'll still need a dog-walker.

GOLDSTEIN: I should have said, "no", when he says he'll come roun' an' talk about it. I must get my suit out. He'll be comin' quick. Not for years I haven't worn this suit. It's a real respectable suit like most people wear. Good for funerals. Three piece, including the trousers. I'll go an' get it on. Three tousan', I could go to America, first class. Yes, a man can be tempted to become like other people. Next thing I'll be changin' my name. Already, tinkin' of the money, I don' feel like Goldstein no more. It makes me feel like a Mr Goldsmith. Oi. What's right? I got responsibilities. A do-og for instance. I'll ask Abie if he'd like to go to America. Come into the back and meet Abraham.

DANIEL: All right.

GOLDSTEIN: You'll get on with him, a humble fellah like you. I tell you, this is a problem. How long can a man hold out against uniformity and change? (*they begin to go*) I'll put it to Abie. A dog can eat well in the U.S.A. (*Now no one on stage. GOLDSTEIN off stage is heard putting the question to Abie. There is a terrific sound of a dog growling and barking. After a short time DANIEL re-enters in a hurry. GOLDSTEIN follows slowly after and shouting off "Schweig, Abie. Schweig"!*) Come back. Don't be afraid. You'll never make a dog walker if you're frightened. Where's your ambition? Abie, believe me, is not fierce. He's got gentle eyes.

DANIEL: It's his teeth, not his eyes, that worry me. It was hate at first sight as far as he was concerned.

GOLDSTEIN: Lies. Fabrications. It was nothing to do with you. It was the idea of America. He's a dog that don' like hot dogs.

DANIEL: Then you're not going to the U.S.A.?

GOLDSTEIN: Am I Columbus? Abie turned down the proposition flat, didn't he? That dog's got integrity.

DANIEL: So you're not selling out.

GOLDSTEIN: Course not. It's just plain dog sense. I can't let down my Abe. (a *well-dressed customer comes in*) Yes?

CUSTOMER: Twenty Abdulla, please.

GOLDSTEIN: Certainly, sir.

CUSTOMER: And a box of matches. (*GOLDSTEIN is about to serve him.*)

DANIEL: But Mr Goldstein, you just said you're not going to sell the shop.

GOLDSTEIN: That's right, too true. (*to CUSTOMER, advancing towards him with Flit pump menacingly*) Abdulla? Where you been living? Aren't you a Britisher? (*CUSTOMER is backing towards door as GOLDSTEIN bears down on him.*) You have to go to Jordan to get Abdullas. An' matches? They don' sell 'em any more in this country. Don't you read the papers? Been out of town, eh? Queening it maybe in Borneo or Bulgaria. (*CUSTOMER is now at the door and goes out quickly*) What are you, a pyromaniac? (*GOLDSTEIN turns back round, squirts Flit in the air and faces DANIEL, and they are both smiling triumphantly. Music up and curtain.*)

DUNCAN BUSH
Sailing to America

Duncan Bush (b.1946) was born in Cardiff and educated at universities in the U.K. and U.S.A. He is a noted novelist (*Glass Shot*), and a prizewinning poet. His most recent collection of verse, *Masks*, was The Arts Council of Wales' Book of the Year for 1995. He is becoming more involved in writing drama for the stage and screen, including a recent BBC documentary about the origins and history of cinema in Wales and a commissioned T.V. play. He currently divides his time between Wales and continental Europe. Written in 1989, *Sailing to America* is set in a stark hospital ward where two very different women, through a lengthy and diverse conversation, discover each other's dreams, disappointments and desires.

CHARACTERS
Josie
Evelyn

(*A terminal ward in a hospital. Three Beds. The middle bed is empty, stripped to a rubber sheet. JOSIE and EVELYN occupy the beds at either side. JOSIE is middle-aged, EVELYN somewhat older. The three beds are separated by bedside tables. The runnered curtains on either side of the empty middle bed are still partly drawn preventing JOSIE and EVELYN from direct sight of each other. As we open, JOSIE is reading a magazine and EVELYN is quietly sobbing. JOSIE looks up from her magazine several times, listens to EVELYN [she sits forward but cannot see her], hesitates, tries to continue reading. EVELYN continues to sob and snuffle. Finally*

JOSIE lays down the magazine.)

JOSIE: Hello? (*pause*) Eh? (*pause*) You alright? (*silence. Evelyn sobs*) We're one less today in here. (*pause*) Till they put somebody else in there. (*pause*) Poor old bugger. She's better off out of it. (*pause*) Was you expecting them today?

EVELYN: What?...

JOSIE: Your girl and the little boy.

EVELYN: Oh I just thought, you know, it's been a few days since they were in.

JOSIE: Haven't they been in since?

EVELYN: Only the other day they were in.

JOSIE: That's what I said. They haven't been in since then? (*pause*) What day was that? Last Thursday?

EVELYN: It's a handful, a small child. (*pause*) Particularly your own. You don't get a minute to breathe with them. (*pause*) I ought to know. I brought one screaming into the world. And I never had a minute's help with her, or a minute's peace from that day on. (*silence*) Perhaps it was Friday. It might have been Friday. I think it was. (*pause*) What's today? Monday, is it? Or Tuesday? (*pause*) You lose track of the days. After a bit. Just lying here.

JOSIE: They're all the same in here, love. Like leaves off a tree. (*pause*) Kids. You sweat your guts out to bring them up. And that's the bleeding thanks you get. My eldest boy's the same. Everything's too much trouble for him. Except his bleeding motor-bikes. Out the back building them up. Or taking them apart. That's all he ever gets time for. Anything else, he can't afford the time to piss. He've always been the same. But it's our fault. We brought them up too soft. They don't know they're born.

EVELYN: You don't know what you're doing, half the time. Let alone who comes in and out of the ward. (*pause*) It's that stuff they give you. You don't know if you're coming or going, if it's day or night. (*pause*) Sometimes you wish they wouldn't bother. Or that they'd slip you something else instead. (*pause*) It's like you're all day in a fog.

88

JOSIE: The Chemical Cosh Nurse Carey calls it. (*pause*) You think yourself lucky, love. You could be like some of them down the ward. You could be lying there crying out. (*Pause. She looks at the empty bed between them.*) You could be like her. (*silence*) I had a look in on her this morning, and they'd already stripped the bed. She must have gone in the night. (*silence*) You been yet? (*pause*) I said, you been yet?

EVELYN: Not yet. No.

JOSIE: I know how it is. Believe me. You can be lying there dying to sometimes. It can be weeks. (*pause*) You want to try and get up and move about more, if you ask me. If it's only on the zimmer. Just down to the Day Room and back of an evening. See a bit of the old telly.

EVELYN: I can't seem to watch it any more. (*pause*) It's not like the old films used to be.

JOSIE: I thought most of it was old films.

EVELYN: I can't seem to follow it any more. (*pause*) Then suddenly I'm watching it, and someone else is in it now, and they're in Hong Kong or somewhere or Hawaii and I think, what are they talking about? (*pause*) It's like somebody's gone up and switched channels. And all they ever do is talk. You watch television, and that's all they ever do. That, and crash their cars into each other. And change their dresses every five minutes. You ever notice that? Every time you look they got a different dress on.

JOSIE: Oh, I love the old telly, me.

EVELYN: I always used to wonder if they got to keep them. (*pause*) Like that one Hedy Lamarr wore, in "Casablanca". (*pause*) Long and black and glittery it was. And with a long train. All black sequins, it was. Thousands and thousands, it must have taken. All sewn by hand.

JOSIE: Black never suited me. I always looked washed out in black. Like I was going to my own funeral.

EVELYN: And she came down these white steps. Marble. And that starry train poured down them after her like water. (*pause*) It was the most beautiful dress I ever seen. (*pause*) I can see her in it now. (*pause*) And I always wondered, did she get to keep it afterwards? (*pause*) Though where on earth would you wear a dress like that, but in a film? (*pause*) She had a lovely face, I always thought, Hedy Lamarr. They always used to say Ingrid Bergman was the most beautiful woman in films. But I never really liked her nose. (*pause*) She had a nice face. But not beautiful. (*pause*) I always thought you could see up her nostrils. (*pause*) You know, at certain angles. (*pause*) No, for me, it was always Hedy Lamarr. To me, she was the loveliest of them all.

JOSIE: What are you on this morning? (*pause*) I think they must have given you the wrong pill. Or wound you up. (*pause, laughs*) Remember them? The old wind-up gramophones? And them scratchy seventy-eights? "Chiribiribin", Slow Foxtrot. Ambrose and his Orchestra. (*pause*) Or "Begin the Beguine". Remember that? (*sings*)

When they begin the Beguine
It brings back the sound of music so tender,
It brings back the nights of tropical splendour,
It brings back the memory evergreen...

Remember? (*laughs*) Seventy-eights? I bet you go back to the old cylinders. (*sings*)

To live it again is past all endeavour,
Except when that tune touches my heart...

EVELYN: Is she dead now, I wonder, Hedy Lamarr?

JOSIE: I see William Holden passed away, the other month. Sudden, it was. He was still quite a young man. Heart attack. They all seem to go that way, these big stars. (*pause*) I think it must be the life they lead. Look at Errol Flynn. Only forty-eight he was. (*pause*) Well, I'm not surprised, with him. You know, all them women. (*pause*) I always liked William Holden, did you? I always thought he had a kind face. He always looked as if he was, you know, a nice man. (*pause*) I suppose they're all dead now. Or near enough. All the old actors. All the great stars. (*silence*) Hedy Lamarr. (*pause*) What was she in?

EVELYN: She was never what you'd call a big star. But you'd know her if you saw her. She'd had a lovely face.

90

(pause) Not that I think it did her much good. According to the papers. I think it was, you know, men. *(pause)* I suppose looks is nothing out there. In Hollywood. *(silence. JOSIE looks at the empty bed.)*

JOSIE: I wonder who they'll put in there. *(pause)* Well, it won't be Hedy Lamarr. *(pause)* I don't suppose it'll stay empty long. There's people crying out for beds. Like Sister always says, you'll have to get better quicker, we need the beds. *(pause)* Die quicker, she means. That's how it usually turns out. *(pause)* I expect they'll put somebody in there by tonight. *(pause)* I hope it's someone a bit younger. They're all so old and gaga in this ward. *(pause)* Someone with a bit of life left in them. A bit of personality. Brighten the place up a bit.

EVELYN: Don't say that. Don't wish it on the young. Let them live their lives out first. *(JOSIE looks at the empty bed.)*

JOSIE: Not another one like her was all I meant. *(pause)* I know she couldn't help it. And far be it from me to speak ill of the departed, wherever she is now. But she was hardly the bleeding highspot of the evening, was she? *(pause)* It makes you ill sometimes, it do, just to see some of the cases they got here. *(pause)* It's like that film on the telly the other afternoon. Where he's in prison for a murder he didn't do. On the word of that bitch. She's as good as laughing at him in the dock as they drag him away. And that metal door bangs shut on him, and you know he knows that's it. It's like a nightmare to him. But it's not. It's really happening. And he's there for the rest of his days. *(pause)* Sometimes that's how I feel. Like they got the wrong person. Like, what did I ever do to anybody to deserve to end up here? *(pause)* No wonder nobody's keen on visiting. *(silence)* She's better off out of it, if you ask me. *(pause)* You know, once they get like that. *(pause)* I know it's a terrible thing to say, but it was a relief when she went. When you realised it had stopped, you couldn't hear her no more. *(pause)* I don't think I could have stood another night of lying here and listening to her. That terrible snore or dragging rattle or whatever it was, like every breath she managed to draw in was going to be the last. Only, it went on. All day, all night.

EVELYN: I blame the food.

JOSIE: Eh?

EVELYN: It's not just the being bedridden. I was bedridden at home. I blame the food. (*pause*) I'm not saying it's bad food, or badly cooked. And they keep those kitchens spotless. (*pause*) They give you too much of it. Three big meals a day. Like you was a navvy or something. When, in here, you didn't ought to eat more than a cage bird strictly speaking. If they gave you less you'd feel the better for it, don't you think? You're not using it up, are you, as energy? Not in here.

JOSIE: Christ, meals are the only thing you got to look forward to. (*pause*) Not that it's all that marvellous, the food. But it's something to do three times a day. You know, managing the tray. (*pause*) Try cutting down. Or going vegetarian. After a day or two you'll probably find you want to go. And at least you won't feel so heavy.

EVELYN: Heavy? Sometimes I feel so light it's only the sheets keep me from floating off. (*Silence, in which Josie closes her eyes as if for a doze.*)

JOSIE: It's only when you shut your eyes that you hear all the noises. (*Silence. Evelyn closes her eyes too.*) All the clanks and footsteps and trolleys out in the corridor. And that hum, it must be the central heating, and the systems. (*pause*) It never stops, that hum. (*pause*) I say hum. It's worse than a hum. It's more like a big wheel grinding round and round. Or some massive big machine vibrating somewhere a long way away. That's what a day is, here: the noise of that machine going. (*pause*) You can lie here at night for hours, just listening to it. No, trying not to listen to it. But hearing it, no matter what. (*pause*) It's the same if you try shutting your eyes for a nap. You can lie here for hours and not notice it, that noise. But soon as you shut your eyes to go to sleep it's back. (*pause*) It's like you're going somewhere on a ship, the noise of the engine room. (*pause*) Sometimes even when I'm asleep I hear it. (*pause*) I can feel the movement

92

under me. The ocean. And then I know it is a ship. And it's taking me somewhere. It's like the whole hospital, all those wings and floors lit up, and me on my bed in it, is steaming off into the dark. Like a big transatlantic liner sailing off to America. (*pause*) And I think, this is it, I've always wanted to see America. (*pause*) And I know this is a trip I won't wake up on. (*pause*) Then I do. (*Pause. Josie opens her eyes and stares upwards.*) And you open your eyes, it's the middle of the night, and you're in the ward and you got that bleeding ceiling light still on. (*silence*)

EVELYN: Like in "Casablanca". They're out on deck. You can see the rail and the sea behind them with the moonlight on it. And Paul Muni's in a white dinner-jacket with a dickie-bow. And Hedy Lamarr's got a shawl on, because it's cooler at night. (*pause*) And Paul Muni puts two cigarettes in his mouth and lights them. And he has to shield the match because of the breeze off the sea. And he takes one of the cigarettes out of his mouth and puts it in hers.

JOSIE: Paul Muni? Was he in that?

EVELYN: And you know that's not really the sea behind them. And they're not really on the deck of a ship. It's just a bit of rail, with some kind of film on a screen, or whatever it is they use, to show that twinkly shimmery look of the sea. (*pause*) It's like in the South Seas or somewhere. You know, with the moon on it, and the night so clear. (*pause*) And you can see it's not real. It's just a background. But it always used to make me think, I'd love to be there. To be out on deck. With the moonlight shining on the sea like that, right out to the horizon. And them not even noticing it because they only had eyes for each other. (*pause*) And then they'd show you just her face as he was going to kiss her. And she smiles as she waits for him to. And even her eyes and teeth and hair and jewellery would have that soft twinkle, like the sea.

JOSIE: How did they do that? (*laughs*) In the old films. (*pause*) I remember the first boy I ever really went out with. I must have been seventeen. We went for a walk in Ely woods. It was hot in the sun. But it was all cool in the woods, and green. And after a while I could tell he wanted to kiss me, from the way he'd stopped talking and kept swallowing. And my mouth was dry too. And when he turned and stopped me and put his hands on my shoulders I remember looking up at him and trying to make my face suddenly go like that. All soft and misty and gooey-eyed. You know. Like in the pictures. (*laughs*) Billy Trott. Christ, I can see him now. And I can still taste how dry my mouth went. (*pause*) I don't know if my whatsit was wet or not. But my mouth was as dry as a cork. (*pause*) Billy Trott. He was the first I ever let do anything. Though I only ever let him put his finger in me. Craddock Street he lived. I knew his sister well. What was her name? She was a common little bitch.

EVELYN: And then you'd come out after the film and it was night there too. The moon might even be out. And the streets would be drying and they'd have that dull shine after the rain. That's how it was after the War. During the war everything was dark at night. Because of the blackout. But afterwards, everything had that moonlit sort of sheen. Life was so drab by daylight. Everything was on ration. Except for the pics. Your life only started at night, in the queue to those films. There was always a queue. You had to queue for everything in those days. (*pause*) I had my twenty-first birthday the day after the war ended. (*pause*) He went all through the last years of the War out in Burma and got killed in an accident in work. He worked down Guest Keen. In the steelworks. (*pause*) We hadn't been married a year. Kath wasn't even born. She never even saw her father. I ached over him for three years while he was away. I mean that. I ached. And then he comes home. He been two years in the jungle, and he gets killed in an accident at work. (*pause*) And then it was like I never stopped aching, all this time. Because nothing was never no good afterwards. (*pause*) I was twenty-six. (*pause*) But everybody else was just men. (*Silence. Optional blackout.*)

JOSIE: I'm starving. Again.

EVELYN: There's some biscuits in my drawer. (*pause*) Go on. They'll only go stale. I can't eat biscuits. Not when I can't move my bowels.

JOSIE: I might have just one. (*She puts back the bedclothes, gets out, comes slowly around to EVELYN'S bedside table. She takes the biscuits from the drawer.*)

EVELYN: What are they? Garibaldi? My Kath brought them in last time. (*pause*) I expect they're stale by now. (*JOSIE takes a biscuit, returns to her bed, sits on it.*) You're lucky to find one left, with little Dean. He loves a biscuit. Kids do, don't they? Anything sweet. (*pause*)

JOSIE: What happened to her... husband? (*pause*) Your Kath's. I never see him in here.

EVELYN: What? Oh, he works away. (*pause*) Actually, they're separated now. (*pause*) I don't think she sees a lot of him now. (*pause*)

JOSIE: Oh. (*pause*) Where's he from?

EVELYN: From? (*pause*) Oh, Moorland Road, I think. Somewhere down that way.

JOSIE: Moorland Road? (*pause*) Like Shirley Bassey. She was from down there. (*pause*) Shirley Bassey? Don't tell me about Shirley Bassey. She used to scrub the steps. Down Orbit Street. I've seen her do the front step for our Winnie many times. (*pause*) Look at her now. Hollywood. Las Vegas. Royal Command Performance. Curtseying for the bleeding Queen. (*pause*) I have, I've seen her scrubbing on her knees. (*pause*) What was his name, that bloke? That actor. (*pause*) Peter Finch. You must have read about it. Her and him. It was in all the Sunday papers. A few years ago this was, now. (*pause*) I suppose she's only doing what thousands would have loved to. Gallivanting off all over the world like that with men. With actors. (*pause*) Let's face it, we're all pink inside. (*pause*) She wears a wig, of course.

EVELYN: A wig?

JOSIE: You never see one with wavy hair like that, do you? (*pause*) I know they used to use the old hot comb and all, in the old days. But that's a wig she wears. (*pause*) They do wear wigs, these days, a lot of them. Particularly all these singers and dancers. There's a lot of them, in show business. (*silence*) Oh, so he's from down the Docks, is he? (*pause*) Where's he from, you know, originally?

EVELYN: Oh, I don't know. I think his family live in Moorland Road. Round there. He was born there. (*pause*)

JOSIE: Perhaps I'm old-fashioned. (*pause*) I mean, it's all very well for the parents. But it's the children who suffer.

EVELYN: Little Dean? How do he suffer?

JOSIE: Not as kids. I don't mean that. Nobody'll blame a kid.

EVELYN: Blame? Blame for what? (*silence*)

JOSIE: Kids. They weigh your arm down when they're little. Then they weigh your heart down when they're big.

EVELYN: Little Dean? He's beautiful.

JOSIE: Oh, he's a lovely child. I never said that.

EVELYN: What are you saying? Only what other people say. (*pause*) I used to say to Kath, I don't know what you're going out with that Roy for. Can't you find one of your own? "I love him, Mam," she'd say. (*pause*) But you know what it's like. The more you try to tell them not to do something, the more you force them to it. (*pause*) Then, when she told me there was a baby on the way, I thought, oh my God, is it his? And she said "Yes, it is". "What a thing to say to me", she said. "What do you think I am?" And I thought, well, that's it, now everyone will have to know what you are and what you done. Even when she goes out with her baby on her own. Or just walks him to the shops. They'll take one look at her and look at that little baby lying in the pram and know. I ate my heart out over that. (*pause*) But now I see little Dean and I don't even notice it. All I think is he's beautiful. Thank God he come out the way he did, with nothing wrong with him, because he come out perfect. (*pause*) He's the only grandchild I'll ever have or be here to see, anyway. (*Pause. Josie has closed her eyes.*) I sometimes think, I never had much joy out of life or out of marriage. I was only married a twelvemonth before my husband died.

96

But at least he left me Kath. If it wasn't for having a baby to look after I never would have carried on. And now she's give me Dean. (*pause*) That's the only reason people have kids, really. Black or white. So that whatever happens to you, you know, well, at least the world will go on. (*Pause. JOSIE opens one eye.*) Don't you think?

JOSIE: I don't know about the world going on. But Jesus Christ, you don't half do sometimes. (*Pause. JOSIE closes her eyes again. EVELYN lies there, then puts the bedclothes back. She gets out of bed very cautiously. EVELYN puts on a dressing-gown.*)

EVELYN: Anyway, perhaps she'll bring little Dean in later, or tomorrow. (*pause*) But it's such a long way out here on the bus. (*pause*)

JOSIE: I wonder where that tea is? It must be getting on for four. (*pause*) I got to wet the inside of my mouth with something. (*She reaches to the bedside table, pours water into a glass, drinks.*)

EVELYN: I can't drink the water in here. You can even taste it in the tea. It must be something they put in it.

JOSIE: Bromide, I expect.

EVELYN: Isn't that what you put down for slugs?

JOSIE: It's what they give you to stop you getting, you know, ideas.

EVELYN: Ideas?

JOSIE: You know. (*pause*) Wetting your knickers for a little bit of what you're missing. Getting cock-happy.

EVELYN: Oh. (*EVELYN goes to the window, stares out.*)

JOSIE: I think they used to give it to men in the nick. Or in the army. To stop them thinking about it too much. (*pause*) I suppose they'd be flogging themselves raw, some men. I suppose it's all they ever have to think about, in jail. (*pause*) There was this terrible story Nurse Carey told me when she was bathing me. About this boy in Stoke Mandeville, when she was a nurse there. He had both his hands blown off in the Falklands. Well, both arms, really. All he had left, she said, was two stumps at his shoulders. (*pause*) A boy of twenty, she said. (*pause*) And he used to get these terrible headaches and depression. But the worse thing, she said, was when he used to complain that he could still feel the pain in his hands. All that time, she said, after he'd lost them. (*pause*) Can you imagine that? Anyway, she was doing something for him, smoothing his bedclothes or whatever. And she said she could, you know, see him getting bigger.

EVELYN: Getting bigger?

JOSIE: Coming to attention. (*pause*) Down there. (*laughs*) Getting the stiff one. The gander's neck. What did they used to call it in your day?

EVELYN: Oh.

JOSIE: He was embarrassed by it, she said. He went red as a beetroot. "I'm sorry, Nurse," he said. "I can't help it. I don't mean to offend you." "I know you can't" she said. "And I'm not offended. I been a nurse too long for that." After three years nursing you get so you seen it all. And as to that, she said, you soon get used to seeing someone's Old Boy stood up. From seventy- and eighty-year olds even. Like she said, you'd rather see that than be blind. You just learn to take it in your stride, or make a joke about it if you have to. (*pause*) But when I looked at that poor boy, she said, lying there with the stumps of his arms no longer than the sleeves of his t-shirt, she thought: How can you make a joke about this? How can you even pretend not to notice it? (*pause*) I mean, what could he do about it? Lying there with no hands. Nobody to give him his relief, she called it. And he couldn't ever do it for himself. I suppose it could have cost me my job, she said. But I felt so sorry for him. I couldn't just change his clothes and then go away and leave him with it twitching. I suppose you need a lot of pity to be a nurse. (*pause*) But it's strange to think of him still feeling pain in his hands. After all this time. Like there was still the nerves in them.

EVELYN: It's only like grief. Bereavement. He couldn't understand his hands weren't there. Like you can't believe someone you just lost isn't there. You keep thinking you can hear them in the kitchen. You keep expecting them to come in through the door. It takes people a long time to die in that way. It's only like that. It's only the memory of having hands all those years. He still couldn't believe they were gone. (*pause*) But look at us. When you're old and infirm it's as if you've got no hands. You can't even have a shit for yourself. Somebody has to do everything for you. (*pause*) And in your heart you're still a girl. (*pause*) When something goes it's gone in a minute and for ever. But you can't let things go, you can't forget how they took a long time growing or just being there. And it's like it was yesterday. (*pause*) It's like it's now. (*silence*) But that poor boy. (*pause*) At least they don't have to worry about us in that way any more, bromide or no.

JOSIE: Us? (*laughs*) Oh, we've seen the last of that alright. The nights of tropical splendour and all that. Them days are gone for good. The old cosh in his pocket pressing against your leg? We won't feel that no more. (*sings*)

To live it again is past all endeavour
Except when that tune touches my heart...

(*Pause. EVELYN is staring out of the window.*) I suppose they're all dead now. Hedy Lamarr. William Holden. Ambrose. And his Orchestra.

EVELYN: The bus is in. Now it's come. It doesn't look as if there's anybody on it. (*pause*) Perhaps they'll be on the next one.

JOSIE: I expect they will. (*pause*)

EVELYN: I feel sorry for the bus. All the way out here it comes. And nobody hardly ever on it when it gets here. (*pause*) But what for? Why do it bother? Nobody hardly ever comes here. Only on a Saturday or Sunday. And then a lot of them got cars. (*pause*) When I was in the Heath it was different. I used to like watching the buses come. I could see them from the ward, down in the car-park there. Families, kids, they all used to be on them. It was like it was a proper trip out there for them. A day out. I know they were only coming to visit somebody in hospital. But it was like it was a happy bus. Not sad. Like they were all going down Lavernock or Barry Island on a

Whitsun treat. Like in the old charabancs. (*pause*)
And the kids running about the ward. (*smiles*) It's as
if you can only keep them quiet for five minutes.
They don't know how to behave in a hospital.
Because they don't know what a hospital is. Or
sickness. They don't know what it means. (*pause*) But
when you're in here that's what you want to see, a bit
of young life. Not long faces, sitting there with that
bottle of Lucozade they brought, as if they can't wait
for sister to come through the ward and tell
everybody it's time. (*pause*) Why does everybody
always talk to you so polite when you're in hospital?
Do you ever notice that? And in that quiet voice?
(*pause*) It's not natural. (*pause*) I wish he was a bit
older, Dean. (*pause*) He don't know who I am now,
really. They don't at that age, do they? (*pause*). He
don't know I'm his Nana. He can't even say Nana yet.
Only dada dada. Everything's dada to him now.
Kath says "It don't mean nothing, Mam. It's just a
noise. They all say dada when they're starting to
talk." But it upsets me sometimes. When I see his
little face. Because I know he haven't got a Dada
really. (*pause*) And of course he gets bored. Or he'll
start grizzling. (*pause*) But I could be like that Beattie
down the ward. She don't get nobody, no visitors. I
feel sorry for her. I do. (*pause*) Particularly on a
Sunday, when they get her smartened up like all the
rest. (*pause*) They got to do that, I know. So you can
still have a bit of pride in yourself. Mutton dressed as
lamb, that's all it is, we all know that. But what's the
point if you're just sitting there in bed while
everybody else got family round them? That's why
she cries. It's terrible. (*pause*) Then they have to pull
the curtain round her. Or she won't let Nurse make
her up. "Keep your effing hands to yourself" she
says. "I'm not an effing stiff yet. You can stuff you
effing make-up." She got a terrible mouth on her.
(*pause*) But they do. They make you up when you're
dead. (*pause*) And it feels like that sometimes. When
they put your nice bed-jacket on you, and some
powder, and do your hair for you. Or a bit of rouge,
just to give you some colour in your cheeks. When
you can't do it for yourself, no more, it's like you're

already in your box. (*pause*) Well, you are, as good as. (*pause*) What I can't stand is the way they never mention it. When someone... you know. Passes on. (*pause*) They just pull the curtains round the bed. Then it's as if they sneak them out on the trolley. Like they were smuggling it out past you. As if you didn't know. (*pause*) Then it's just the bed there, stripped. (*pause)* And sometimes it's as if you can't even remember who was in it. Once they're gone. (*Silence. She stares out of the window.*) It looks lovely out there now, all the daffs, and the grass. They keep it lovely, the grass. I expect they'll let us have our tea out there again soon, if we get a nice day, and no wind. (*pause*) But I do, I feel sorry for the bus. (*pause*) It's the only thing that makes me cry. All the way out from town it comes. It turns round here. Then it just waits. (*pause*) It's sad to think of it coming all the way out here. It's like it do try. But nobody comes out this far, not in the week. (*pause*) And nobody gets on it, unless one of the nurses. Nobody goes from here. Not on the bus. (*pause*) But sometimes I think I will. As if it's been coming here and waiting just for me, all this time. (*pause*) And that's what it'll be like. Not like an ambulance, with those horrible black windows, or a big slow hearse. But on that orange bus. So you can look out at the houses, parks. And sit. With people. (*pause*) He won't ever remember me, little Dean.

(*Silence. Fade to black.*)

ALAN OSBORNE
Redemption Song

Alan Osborne, (b.1942) was born in Merthyr Tydfil and now lives in Cardiff. Osborne wrote a great deal of drama in the 1970s and early 1980s that directly reflects the troubled tenor of post-industrial Wales. His characters are often damaged young men disenfranchised by society and prone to violence and drugs. *Redemption Song,* an unflinching portrait of two failed entrepreneurs, is typical of Osborne's work at this time. His full-length plays include: *Terraces; Johnny Darkie; Tiger Tiger; Forbidden Hymn; The Rising; Bull, Rock & Nut; In Sunshine and in Shadow;* and *The Tuscan.* He has also written for radio and film. *The Whistling Boy,* a BBC film, was nominated for a BAFTA in 1995. His work has had a substantial influence on the succeeding generation of young playwrights from Wales.

Author's Note

Mick is a craftsman. He has designed and constructed a toy for children. Bob has laboured for him. Mick hopes the design will win great acclaim and he may win back his wife and children. Bob is a drifter, comical and supportive. Both men are committed to dope smoking. Bo Bo and Bunny are heavies, local street-wise protectors. Bo Bo has supplied Mick with his drugs and feels justified in claiming half of Mick's dream were it to be a successful economical venture. Bo Bo and Bunny have threatened Mick and Bob. Mick and Bob retaliate. Holed in the filthy warehouse room with the crate containing the toy and a gun from the violent conflict with Bo Bo and Bunny, they prepare for the siege. Mick's spirits are kept alive by an inspirational book he has read, and by luck, a huge supply of draw. They often find it difficult to separate "head" thinking and reality — wishful thinking and the cold light of violence. Maybe these periods of abdication from their true selves is why they are life's losers with only a dream? Maybe. Maybe they have some sense of serenity and passion they could teach us? They claim only self defence.

CHARACTERS
Mick
Bob
Bo-Bo
Bunny

(The warehouse room is a tip: runs of torn wallpaper, a work bench, saws, hammers and a vice. Broken curtains on a barred window give a homely effect. The floor is littered with woodshaves. There is a ragged settee and a chair. There is also a cot, a rocker and a small Welsh dresser, all in fresh pinewood. A large crate lies at the back of the room. It is padlocked. MICK is rolling a joint.)

BOB: *(dancing and singing)*

We're in the money, we're in the money!
Da da, da dee dee da da dee dee da dar...
We've got the patent, we've got the patent... *(etc.)*

MICK: *(singing)*

We gonna make some big money
and get out of here...

Bob! Get this... I move to the door... I dress exactly like this.. a little dirty... dirty hair. She says "Dirty bastard, what you want?" I say, "Can I see the kids?" She says, "Piss off, Dwarfy!"

BOB: You got the Roller outside, yeah?

MICK: Nu! Not yet... I says, "Please, can I see the kids?" She says, "Oh no... not again... out!" I give her five grand — smack — fresh. She looks stupid, right? I says, "See you next week. I'll give ten grand to the kids. You thought you married an arsehole? But this arsehole... is a genius. Number one...." Then! I whistle for the Roller... *(lights up, drawing in)* One-half pound of Lebanese is the difference... between... First Avenue snake dance gripe shit... And the big world up there... *(points up, eyes close)* One little baby of a

103

dream and you float up there like a God looking down on all the crap... and I'm in that heaven-haven. (*touches his lips and kisses the joint*) Kisses Maloney... Kisses Mickey Maloney, that's his name.

BOB: Jesus walked in a hotel carrying nails. Put me up for the night, Butt? (*Smiles all round. Like Frank Spencer.*) I'm so unlucky with women... if I fell into a barrow of nipples, I'd come out sucking my thumb... (*small laughter*) I'd buy a horse.

MICK: Remember Bob, Neck and the head of a swan...

BOB: Into... the four ducks protecting the sides...

MICK: Into... the kid sits on the Gingerbread man...

BOB: Rocks on snails...

MICK: Back is an elephant...

BOB: And we've got the world by the curlies...

MICK: This is the once... just one... wait till the next. Everything a kid wants, go-karts into ships, every-thing within two feet of his arms. This is the one. It goes in the crate. Nobody sees it!

BOB: Get your drawings back from Swansea?

MICK: In the box... stamped! Numbered!

(*BOB reaches for the draw off Mick. He takes it. MICK rolls another from his wallet. BOB goes to the crate, dancing silently.*)

BOB: It's locked...

MICK: Yeah...

BOB: We haven't varnished it....

MICK: Fuck it!

BOB; Where's the key?

MICK: (*busy*) Round my neck... for keeps. I was going to be a priest once... and Barbara came in. She used to be a Hell's Angel next flat — cuts here, cuts down there. I wouldn't let her sit on the chair of God. No kid now. I'd sit erect at the table, polite, and talk to the furniture.

MICK: (*drawing in*) Bo-Bo'll get a mouthful off the Angels! Shitty place anyway. Full of rats and lice....

BOB: The rats were polite, mun. "Hallo Bob", they'd say,

"gor any filth on you?" (*both titter, silence*) Bo-Bo took my record player, you know the one, the plate. I use to spin it on my finger and put my buck tooth on it. (*demonstrates*)

(*MICK looks at the door as BOB demonstrates. Two men in dark clothes appear. One of them has a trilby cocked down over his eyes.*)

MICK: (*not looking at the demonstration*) Hallo Bo-Bo. Hallo Bunny. I didn't hear you breaking the door down.

BOB: (*responds: he is caught between fear and laughter*)

BO-BO: (*monstrous in trilby*) Where's the toy, Creep?

(*BUNNY with a shotgun, pointing*)

MICK: Gone...

BO-BO: Get it then...

MICK: It's in Swansea. In the office...

BO-BO: Tell you what... get the toy from Swansea. I'll give you four hours, Kid, or so help me... I'll kill you. I'll do it myself. I'll kill you, right? You'll be dead.

MICK: Get stuffed, Bo-Bo! My brain... my thing... and his!

(*BOB cringes. BUNNY goes to BOB, cocks both the triggers*)

BUNNY: Dead. Oh! You're dead, Beauty. You're out of it.

(*BOB is rolled up in a heap on the floor*)

MICK: (*looking at his joint*) This joint keeps going out.

BOB: (*looks up, terrified, and slowly stutters:*) Matches were damp...

MICK: Bo-Bo! Matches were damp...

(*BUNNY looks at BO-BO. BO-BO goes to MICK and sits with him, like he is going to tell him a story, arm securely around his neck*) Where's the toy, Hard Man!

(*BUNNY puts the rifle in MICK'S mouth*)

MICK: Right! Right! (*falls on his knees at the side of a crumpled BOB and holds BOB'S head*) Confess, you Bastard! Confess!

BOB: (*weeping*) You put it in your mother's iron lung. I saw you do it. Tell 'em. Please. One life we've got, one moment to walk the Earth, to touch the sun, smell the autumn leaves. I saw you take it out of

	your Sister's coffin and put it in the lung. Tell 'em, please, for me. Feel clean. Please. Walk again and love the raindrops. Tell 'em.
BO-BO	(*standing, snatches the gun off BUNNY and rams it hard against MICK'S head*) I gave you the draw, Pig's Arse. You told me the idea on the draw. Half of what you got is mine. Four hours, Pig's Arse, you got!
	(*BUNNY kicks them both violently. BO-BO and BUNNY go to the door.*)
MICK:	(*coughing and in pain*) Bunny... is it true you were caught... killing the Queen's deer in Windsor Safari Park?
BUNNY:	Yes, Arse. Why?
MICK:	Good job....
BUNNY:	Just do the job, Kid. And live.
	(*exit BUNNY and BO-BO*)
BOB:	(*laughing and sobbing*) I saw the land of tables and chairs... (*doubles up laughing*)
	In... the... iron... lung... (*they both struggle to their feet. MICK laughs his way to the crate and drapes himself over it*) Oh my little lovely. They all want to ride on you.
BOB:	(*crawls over the floor, over the settee and falls*) Mick!
MICK:	Yeah....
BOB:	I've passed over... (*laughing*) to the... other side!
MICK:	(*laughing*) Listen, mun. Stay cool. We still got this. They can beat me black and blue but I still got this. This! (*bangs the crate*)
BOB:	(*crawling*) Gis a ride, Mick.
	(*BOB wraps himself around the base. Both young men hang on the crate like the raft of the Medusa. Time passes and they hang there silently.*)
BOB:	Mick?
MICK:	Mm?
BOB:	Will Sharon come back, do you think?
MICK:	Yeah...
BOB:	Where will you live?
MICK:	Ssh... I don't know. Somewhere quiet.

(They hang there, in silence. Time passes.)

MICK: I don't think there'll be a reconciliation. But I'll love her to death. I could walk around forever, crying out for her.

BOB: I don't think women are worth it.

MICK: They get right inside you. And you can't shift the bastards. You just hold on and on... terrified....

BOB: Find someone else. You got the money now.

MICK: *(silence)* I miss Simp, mun.

BOB: Who's Simp?

MICK: A dog in a fucking story in a kid's book. *(weeps silently)*

BOB: Remember Barbara? I was doing my head in one night and I told her I was the force. The force of the whole eternity and if I touched her I could cure her of all little problems on earth and heal up her cuts.

MICK: What she say?

BOB: She was doing her head in herself, thinking she was the devil.

MICK: Didn't get on then?

BOB: No. *(laughing)* Couldn't stand the bastard! It was Star Wars!

MICK: What did the rats think?

BOB: She killed them. They turned white.

(Silence: Hang in There! Time passes.)

MICK: *(stands)* Hey! In this box. You can't see it, right? Inside, and you can't see it. Believe it, right? Is everything I ever hoped for. Here. Everything. I've done it. I've contained... the force. I don't want anything else. Offer me three houses on Seventh Avenue. A Roller, pile of girls, mats, food, nothing... I got it! *(turns, amazed with himself)*

BOB: *(standing)* Mick?

MICK: *(distracted)* Yeah....

BOB: If I did the Gingerbread Man....

MICK: *(turning)* Yeah?

BOB: I got it as well.

107

MICK: Got what?

BOB: The force.

MICK: Those bastards will be here every hour, checking if we gone to Swansea. (*walks forward*) Listen! What was the idea?

BOB: The toy?

MICK: Right....

BOB: Everything is something and something is everything. Multi-dimensional toy.

MICK: What did I teach you?

BOB: Um... What it looks like, right? Appearance... um... What it does, right? Function... um... What it cost... money.

MICK: Last one....

BOB: Um... let me think... right! Could it be mass produced?

MICK: Right! (*thinks*) They are coming to see... eyes! Pass through the door... function! After the money... money! Keep coming till they get it! Mass! (*shakes his head*) I'm a dope head...

BOB: You've lost me, Mick....

MICK: Pass the problems... out of our hands... into something greater....

BOB: Uh? I don't get it now!

MICK: Sharon's father is an Indonesian banker. He's got stacks, house in Surrey, house in London....

BOB: I don't get it. Why not get Bo-Bo in with a gun. Tell him the rules of the toy. Send him to Sharon's father.

MICK: No. (*sits, rolls a joint*)

        (*BOB is confused. Silently, with a chisel, he prises open the slates of the crate and peers inside.*)

MICK: (*lighting up, drawing in*) Process! (*inspired*) Make a toy. Photograph it. Take it to Mothercare. Get a contract for a few grand. Thirty quid a piece rocking horses. Sixteen rockers at thirty quid. Four hundred and eighteen quid. Go to a work unit. Have a thousand made up. Get a price. Get delivery. Work unit to Mothercare. (*staring at point in space*) We just

108

	pick up the cheque.
BOB:	Remember the rocker at Mothercare. Four kids fighting over it. Broke it first day.
MICK:	Shut up! (*staring*)
BOB:	(*joins him, staring*) Join forces. Fix a point.
	(*MICK staring, without a flinch*)
BOB:	Which point are you staring at?
MICK:	Rip on the curtain.
	(*both stare*)
BOB:	Which rip?
MICK:	Under the fold.
BOB:	(*shifting his stare continuously*) Got it!
	(*both stare at different points*)
MICK:	Believe in the power. Believe. Believe that there is a force that directs us all.
BOB:	Oh yes... I feel it. Can you feel it?
MICK:	Lose all sense of self and time.
BOB:	Incredible... I'm floating in space...
MICK:	Let the force... sink inside... NOW! (*stops and turns to BOB*) Got it! Feel it! Inside! We made the toy before because we believed in the force! It made the multi-dimensional toy! We were just labourers... funnels... for the power to come down through. I'm fusing....
BOB:	And me....
MICK:	Stare... and reach out... bring it here.
	(*Both stare at their points. BO-BO and BUNNY enter and see the young men staring.*)
BUNNY:	(*carries the stag's head and sets about prodding and stabbing BOB mercilessly until he screams in pain*) I'm not doing it, Kid. The animal is doing it. I'm not doing it. Look, the animal's doing it!
BO-BO:	(*grabs MICK by the hair*) Swansea, I said! (*BO-BO beats him harshly. Both men are satisfied with their warning and exit.*)
BO-BO:	Three hours!
MICK:	(*staggers up, beaten and bent, he slouches onto the crate, moaning*) Oh... God... Oh... Dear....

BOB: (BOB *crawls to the crate. Attempts to use it to stand but falls on his backside against it. He holds his stomach and his face.*) Oh... God Almighty, mun! Why don't we fuck off?

MICK: They can kill me if they like, I don't care. Even if they maimed me. I still got my joy, in here... (*silence*) I haven't got the bus money to Swansea. Have you?

BOB: (*in pain*) Yeah. But I'm not dressed for it... (*tries to laugh, MICK tries to laugh*) Phone the cops, is it?

MICK: (*laughter makes him puff and cringe*) They've... been van.... (*can't finish*)

BOB: Dullised... (*painful, soft laughter*) Vandullised.... The telephones have been vandullised. (*silence*) Give them the patent. They can have my half.

MICK: Nu... they don't know what patent is... Bob....

BOB: What?

MICK: I want to live.

BOB: And me.

MICK: Have you got anyone?

BOB: Girl, you mean?

MICK: Anyone... family?

BOB: No. I got a brother Mike. He's got a motorbike. He went around the Gower, in a quarter of an hour....

(*Both find giggling painful. Light dimmer. Both hold on. Hang on in There! Time will heal!*)

Lights to black. Lights to dim. Lights.

BOTH: (*singing in the darkness*) Will they make it? Will they take it? Will they make it? Will they take it?

(*Blackness. Time passes. MICK is in his chair, rolling up. BO-BO and BUNNY sit opposite. BUNNY swings his gun and admires it.*)

BO-BO: When did he go?

MICK: About an hour... He's got a lorry driver's tachograph. He'll get a lift fast there and back. (*lights up*)

BUNNY: What's the shit?

MICK: Yours....

BO-BO: What's it worth?

110

MICK: The shit?

BO-BO: The toy.

MICK: If Swansea like it, fifteen hundred quid. On the nail.

BO-BO: Anything after?

MICK: Sales. Thirty quid apiece.

BUNNY: I don't see you with that scrawny piece lately.

MICK: That's my wife.

BO-BO: She pissed off?

MICK: Gone on holiday.

BUNNY: She's in care. In the Hostel. Seen her... and your kids, liar!

BO-BO: She was drinking with Lance.

MICK: Liar.

BUNNY: Lapping him up, she was. Dirty cow.

MICK: (*stares at BUNNY*) She didn't like my pornography collection.

BUNNY: Boys don't have that stuff.

MICK: I got the best, Bunny. It'll upset you. You! (*points at BUNNY*) It'll upset your guts!

(*BUNNY rises in temper, goes to stand*)

BO-BO: (*holds him back*) Stirring the shit, Bunny. (*stands*) You got less than two hours, Kid.

MICK: Scared Bunny? Leave him go, Bo-Bo. He's a big boy. But I'll tell you what, a big boy like, ain't seen nothing like I got. Take it, Bun, wank yourself to death. Pubs are shut. (*looks away*) Have it. I'm sick of it. Blue films. Two hundred quid's worth. And don't... don't split on me. Don't use the mitts again, O.K.? In the back room, blue cardboard box, marked eclairs. That's chocolates, Bo-Bo.

BUNNY: (*moves past MICK, points down at him*) Two miles of Taff. Three times a day. And I'd pour it down your guts, personally. (*walks to the backdoor*)

MICK: Ungrateful bastard...

(*BUNNY disappears inside.*)

MICK: Don't mind me asking, Bo-Bo, but do you believe in Jesus? Since I saw your ugly mug around town I've been dying to ask you.

BO-BO: (*storms to MICK*) You've had it now, Boy!

(*BUNNY screams and enters with a bill hook stuck in his head. BOB follows him with the gun. BUNNY rushes in pain, his hand clutching the point at which the hook entered his head. The loose end waves like a horn. He smashes into furniture blindly, raging.*)

MICK: (*takes the gun*) Out! Out! Or I'll blast you to kingdom come! Get out!

(*Lights go black. Time passes. Lights rise up slowly. MICK and BOB and gun are with their backs against the crate. They are seated on the floor, sharing draw.*)

BOB: I was shouting....

MICK: Where?

BOB: Glastonbury. Five minutes conversation, fifty pence! Answers to life, thirty pound each!

MICK: I'm gone... bushed....

BOB: And me....

(*Dim lights to night. BO-BO and BUNNY stand in front of them.*)

BO-BO: (*posh accent*) Brilliant. I was foxed throughout. Bloody clever the way you got Bunny inside.

BUNNY: (*equally posh, stag's head on his head*) Jesus, was I surprised. Speed? Bobo just flipped like an acrobat.

BOB: (*mumbles*) Gymnast.

BUNNY: Gymnast. Oh yes. Swipe! He made it seem so easy. Look, hardly any blood at all. How does he do it?

BOB: (*mumbles*) Practice. Days and weeks at the lathe.

BO-BO: Anyway boys, we're off. We've got a lot to tell the gang. You're good, fucking good. (*walk off*)

BUNNY: (*turns*) Hey, you two take it easy now! (*silence*)

BOB: What did you say, Mick?

MICK: Nothing. Thinking. You been talking mostly, mun.

BOB: What was in that stuff?

MICK: Paranormal bush.

BO-BO: (*reappears at the room door*) Mick? Sorry to disturb you, Mick. But I didn't mean it when I said I wanted half shares in your dream, O.K.? And another thing, it wasn't true about Sharon being with Lance. We made it up.

MICK: (*mumbles to himself*) I knew you were lying anyway.

BOB: What? I'm freezing ai... and starving. Got any chocolate biscuits, Mick?

MICK: (*slowly*) Yeah.. hold on, Bob boy... I got a couple behind my yers...

(*In MICK'S head: lights pass through the window: like torches, like cars, like the moon. Blue light illuminates the room door and smoke is apparent. Light flickers like an old silent movie.*)

(*BUNNY, half beast, half man, posing, in staccato movements, like a Bryan Mills catalogue. Casual with cigarette advertising pyjamas. Surprised and waving to those on a beach. Keep fit. He reverses back into the blue...*)

MICK: See that, Bob? (*nudges him*)

BOB: Where?

MICK: By the door. In lights...

(*BOB stares. The lights are red. BO-BO appears in a white t-shirt and white trousers, a large XO printed on his shirt. He makes a movement to his mouth continuously.*)

BOB: XO... EXO... EX... OOH...

(*BO-BO signals good, like charades, signals to watch him as he turns. He turns, a large O on his back, turns back, waits.*)

BOB: OH... EX... O...

(*BO-BO mimes eating.*)

BOB: Got it... Oxo...

(*BO-BO hands are undulating the air like waves.*)

BOB: Gives a meal a

(*BO-BO mimes "Come on! Come on!".*)

BOB: A beefy taste...

BO-BO: Gives a meal a beefy taste!

(*silence*)

BOB: Pity, mun.... (*shakes MICK*) Pity, mun!

MICK: (*sings*) Take the world and turn it upside down so that everyone can wear a crown....

BOB: Is Bunny dead, Mick? Do you think?

MICK: (*shakes his head*) If he does right, his gun goes marching on.

(*Black out for a few moments. Time passes.*)

(*Morning. Lights. BOB is draped from the back of the settee, his arms over the broken back, asleep. MICK is still propped up.*)

BOB: (*Wakes up, looks around, stands, walks uneasily to the room, reverses slowly, rubs his eyes.*) Mick! See that! (*no response*)

BOB: (*Walks into the room. A water tap is heard. He reappears drinking.*) Water, Mick? Water? (*MICK stretches his arm while his eyes are closed.*)

BOB: (*Walks over to him and gives him the water. He guides it down to MICK'S mouth.*) I wish it didn't happen, Mick. This is just a new day like... ordinary. Go up the mountain, riding Cleary's horses. Nice day, you know. My head's just... and ugly past... ugly... full of blood.

MICK: We did everybody a favour, mun! (*staggers up, holding on to the crate and drapes himself on it*) There'll be street parties. Jack Shit will be the new protector. Long live Jack Shit!

BOB: Mick. Who's this? (*puts his glass on the crate*) My Frank Spencer imitating John Wayne.

MICK: Frank Spencer.

BOB: (*laughing*) Yeah! No... listen... (*stands, posing like John Wayne*) Chuck away my beret, chuck beret. (*Both double up laughing. Poses again: tough-Spencer-voiced:*) O.K., Stumpy. I get offa my 'er hoss an' drink a my milk a... oh....

MICK: John Wayne.

BOB: Right!

MICK: (*points at BOB*) We do the whole human race a favour. They'll give us respect. And Bo-Bo... and Bunny... it's the language they understand. They won't hide behind cops. They'll be a laughing stock

114

to their mob. (*smiles*) Bunny'll have six stitches, O.K.? We keep the Avenues clean. Exterminators. Vermin. When I come up trumps I get a yacht in Siberia. Two yachts. I don't doubt it. Right. I believe in that crate. And if they cut me up, sonny boy, I come bouncing back in bandages. Because I still got this. (*points to his head*) And I'll put this in Mothercare. In Habitat. Work units and fifty staff. Focus! Focus!

(*Both stare. Bob Marley plays their Redemption Song. They sing along together, inspired. Gesticulate.*)

MUSIC: Why do we kill our prophets
While we stand aside and look
Some people say it's part of it
We've got to fulfil dee book...
O' won't you help me sing
Dees songs of freedom
Is all I ever had
Emancipate yourself
From mental slavery
None but ourselves can free our mind OOOO!
Have no fear from atomic energy
'Cos none of them can stop the time
O' won't you help me sing
Dees songs of freedom
Is all I ever had
Redemption songs...

(*MICK is moving now to his mental music, silently, on the spot.*)

BOB: (*arms outstretched, shouting and singing*)
I'm here in America
On a cobbling course
My father sent me
Because I'll show you the broken
Twisted time warp you live in...
All will come true...
At the end of time...
Children will walk with Gods
And the injured with the dead....
It's all broken now...
But you'll see the picture in
Twenty ninety nine...
In twenty ninety nine...

Rats will walk in peace
Bunnies in the field... (*stops*)
I might have to live all my life
Knowing that I killed a man...
Took his human life away...
I dowsed his spirit...
Me....

MICK: Six, seven stitches. We won! Jack the Giant Killers... (*walks to BOB*) Accept it. They put you down. Accept it kid. What you did was with Honour. It was meant to be. You fulfilled the meaning. (*sings to BOB, holding BOB'S face:*)

O' won't you help me sing
Dees songs of freedom
— Is all I ever had
Redemption songs.... (*stops suddenly*)

(*MICK and BOB look up to the ceiling, listening.*)

MICK: (*stares at BOB*) They're in.... (*points up*)

(*They both walk around on tip-toe listening and looking up. BOB points up. MICK follows a noise with his finger. BOB indicates a noise directly above. MICK indicates to BOB to get down. Shows a climbing action with his fingers. BOB bends. MICK climbs on his back. BOB stretches up. MICK stands on BOB'S shoulders, taps BOB's head and points to the glass of water. BOB walks over, collects it and passes it up to MICK. MICK drinks the water and then listens with the empty glass.*)

MICK: Can't reach! (*He passes back the glass and hauls himself out of reach. Silence.*)

BOB: (*quietly*) Mick...? Mick...? Mick...? Anything...? Mick...?

(*Silence. A large figure of a swim-suited girl advertising holiday snaps is lowered down slowly.*)

BOB: (*undoes it, laughing loudly*) Have you got one up there?

(*The rope disappears. Figure falls flat. An oil drum is beaten... thump... thump... like war drums... Jaws Film!*)

MICK: (*Slides down with bird's feathers in his hair. American accent:*) I dun like it Lootenunt... It's too quiet....

BOB: (*laughing: Frank Spencerish*) Is that your hoss outside, ooh! Wella, sumbuddies painted it yella... (*pulls on the rope, jumps up, the rope falls down and BOB falls down laughing.*)

MICK: Indian... rope... trick....

BOB: How did you do it?

MICK: I only did a bow.

BOB: A bow!

(*Both laugh, in stitches. They stand, walk over to the settee and sit.*)

MICK: (*Pulls out his wallet and draw. Rolls up, giggles:*) I done a bow....

BOB: Indian brave
Needed shave
Tomahawk slipped
Brave in grave.....

MICK: (*laughing*) I-only-done-a-bow. (*shakes his head*) Hang loose... stay cool....

BOB: What's up there?

MICK: Nothing... dust.

BOB: No windows?

MICK: Nu... (*lights, draws in, hands to BOB*)

BOB: (*takes it: Indian pipe of peace*)

Bumpa Dumpa
Bumpa Dumpa
Bumpa Dumpa

(*draws in*)

The poet and the planner
Stood side by side
The poet wrote his poems
The planner did his plans
Can't remember it...
The planner saw destruction...

(*hands it back*)

Something about God...

MICK: Think Sharon will come back to me?

BOB: I don't know.

MICK: She got dough... her father's dough.

BOB: Indonesian Banker is he?

MICK: Ai... as opposed to a Welsh banker. (*Silence. Mick draws in*) What she say when you saw her?

BOB: When?

MICK: When you saw her... in town.

BOB: She walked straight past.

MICK: Say nothing....?

BOB: Nothing. To say the God's truth, Mick, she looked thin, teeth were black...

MICK: She smiled then?

BOB: She was screaming at the kids.

MICK: What did she say?

BOB: Um? (*thinks*) Fuck off or something...

MICK: To the kids?

BOB: She's no good, Mick. When you're not around her language is foul. Say you get hundred thousand. World wide, I mean. You know, for the rights, the toy. You could have your pick.

MICK: No good, Bob. I want Sharon.

BOB: Think she's with Lance?

MICK: He was lying. Using the old psycho torture. Freaking me out. (*silence*)

BOB: Mick?

MICK: (*staring forward*) What?

BOB: What's the crate doing there?

MICK: It's safe....

BOB: No.... but... shouldn't we send it off? Swansea... or, wherever you can send it... off?

MICK: I don't want to be without it... like a baby. (*turns to Bob*) What do you do when you catch a train... important train?

BOB: Catch it....

MICK: But don't you always... sort of... feel the ticket in your pocket... make sure it's there?

BOB: Yeah. I done that.

MICK: Get the crate, Bob. Let's look at it.

BOB: (*stands*) She still calls you apathetic.

MICK: Among other names. If I go there with the toy, she'd say, "Hashish heads don't change their spots, toy or no toy."

BOB: (*touching MICK'S shoulder*) I'm young, you're young. We're at the prime of our poverty. (*walks to the crate*) They don't know it's inside, Mick. (*turns: face lights up*) They don't know. Mark it with another name.

MICK: Liquid nitrogen like....

BOB: Boot... shoes... um fragile... broken glass. Right Mick, I got it, the rope... up! Put it up there... and us!

MICK: Too heavy... too dusty. We got the gun anyway.

BOB: Put the gun up.

MICK: No, no, Bob. Gun to defend us.

BOB: (*cracks up*) Put the gun up. Just the gun. And we all hang around, confident, you know. Fucking gun's up the attic. Bo-Bo and Bunny come in... O.K. Pig's Arse. This is it! — Just smile... (*cracks up*) Secure-in-the-knowledge-of-the-gun-fifteen-feet-out-of-our-reach.

MICK: (*cracks up*) Remember the time you used my razor, old razor blade....

BOB: (*cracks up*) I come down stairs, worse shave I've ever had....

MICK: And Sharon pulls the new pack of blades out of her bag... (*laughs at the personal situation humour until they collapse*)

BOB: Knock-knock....

MICK: Who's there?

    (*BOB whispers and laughs.*)

MICK: Who?.... (*laughs*)

    (*BOB whispers*)

MICK: Who, mun?

BOB: (*loud whisper*) Secret police.... (*seeing through the curtains*) Mick, you're not going to believe this... (*watching, his head slowly following something*)

MICK: (*standing on the settee*) What!

    (*A letter comes through the door.*)

BOB:	(*picks it up*) From Sharon.
MICK:	How do you know? Was that Sharon? (*climbs over*)
BOB:	(*holds him at the crate*) Don't go out Mick! Don't go out! It's a trick!
MICK:	Sharon! Sharon! Sharon!

(*They struggle and wrestle and the actions turns aggressive until they fall, exhausted.*)

MICK:	Sharon... Sharon.... (*breathless*)
BOB:	Bo-Bo's trick! (*hold around MICK*) Cool it... easy... Mick....
MICK:	(*sees the envelope, picks it up, tears it open*) A card with an ape man.... (*shows BOB*)
BOTH:	(*reading the verse*)

Dear Jack Shit

You smoke so much
Because you're guilty
And you're guilty because
You smoke so much
Because you're guilty
And you're guilty because
You smoke so much

BOB;	No kisses... turn back....
MICK:	(*turns it*) Hash head on Mars....
BOB:	She came. That's a start.
MICK:	(*turns the card over, checking*) Rubbed the price off. (*scrutinises*) Does that say "Lance" under those scribbles?
BOB:	(*with his finger, tracing*) No, stupid. Thirty-five pence, "New-World-Art-Prints". Hey! It's your birthday. What would you like?
MICK:	Sharon and the kids.
BOB:	(*thinking*) Something second then.
MICK:	A stand in the British Trade Fair.
BOB:	You'll have all that if you believe in the force.
MICK:	Hey! If the Universe is us... then I am the Universe... all things are possible.
BOB:	Same as me. And the Universe is inside us.
MICK:	We'll get through, see. Just fifty-one per cent to forty-

nine. Score, thirty-three to thirty-two. We'll come through.

BOB: (*shaking with laughter*) And the good die young.

MICK: I got half a pound of shit. Today is my earth birthday. I don't care, see, Bob. I got stuff, I got the toy....

BOB: (*mumble singing*)

Warder threw a party
At the county jail!
Da Da Da DA Dee Dee...

(*Blackout. Silence. Two red spots of cigarette lights. Some moon, car and street.*)

BOB: What do you do then?

MICK: Shop-fitting... then pub decor... with a team.

BOB: Then "The Incredible Psyche", the book?

MICK: No. I hadn't read it then. Did some hobbling... private jobs. I built a house once and forgot to put in the kitchen. It was in the paper, me scratching my head. Then I read "The Incredible Psyche": Part One, "A Lazy Man's Way to Riches", Part Two, "Authenticity and Simplicity", Part Three, "You are Providence", Part Four, "Immortality Begins at Home", Part Five, "Fulfilling Wishes".

BOB: We're bringing good things to earth... "The Incredible Psyche"... O.K!

(*Silence. The smoke thickens. BOB and MICK cough and hold on to each other.*)

MICK: (*weeping*) They'll get us....

BOB: (*hands him the Kodak girl*) Sharon... Mick....

MICK: Sharon... Oh Sharon.... (*holds her tight*)

BOB: I can't make kids.... (*sits in isolation, desolate*)

MICK: Give them the toy when they come....

(*Smoke thickens. Blackness.*)

121

FRANK VICKERY
The Drag Factor

Rhondda playwright Frank Vickery (b.1951) is Wales' most popular contemporary dramatist. With some twenty-five published plays to his credit, he writes full time for theatre, television and radio. He is also an actor, director and producer. His television work includes episodes of *The District Nurse*, *Wales Playhouse*, and *Lifeboat*, all for the BBC. *The Necktie Party* and *Killing Time* are just two of the series Vickery has written for the radio. He has also written a sitcom based on his stage play, *Family Planning*, for S4C. Though best known for his comedies, there is usually a dark seam woven into his work, an obsession with social taboos and unsavoury secrets. *The Drag Factor*, written in 1994, demonstrates these aspects of his style. It is a *tour de force* for two actors.

CHARACTERS
Ruby
Griff
Nurse

(*The play takes place in a corridor outside a small hospital room. Outside this room is a door and part of a wall. Against this wall are two chairs. Ruby, a woman in her mid-fifties is sitting in one of them. She is wearing the uniform of a lollipop lady. Her hat is on the chair next to her. She has a shopping bag on her lap and a large, white man's hanky in her hand. She is wiping her nose as the lights come up. We know instantly though that she is not doing this because she has a cold. There are jangling instrument noises and a male nurse comes out of the room carrying a tray covered by a white cloth.*)

122

NURSE: Back in a minute.

RUBY: Is that it? Can I go in now, nurse?

NURSE: (*shaking his head*) Not quite finished with him yet. Shouldn't be long, though.

RUBY: How is he this morning?

NURSE: A definite improvement on yesterday, I'd say. (*pausing slightly before making to leave stage right*)

RUBY: I heard somebody laughing just now. What it him?

NURSE: No, it was me. He's a real live wire once he starts, isn't he?

RUBY: He's a hell of a boy, mind. He's never happy unless he's making people laugh.

(*RUBY laughs and so does the NURSE.*)

NURSE: Ten minutes and he should be ready for an audience.

RUBY: Good God, he's told you as well, has he?

NURSE: Sorry?

RUBY: That's the best way to be though, I suppose. I keep telling Griff, that's my husband, things will be much better now it's all out in the open, I said. He's only just recently found out. I've known for a while. It's not so bad when you've had time to get used to the idea.

(*The NURSE suddenly realises what RUBY is on about. He smiles before leaving.*)

NURSE: Be back in a minute.

(*After a second or two RUBY gets up and looks into the room through the round hole in the door. She can't really see anything so she sits back down. She dries her nose again. GRIFF walks on from stage left. He is about the same age as RUBY. He is wearing his Guard's uniform complete with hat. RUBY looks up and sees him.*)

RUBY: (*wiping her eyes*) Griff. You came after all.

GRIFF: Let's get this straight now before we start, right? I'm not here for him. It's you I've come for.

RUBY: Shshsh... You can't say that. He's our son.

GRIFF: He might be your son, Ruby, but I told him Saturday night, if he was going to carry on with all that nonsense he'd be no son of mine. I meant it then, and accident or no, I mean it now.

RUBY: (*raising her voice*) Don't talk like that. He might never come out of there.

GRIFF: (*shouting back*) He's got a couple of bruises, a few fractured ribs and he's had a knock on the head. He's not going to die, Ruby. He'll be out of this place by Thursday. You take it from me.

RUBY: Look here, he didn't come round hardly at all yesterday. He talked nonsense for a solid hour last night.

GRIFF: He's been talking nonsense since last Saturday if you ask me.

RUBY: Well, I'm not asking you. And I told you this morning, you've got to forget last Saturday...

GRIFF: I can't.

RUBY: Well, you're going to have to. For the moment, anyway.

GRIFF: It's like a bloody nightmare. It keeps playing over and over in my head.

RUBY: There's no way he'll be out of here this weekend. He's in no fit state. (*she has a thought*) They're hiding something from me, I'm sure of it.

GRIFF: Don't talk rubbish.

RUBY: They are, I can tell.

GRIFF: They've said he's all right.

RUBY: Yes, but they're not going to tell me everything, are they? And you must be concerned as well, if the truth be known, because nothing couldn't shift you to come here with me this morning. (*she has an idea*) They haven't sent for you, have they?

GRIFF: No.

RUBY: They haven't rung you from the hospital to come here, have they?

GRIFF: Would I be dressed for the afternoon shift if there was anything wrong?

RUBY: Tell me why you changed your mind, then?

GRIFF: For you. I changed it for you. I didn't want you to be on your own.

(*A slight pause. GRIFF sits down and takes a pack of sandwiches out of his bag.*)

RUBY: (*a loud whisper*) There was a policeman here earlier on. He confirmed there was no other car involved.

GRIFF: So what do they think happened, then?

RUBY: They know what happened. He fell asleep at the wheel.

GRIFF: Well, I'm not surprised. He should never be doing two jobs. I don't know anyone who can survive on three or four hours of sleep.

RUBY: Yes, he's been over-doing it lately.

GRIFF: Sandwich?

RUBY: Good God, no. I can't eat.

GRIFF: (*pause*) When he gets out later this week — perhaps you'd better suggest him giving up that "club" lark.

RUBY: I'm not suggesting anything of the sort.

GRIFF: Well, he's hardly going to listen to me, is he?

RUBY: You still don't get it, do you, Griff? If Nigel decides, for whatever reason, to give up one of his jobs, it'll be his day job in Cardiff. It's not going to be the clubs, Griff. You can put money on that.

GRIFF: Let's be honest. You wouldn't talk him out of doing it anyway, even if he would listen to you.

RUBY: No, you're right. I wouldn't.

GRIFF: God, you must be as proud as he is.

RUBY: I am. He's damned good at what he does and you thought so too before you realised who it was.

GRIFF: (*Pause. He looks at her.*) I'll never forgive him for that — or you either.

RUBY: How else was the boy supposed to tell you?

GRIFF: Like any other normal person.

RUBY: Griff, if he was normal, he'd have nothing to tell.

GRIFF: Am I that bad a father that I couldn't be told in the privacy of my own house?

RUBY: In a word, yes. You know what you were like when he wouldn't take that job with you on the railway.

GRIFF: That was a damn good job.

RUBY: But he didn't want it.

GRIFF: No, he'd rather go and dress windows in Cardiff. The writing was on the wall, even then. (*slight pause*) Well, that's it as far as the club is concerned, you know that, don't you?

RUBY: What do you mean?

GRIFF: We're in every Saturday night from now on because there's no way I can show my face in that place again.

RUBY: Oh, for goodness' sake. Anyone would think he robbed a bank or murdered somebody or something.

GRIFF: I think I could cope better with it if he had.

RUBY: Look, it's not easy for me either, mind.

GRIFF: I was the butt of all the jokes in work yesterday.

RUBY: Well, that's just great that is, isn't it? There they all were in the club Saturday night...

GRIFF: Exactly...

RUBY: All your workmates having a marvellous time, and today? Today they mock him for it.

GRIFF: It's not Nigel they were mocking — it was me.

RUBY: You think you're by yourself in that? I get it. I get it in supermarkets and in bus queues. I get it when I stop them in their cars to let the children cross the road. It happened last week. The car window was rolled down and I actually heard this woman say, "See her by there? Her son dresses up in women's clothes." I waited 'til the last kid was across the road then I stood right in front of her car. "My son is a female impersonator," I said. "He does it for a living. I heard your husband does it for kicks." With that, the car revved up and I swear to God, if I hadn't stepped out of the way when I did I think she'd have run me over.

            (*pause*)

GRIFF: It sounds like everyone knew except me. (*pause*)

RUBY: He tried to tell you...

GRIFF: So when did you find out?

RUBY: Well, I was down his house and I went in the bedroom dusting and saw he'd left the wardrobe door open. There were all these beautiful dresses in there. So I asked him about it and he told me.

GRIFF: He'd have told you eventually, anyway. You've always been close, and that's half the trouble. (*she looks at him*) Don't look at me like that, it's true. (*slight pause*) Me and him... we've never had anything going for us. He's embarrassed me all his life.

RUBY: The trouble with you is that you've got a short memory. You want to think back to Saturday night in the club.

GRIFF: I don't have to think back to it. I can't get the bloody thing out of my brain.

RUBY: You were having a marvellous time.

GRIFF: And that's what hurts the most.

RUBY: Tell me why you like drag acts, Griff?

GRIFF: I don't know... they're a bit of fun, I suppose.

RUBY: Exactly. You thought "The Dolly Sisters" were the best act the club had booked in months. You were killing yourself laughing. I know because I watched you. You laughed so much I thought you weren't going to stop.

GRIFF: And the fact is, I haven't laughed once since.

RUBY: They were marvellous. Nigel and his friend. Everybody loved them, they were so professional. All right, maybe it was cruel to call you up on the stage with them but you were glad to go at the time. You were having a ball. (*slight pause*) Until Nigel took his wig off.

GRIFF: I wanted to die.

RUBY: I swear to God I didn't know he was going to do that. And in fairness I don't think he had planned it either. I think he just seized the moment when he could.

GRIFF: (*quietly*) I just wanted to crawl in a corner and die.

RUBY: You hid your feelings pretty well, then.

GRIFF: No, I didn't. (*pause*) When I wiped my eyes everyone thought, including you, it was because I was laughing so much and it was... until I realised it was my boy up there. (*slight pause*) You can't imagine how I felt.

RUBY: Of course I can.

GRIFF: No, you can't. It's different for a father.

RUBY: In what way?

GRIFF: I can't explain it.

RUBY: Try.

GRIFF: I felt so...

RUBY: Disappointed?

GRIFF: (*He tries to find the words.*) Cheated.

RUBY: Even after all the laughter.

GRIFF: Because of all the laughter.

RUBY: You're saying you'd have taken it better if they didn't like him so much?

GRIFF: It would have been a lot less embarrassing for me, yes.

RUBY: So you'd rather he had died up on that stage?

GRIFF: (*quietly*) Yes.

RUBY: Is that what you are saying?

GRIFF: (*shouting*) Yes!

RUBY: (*slight pause*) Nigel didn't do anything that you haven't done in the past.

GRIFF: What are you talking about?

RUBY: You've dressed up as a woman before now.

GRIFF: I have not!

RUBY: What about that Blackpool trip we went on?

GRIFF: That was a long time ago.

RUBY: I can remember you prancing up and down the aisle wearing my green lurex dress and Mary Morgan's hair piece. And I'm sure Nigel can. There's a photo of you too, somewhere.

GRIFF: That was only a bit of fun.

RUBY: And last Saturday night wasn't?

GRIFF: That's a different thing altogether.

RUBY: But it's not, not really. The only difference is that you entertained forty people on a bus and he entertained four hundred in a club.

GRIFF: No, no... now you can say what you like, there's a lot more to it than that.

RUBY: Tell me why you did it, Griff?

GRIFF: (*slight pause*) I don't know... I was probably drunk.

RUBY: Come on... you can do better than that.

GRIFF: I can't remember.

RUBY: I can.

GRIFF: Then what do you want me to tell you for?

RUBY: I want to hear you say it. (*slight pause*) O.K., I'll help you out. You always saw yourself as a bit of a lad, didn't you? Hard to imagine looking at you now, but you still like attention, Griff. Nigel follows you for that. That's why you were quite happy to join the drag queens up on the stage. You like making people laugh. The trouble is, you think that last Saturday the joke was on you.

GRIFF: It was.

RUBY: Then it was on me, too.

GRIFF: No, it wasn't. You knew who you were looking at. You knew why you were laughing.

RUBY: I wasn't laughing at you, Griff, and neither was anyone else.

GRIFF: They might not have laughed at me at the time, but they've laughed at me enough since. I'm the talk of the place. We all are. (*slight pause*) I shouldn't have found out the way I did.

RUBY: No, I know, love. Only last week I said to him, "You'd better tell your father, quick," I said. "You take that booking at the club and sooner or later, he's bound to find out." (*slight pause*) I think the plan was to tell you after his spot. Or later when we got home, but you were enjoying the show so much...

GRIFF: (*slight pause*) Do you think he's...? He isn't, is he...?

RUBY: What?

GRIFF: You know what I mean.

(They look at each other for a brief moment.)

RUBY: They say it doesn't go hand in hand, but... yes, he is. *(slight pause)* Do you know what hurts me the most? Not that he'll never get married, but that I'll never show a little grandchild over the crossing and in to school. *(slight pause)* And then I thought, well, there's nothing I can do about it. You can't have the penny and the bun. I'm going to have to settle for the fact that my son is a cabaret artist and a very good one at that.

GRIFF: I wish it was that easy for me.

RUBY: It's not a question of it being easy, Griff. Our hands are tied. We play the game with the cards we're dealt. We either accept him for what he is or we don't. *(slight pause)* Do you know how he told me? *(GRIFF shakes his head.)* Do you want to know? *(he nods)* I suppose it was about two years ago now. It was a Saturday morning and you were in work.. I knew there was something up. He was hanging around my feet and you know, generally getting in the way. In the end I said, "Come on, what is it? You've obviously got something on your mind, so spit it out". He was at the table and he told me to sit down. I did and the atmosphere changed. The sparkle went from his eyes and he came over all serious. I didn't like it at all. "What is it" I said, "you're frightening me". He held his arms out across the table and grabbed me by the hands so tight I could see the whites of his knuckles. He looked me straight in the eye. "I've got a brain tumour" he said, "and I've only got three months to live". Oh my God, I could feel myself floating off. Then he yanked my hands and it suddenly brought me back. "No, I haven't" he said. "It's all right, I'm not going to die. I'm only gay." I could have killed him... but it's a funny old world though, innit? I kissed him instead.

(Pause. At this point the NURSE returns.)

NURSE: *(on seeing GRIFF)* Oh, Mister Gregory. Nigel asked me if you were here. I'll tell him.

GRIFF: Er, no... *(slight pause)* I'm not staying.

NURSE: Oh... can't you pop your head round? I'm not going

	to be very much longer.
GRIFF:	I've got to get to work.
NURSE:	All right, go on, nip in now, then. You've got time to show your face.
GRIFF:	(*shouting*) No, I said! You bloody deaf or what?
	(*NURSE looks at RUBY before going in to NIGEL.*)
RUBY:	You're going to be a very lonely old man, Griff.
GRIFF:	You never tried, not once... not once when he was growing up to interest him in...
RUBY:	Hey, you can't blame me. Now, it's not my fault. That's the first thing Nigel said to me. He said, "Now look, Mam," he said, "You musn't blame yourself". And I don't. How he's turned out has got nothing to do with me at all.
GRIFF:	You saying it's my fault?
RUBY:	You're the one who dressed up and entertained the bus from Blackpool. Who's to say what put the idea into his head?
GRIFF:	You don't think that, do you?
RUBY:	(*slight pause*) No, Griff. You didn't make him what he is and neither did I.
GRIFF:	We must have done something.
RUBY:	All I've done is to accept him for what he is because he's my son and I love him.
GRIFF:	I can't think like that.
RUBY:	You still love him, don't you? (*he doesn't answer*) If you don't feel the same as me then I feel sorry, because you're going to miss out. You're going to miss out on something very special.
GRIFF:	Special?
RUBY:	(*slight pause*) You're a hypocrite, Griff Gregory, and not a very nice one at that.
GRIFF:	Is there any other kind?
RUBY:	(*a thought strikes her*) It's Monday. Did you remember to put the rubbish out before you came?
GRIFF:	Have I ever forgotten?
RUBY:	(*slight pause*) Everything will be all right in the end.

(*he looks at her*) We've still got him, that's all that matters. We could have lost him in that car crash. How would you have felt then?

GRIFF: A lot like I do now, I suppose.

RUBY: Look, when you go in there....

GRIFF: I'm not going in there. I told you when I came here it was only for you.

RUBY: I'm sure he wants to see you.

GRIFF: Well, we can't all have what we want.

RUBY: Refusing to see or speak to him isn't going to make it better.

GRIFF: And going in there is?

RUBY: It's not going to make it any worse.

GRIFF: I can't go in there. I can't look him in the face.

RUBY: Why, it's the same face you looked at last week.

GRIFF: It's the same face I looked at last Saturday, minus the make-up.

RUBY: And wig. Don't forget the wig.

GRIFF: It's not funny.

RUBY: Of course it is. It's bloody hysterical. We'll all be laughing about it in a couple of months' time.

GRIFF: I should have put my foot down.

RUBY: What?

GRIFF: I saw it coming. I knew the way things were going right from early on. (*slight pause*) I should have done something... took him to football matches and...

RUBY: Oh, for goodness' sake, what's the matter with you? You don't honestly think watching twenty-two men kicking a ball around would have made any difference? You don't live in the real world, you don't. Buying him a cowboy outfit for Christmas when he was small instead of a Post Office set wouldn't have changed anything, even I know that. (*slight pause*) You're doing what I first did. You're blaming yourself and you shouldn't. You're looking for a reason and there isn't one.

GRIFF: There's got to be.

RUBY: Look, I am what I am, you are what you are, and he

132

is what he is. At the end of the day, thank God we're not all the same.

GRIFF: (*during this speech GRIFF runs away with himself*) What went wrong, then? Tell me, I need to know because something, somewhere went wrong. There must have been a time when he realised he was what he was. I mean, you don't just wake up one day and choose to be something like that. And if it's got nothing to do with you or me and the way he was brought up, then what has it got to do with? Where's the reasons for it? I don't believe it when you say there isn't one. Why didn't he tell us about it at the time? Maybe he could have had help. We could have taken him to see somebody who could have talked to him, who could have listened to him and then all this could have been avoided. (*a thought hits him*) Maybe it's not too late? He could go private — we can pay. I bet it would only take a few sessions with someone who knew what they were doing, someone recommended who could get to the heart of his trouble straight away. I don't think it's as big a problem as it first looks. It's only a question of preference, isn't it? So it shouldn't be difficult to find someone who could straighten him out. Get him to see it's only a matter of choice and once all that's sorted, I'm sure the other thing, the dressing up thing, will right itself. What do you think?

RUBY: (*slight pause*) Look Griff, I don't know much about it. I suppose there are books you can get on it, but I'm sure as hell not going in to the library to ask for one. All I know are the few bits and pieces that Nigel has told me. From what I can gather it's not a life-threatening disease, apart from this AIDS thing, and it's not something you can go have "straightened out" either. It's not like having a tooth pulled and then that's it, it's gone, everything back to normal. (*slight pause*) If it's only a matter of preference, like you say, is it really that big a deal he prefers something else? I know it's disappointing and I know it's not what we want.... but we don't have a choice... and although you'll find this hard to believe, I don't think Nigel had much of a say in it, either. You don't choose to be different... you just

133

are.

GRIFF: I can't understand how it's all so "matter of fact" with you.

RUBY: Oh, don't think he didn't break my heart, because he did. I've lost count of how many nights I cried myself to sleep. And what made it harder for me was I couldn't show him or you. I had to cry on my own and carry on as if nothing had happened even though my world was collapsing around me. (*slight pause*) "I'm glad I told you" he said. "It's like taking a big weight off my chest." Trouble was, he took it off his chest and put it on mine. I'm not complaining. That's what mothers are for. (*slight pause*) Do you know what did help me, though? (*he doesn't answer*) I picked up my magazine one week and some mother had written in to say that her son was going through the same thing, and do you know what the advice was? (*he still doesn't answer*) I can't remember it now word for word, but it was something like... There are two things parents should give their children, it said. Roots and wings. Roots and wings, Griff. Our Nigel knows there's always room for him at home and...

GRIFF: Does that mean he's coming to us when he gets out of here?

RUBY: I don't know. I haven't talked to him about it yet but I hope so. (*slight pause*) Whatever he wants to do, Griff, or wherever he wants to fly... it's O.K. with me. I'm behind him all the way. All I want is for him to be happy and there's nothing I wouldn't do to make sure he is.

GRIFF: What if I said he can't come home?

RUBY: What if I said you can bugger off?

GRIFF: He's left home. It's not fair to encourage him back.

RUBY: What's fair got to do with it? He'll need to recuperate. Kevin will do his best, I'm sure.

GRIFF: Who the hell is Kevin?

RUBY: Nigel's friend. The other half of the act.

GRIFF: (*slight pause*) Wait a minute. You're not going to tell me that they live together, are you?

134

RUBY: Well, I was going to, but it's pointless now.

GRIFF: I don't believe this.

RUBY: You're going to have to learn to be more tolerant, Griff. Shouldn't be difficult. You've always said, "Live and let live".

GRIFF: Yes, but not when it's your own flesh and blood.

RUBY: It should apply even more then.

GRIFF: So my son lives with another man. Is there anything else I should know?

RUBY: No, I think that's everything.

GRIFF: You sure? You're not keeping anything back to protect me from having a heart attack, are you?

RUBY: There's the little one they're expecting in June, but apart from that, there's nothing.

GRIFF: I wish I could joke about it.

RUBY: Who says I'm joking? (*He looks at her incredulously.*)

GRIFF: You're not serious? You are serious, aren't you?

RUBY: Kevin used to be married. Wife not up to much, from what I can gather. I don't know what her job is. I take it, it's to do with the military, though, because I heard Kevin say something about her being R.A.F.

GRIFF: Where's all this leading to?

RUBY: Well, they had a little girl together. Now, the ex-wife have picked up with yet another fella and he hasn't taken to her, poor little thing. There's a lot of talk of the little girl coming to live with Kevin.

GRIFF: In Nigel's house?

RUBY: Well, where else?

GRIFF: (*slight pause*) If I don't take in all that's happening, you'll have to appreciate it's because things are moving a bit too fast for me.

RUBY: Too fast?

GRIFF: Last week I thought I had an average twenty-five-year-old son who lived alone and had a mortgage in Pontypridd. Today, he's a drag queen who shares a house and bed with a man who's already married and whose daughter is about to move in. I mean, there's only so much a guard with British Rail can

	grasp.
RUBY:	Oh, I don't know. I think you've grasped it all pretty well, Griff.
GRIFF:	Will you tell me what the hell's happening to us?
RUBY:	Keep your voice down. You're in a hospital, remember.
GRIFF:	I don't care where I am! Up till last Saturday our family was quite... (*he searches for the word*) Orthodox.
RUBY:	Ortho? Orthodox? Christ, Griff, you can call us a lot of things but we've hardly been that.
GRIFF:	On the surface we were. Now all of a sudden everything's a mess.
RUBY:	No, it's not.
GRIFF:	(*shouting*) If people make fun of our son, it's a mess! If you get talked about by women in cars, it's a mess! If my work mates take the piss, believe, it's a bloody mess!
RUBY:	You shouldn't care what people say.
GRIFF:	But I do! It matters when they crack a joke and I can't laugh because we're the butt of it.
RUBY:	I don't suppose we get a fraction of the flack Nigel does. If he can take the slings and arrows, why can't we? If we stick together as a family, Griff, no one can hurt us.
GRIFF:	You don't know what it's like for me. What it was like for me on Saturday night.
RUBY:	All right, I'll admit finding out the way you did that Nigel was a drag artist perhaps came as a bit of shock to you, but you've just got to come to terms with it just like I did.
GRIFF:	It's not as easy for me.
RUBY:	I wish you wouldn't keep saying "It's not easy for you".
GRIFF:	(*insisting*) It's not!
RUBY:	Well, it should be.
GRIFF:	Why?
RUBY:	Well... I mean, you're normal enough now...

GRIFF: What do you mean?

RUBY: When we were courting I used to wonder which side of the fence you were going to fall.

GRIFF: You're all right, are you?

RUBY: Everybody has a mate, you know, I understand that. But you couldn't move without that Richie Thomas. Talk about Tweedle Dumb and Tweedle Dee? He was like your shadow till I put my foot down.

GRIFF: There was nothing funny about me and Richie. We were like brothers, we were.

RUBY: You don't take your brother with you on honeymoon.

GRIFF: (*shouting*) I didn't take him on honeymoon.

RUBY: (*shouting back*) It's a hell of a coincidence then that he ended up in the caravan next to us, don't you think?

GRIFF: It's not fair to throw Richie up. Specially now he's not here to defend himself.

RUBY: I'd have said exactly the same thing if he was alive.

GRIFF: You're a dangerous woman, you are, Ruby.

RUBY: I put it all behind me and didn't think much more about it. But after you made a fool of yourself at his funeral it brought it all back.

GRIFF: How many times have I got to tell you? There was never anything like that between us.

RUBY: Funny how he never got married.

GRIFF: You want to know why he didn't get married?

RUBY: Go on, surprise me.

GRIFF: I will. (*slight pause*) He loved somebody who was already married and it wasn't me... it was you. (*slight pause*) Well, what do you say to that?

RUBY: I knew. (*slight pause*) Now what do you say?

(*GRIFF is speechless. A slight pause before NURSE comes out of NIGEL'S room.*)

NURSE: There we are then. He's all done and sitting up in bed waiting for you.

(*The NURSE makes to go.*)

GRIFF: Er, Nurse...

(*The NURSE turns around.*)

GRIFF: Just now... um... (*he finds it hard to apologise*) What it was... Um...

NURSE: It's all right. Forget it.

RUBY: No! It's not all right, is it, Griff?

GRIFF: I shouldn't have... you know... shouted...er, like that. You all do a good job... deserve better...

RUBY: He's apologising, but it doesn't come easy, as you can see.

NURSE: It's no big deal, you know. You can change your mind and go in if you want to. (*slight pause*) Anyway, I've got to go. (*he smiles and leaves*)

RUBY: He's a nice fella, isn't he? (*meaning the NURSE*) Reminds me of Richie Thomas. (*slight pause*) He came to the house in a hell of a state one day. (*he looks at her*) Richie. He told me how he felt about me... then I told him how he felt about you and the poor bugger went home in a worse state than when he came in. (*slight pause*) I don't believe for a minute you ever got involved, but... you can't deny you didn't know how he felt about you.

GRIFF: We grew up together.

RUBY: All right, so as far as you were concerned, you were close. He had feelings for you...

GRIFF: And you...

RUBY: That he shouldn't have had and you knew it. You accepted it and understood it. Why can't you show something of the same for your son.

GRIFF: It's different when it's your own. And anyway, Richie never dressed up in women's clothes, or wanted to, as far as I know.

RUBY: Good God, Griff, it's only a bit of fun, you've said that yourself.

GRIFF: I can take a joke and have a laugh as good as the next man. But you've got to admit that what our Nigel is into is a hell of a lot deeper than that.

RUBY: All right, so he does take it a bit more serious. He's got to. It's his job. There's nothing more to it than that. At the end of the day all the dresses get put

	away in a wardrobe.
GRIFF:	Who said?
RUBY:	Hell's delight, do you think he walks around the house in a dress, do you?
GRIFF:	It's possible. Who's to say he isn't sitting in there now waiting for us dressed up in a sister's uniform?
RUBY:	(*laughing*) Good, you're making a joke of it.
GRIFF:	I'm dead bloody serious.
RUBY:	(*slight pause*) Would it be so awful if he was? (*he doesn't answer*) It shouldn't matter to us if he wanted to go around naked with a frying pan on his head.
GRIFF:	You can say all you want, I can't like him for what he does.
RUBY:	All right, don't. You can still love him for what he is.
GRIFF:	You mean in spite of what he is.
RUBY:	Whatever. Nobody really cares what he does behind his front door, Griff, and if they do, why should it matter to us?
GRIFF:	You're very good at all this, aren't you? Much better than me.
RUBY:	I've had more time. It'll get easier if you try, I promise.
GRIFF:	But it will never go away.
RUBY:	No, Griff, it'll never go away. You can be sure of that. (*slight pause*) Can I ask you something? (*he looks at her*) Which was the worst for you? The humiliation on Saturday night, or the knowledge that your only son is gay?
GRIFF:	(*shouting*) It's not fair!
RUBY:	Of course it's not, but life never is. (*slight pause*) I want to know what the hardest thing is for you. See, if it's the fact that he's gay, well there's nothing anybody, including Nigel, can do about that. If, on the other hand, if it's the drag thing, asking Nigel to give up the dresses isn't going to change him either.
GRIFF:	Do you know what I've gone and done?
RUBY:	Surprise me.
GRIFF:	You know you brought Nigel's suitcases home with

you after the accident? The suitcases with all the costumes? (*slight pause*) I've emptied them. I emptied them into two big plastic bags and put them out with the rubbish bin this morning.

RUBY: (*slight pause*) Oh my God. You thought that would solve everything and that would be the end of it, I suppose?

GRIFF: I don't know what I thought. (*slight pause*) After Saturday maybe I just wanted to get my own back.

RUBY: There was over five hundred pounds worth of dresses in those cases. Not to mention the make-up and wigs.

GRIFF: What can I say?

RUBY: Well, nothing to me. I'd start thinking about how you're going to tell Nigel if I were you.

GRIFF: I don't know if I can apologise to him.

RUBY: And you won't know unless you try. Anyway, seems to me there's apologies due on both sides. See him. Go on. Go in and...

GRIFF: You don't know what you're asking.

RUBY: I'm only asking the same of you as I ask of myself. (*slight pause*) And you still haven't answered my question.

GRIFF: (*slight pause*) Going round the clubs like he does... it's a bit like having a tattoo on his forehead.

RUBY: So it's not that he's gay, then. It's the drag factor?

GRIFF: Why has everybody got to know?

RUBY: You'd feel better if he tried to hide it?

GRIFF: I'd feel better if he didn't flaunt it.

RUBY: So it's the drag factor.

GRIFF: I'm never going to be able to accept it like you.

RUBY: There's only one way to accept it, Griff, and that's a little bit at a time. The first hurdle is to walk in through that door. The second is to smile, and if he smiles back, which he will... everything will be plain sailing after that.

GRIFF: How can I smile when I feel like knocking seven different colours of shit out of him?

RUBY: You'll smile, Griff. We both will because the chips are down and we can't do anything else. (*slight pause*) When he was a little boy, all I wished was for him to be happy... and he is. I forgot to wish for me to be happy too.

GRIFF: We can always walk away... let him get on with it.

RUBY: (*shrugs*) I can't do that. He's my son. He needs me.

GRIFF: Oh well, there you are then... as long as he's got you...

RUBY: And I need him. And although it's not easy for you to admit, you need him too.

GRIFF: Does he need me, do you think?

RUBY: The answer to that is staring you in the face, Griff. It wasn't me he asked the nurse about. It was you.

GRIFF: He only wants me to condone what he's doing.

RUBY: He's not after your blessing. He needs you to accept him for what he is. That's not the same thing.

GRIFF: What about what I need?

RUBY: Shouldn't come into it. Roots and wings, Griff... roots and wings. (*slight pause*) You can walk away if you want to, but it's not going to solve anything. (*slight pause*) Whether you like it or not, you're going to be his father for an awful long time. (*slight pause*) Closing your eyes is not going to make him disappear. (*slight pause*) I'm going in. I bet he's wondering what's happening. (*She makes at NIGEL'S door.*)

GRIFF: Do you want me to come with you?

RUBY: Of course I do... but there's no way I'll let you. Not with me. You go in there, you go in on your own. (*slight pause*) Well, what's it to be, Griff? Is it time to take your head out of the sand, or what? (*slight pause*) Come on, it can't be as bad as all that. One small step for Griff, one giant leap for Nigel. (*slight pause*) If it makes you feel any better, you'll be killing two birds with one stone. (*he looks at her*) You remember that weight we talked about? You know, the one Nigel took off his chest and put on mine? You can't take it away, I know that... but I'd sleep a hell of a lot easier if you took half. Isn't that what husbands are for?

GRIFF: And sons?

RUBY: (*slight pause*) Kids. They're all the same when it comes down to it... arm ache when they're small, heart ache when they've grown.

            (*They share a moment before she turns and goes into NIGEL'S room.*)

RUBY: (*off*) Hiya luv, you're looking marvellous.

            (*GRIFF stands motionless for a moment. Slowly he turns to look into NIGEL'S room. After staring in for a moment or two he moves away to the chairs where he has left his work bag. He picks it up and slowly walks to the door again. After a brief pause he opens the door and stands just inside.*)

CHARLES WAY
Looking Out to See

Charles Way was born in 1955. He is a prolific and established playwright dedicated to writing for touring theatre companies. Three of his plays, *Dead Man's Hat, Paradise Drive* and *In the Bleak Midwinter*, are collected in *Three Plays: Charles Way* (Seren). His play, *A Spell of Cold Weather*, won the Writers' Guild Best Children's Theatre Award for 1996. His recent work includes a forty-minute film poem for BBC2 called *No Borders* and *The Dove Maiden* for Hijinx Theatre. *Looking Out to See*, written in 1996, is a poignant play written especially for young performers. It was first presented in 1996 by the Sherman Youth Theatre, Cardiff as part of "A Generation Arises".

Throughout the piece dancers represent the emotions
of the characters, the story and elements of the natural world.

CHARACTERS
I   age 18
Idge   age 19
Carol   age 17
Geoff   age 40
Karen   age 15
Sharon   age 13
Darren   age 13
Daz   age 12
Einstein   age 13
A group of 12/13 year-olds.

ACT ONE WALES

Author's Note

The I of the poem is a boy who is 18, and about to go
to college. I see him with longish hair and dressed in
a great-coat, whereas Idge is much more working
class. The poem is the boy's appraisal of a day trip to
Skomer Island off the west coast of Wales. It is
important that he does not dominate the poem but
leads it. The poem can sometimes be spoken chorally
and the lines shared out between all participants, not
just the named characters.

I: At seven in the morning
as we stand in the dirty light
outside the youth centre
waiting for the minibus,
it starts to rain
the kind of rain
that only rains in cities.

IDGE: I feel dead...

I: Says Idge
an' rubs his eyes.
When the world refuses
to come into focus
he closes 'em again
an' stands there on the pavement
swaying
to some music of his own making.

OTHERS: Then we see
that the rain falls only on us
an' everywhere else it's sunny an' dry
an' even Einstein...

I: Thirteen years old an' six o'levels
to his real name
can't reason with reality.

EINSTEIN: We're not meant to be here

I: He says...

EINSTEIN: Wrong time, wrong place,

I: An' we find it hard to to tell
if this is merely true in the cosmic sense
or if there really has been

a cock-up in the arrangements.
But Lo
like a star from the east
at 7:45
the minibus arrives. (*They cheer sadly.*)
We cheered ecstatically.

(*There follows a movement section which abstractly conveys the confusion of a group of people getting on a minibus, out of the rain. They climb over each other, round each other and DAZ ends up on the floor.*)

I: There were fourteen of us that day, including the Dodge family:

KAREN: Karen

SHARON: Sharon

DARREN: And Darren.

I: Darren was twelve last Tuesday
and keeps looking through his pockets
for his childhood.

KAREN: That's his excuse.

DARREN: Shut up, you.

I: There was Idge an' I.

CAROL: And Carol.

IDGE: I'm not sitting next to her.

I: And a bag of youngsters
who all looked exactly different.

SHARON: Except Einstein

I: Who looks like nothing on Earth
but says with a confident air...

EINSTEIN: There's a five to one chance
I'll be sick on the bus

I: An' would anyone fancy a bet.
An' of course there was Daz
with hair cut by his Dad
who's in the T.A.'s
an' once played rugby for Newport.

GEOFF: Daz. Daz. Daz.

ALL: Daz.

I: His name came to him

145

	as out of a dream.
GEOFF:	What's the matter, Daz?
I:	Says our leader, Geoff.
DAZ:	I'm lookin' for me crisps.
I:	Says Daz from the deck o' the bus. An then he stands bites his bitten lips an' smiles the soft smile bullies find so appealing.
DAZ:	I'm looking for me crisps.
I:	Then Carol...
IDGE:	I'm not sitting next to her.
I:	Sits next to Idge.
IDGE:	Fat slag.
CAROL:	Dickhead.
IDGE:	Bitch.
	(*Silence. CAROL moves away.*)
K & SH:	Are we going somewhere nice, Miss?
GEOFF:	Don't call me Miss I'm not in school now.
I:	This remark perplexes even us but I collect our thoughts an' say How far is it, Geoff? With due respect for his idea of authority.
GEOFF:	Like I told you
ALL:	A hundred times
GEOFF:	We're going to an island
CAROL:	What'd ee say?
DAZ:	He said we're going to Ireland.
SHARON:	I'm not going to Ireland. Me Mum'll kill me.
IDGE:	Good.
SHARON:	I don't wanna go to Ireland.
IDGE:	No, not Ireland, not bloody Ireland. You have to get a plane or a boat to go to bloody Ireland.

146

GEOFF: It's called the Isle of Skomer.
           It's a sanctuary for birds.
           It's lovely in the spring
           beauty beyond words.

IDGE: Why don't you shut up about it, then?

I: What's up with you?

IDGE: Nothing.

CAROL: How long did you say, Sir?

GEOFF: A couple of hours, maybe three.

CAROL: You're kiddin' me?

I: Says Carol.

CAROL: Three hours with him?

IDGE: Fat slag.

CAROL: Dickhead.

IDGE: Bitch.

GEOFF: What's a couple of hours
           In the scheme of things?
           An hour is nothing
           in the great wheel of time.

           (*silence*)

I: An' with these words
           he closed his eyes
           crossed his Stead an' Simpsons
           an' nodded off
           into a world
           where happy youth club leaders go
           to reclaim the years
           they've never quite outgrown.

DAZ: Will we see the Sea?

I: Yes, Daz.

DAZ: I like the sea.

DARREN: When I was a kid
           we used to sing songs
           to greet the ocean.

K&SH: A sailor went to sea sea sea...

IDGE: Shut it.

K&SH: (*louder*) To see what he could see see see
           But all that he could see see see

147

was the bottom of the deep blue sea sea sea.

(*This rhyme is repeated as the group move to a new configuration. As they do so we hear again the sound of the sea and birds. Gradually the rhyme gets quieter and quieter until the whole group are staring out to sea.*)

I: An' there it lay

ALL: The sea, the sea,

I: An' the minibus came to a halt
out of sheer respect.

DAZ: What's that then?

I: That's the sea, Daz.

DAZ: Where's the beach then?

I: There's no beach, not here.

DAZ: No beach?

I: We stood on a rock
at the edge of the sea
our backs to the land
facing the breeze.

(*silence*)

DAZ: What's that, then?

I: That's a boat, Daz.
It's different to a minibus.

DAZ: Have you seen my crisps?

(*Once again the group are on the move, this time into a boat, and the movement should mirror the earlier transition onto the minibus.*)

I: From St. Martin's Haven...

ALL: We caught a tiny boat
most of us thought
would never float
with all of us on board.
An' we sat in small
rows of three
under the sky
over the sea.
And the sky was dull
an' the sea grey.
We held out our hands
to catch the spray

148

from over the gunnel,
an' for a moment
no-one spoke,
all were diminished
by space an' colour.
Darren got soaked
an' blamed his mother
for not getting him dressed
like she used to.
Then the island
came into view
and the seagulls
laughed in the sky
at the sight of the boat
and its nervous crew.

(Music. Third movement section which transfers the group from the boat to the island. Once on the island they run madly about shouting, until GEOFF calls them in.)

GEOFF: Stay back from the cliff's edge
don't stray from the path
don't drop litter
stay together
please — don't do anything daft!

(At this, the group disperses wildly and GEOFF repeats his commands as the group spin round him.)

I: We stalked the Isle in groups of five

GEOFF: Groups of five!

I: And the day became its own day
an' no-one behaved in quite the same way
as in corridors, changing rooms or toilets.

GEOFF: Stay back from the cliff's edge.

(silence)

ALL: It was like stompin' about
on someone's head
an' the hair on the head was blue
'cos it was May
and in May
the place is covered in bluebells.
An' as for the weather
all heaven broke loose
on our upturned faces

an' we shivered an' shook
'cos we was no more
than a drawer
of thin socks an' cheap anoraks.
All day the wind came and went
and the sun and the rain
did exactly the same
and nothing was settled.
Once it hailed, even as the sun shone
'an we thought some crazy sod
was playing silly buggers an' chucking grit.
But it wasn't grit, it was ice,
Ice
from a single cloud in a clear blue sky.

(*The group disperses leaving CAROL sitting on a rock, looking out to sea. KAREN approaches.*)

KAREN: Did you feel that?

CAROL: What?

KAREN: Ice.

CAROL: Yeah.

KAREN: Ice — in May.

CAROL: So.

(*silence*)

KAREN: Must be strange.

CAROL: What?

KAREN: Living on an Island.

CAROL: Wish I lived on an Island.

KAREN: The birds would get on me nerves.
Just listen.
And it's worse at night, apparently.
They all come back to the island for a kip
but they don't, they just gossip — all night.

CAROL: You'd get used to it.
You can get used to anything. (*silence*) Karen?

KAREN: Yeah.

CAROL: Do you know — about me?

KAREN: Everyone knows.

CAROL: Great.

KAREN: What did your Dad say?

CAROL: He said nothing at first, for hours.
He just sat in his chair
in front of the telly.
Then called me a prat
but said, not to worry
we'd talk it all out
over a curry.
In the Taj Mahal on Newport Street
I told him straight,
I'm keeping the baby.
He said I was daft.
I should have an abortion
and why the hell
didn't I take precautions.

KAREN: Did he get mad?

CAROL: No, he was tender, loving an' kind,
an' said he and my mother
would help me out
that, "Despite the distance between them
they still cared for each other
and me."

KAREN: So who's the father?

CAROL: That's the problem.

IDGE: (*from a distance*) What are you two gassin' about?

KAREN: It's not Idge, is it?

CAROL: No, that's why he hates me.

KAREN: Well, look at it from his point of view.

CAROL: I know, I know.
(*IDGE approaches.*)

KAREN: Do you want me to stay?

CAROL: No, I'll be alright.

KAREN: Sure?

CAROL: Yeah, thanks.
(*KAREN goes.*)

IDGE: What then?

CAROL: Nothing.

IDGE: What are you staring at?

CAROL: The sea. What are you staring at?

IDGE: (*he looks away from her*) Nothing.

CAROL: Do you want something to eat?

    (*He nods, sits and eats a sandwich rather ungraciously. I watches from a distance. Lights change. Sea sounds.*)

I: And they sat on a rock
looking out to sea
and far away
a ship vanished
and then returned
as if to prove Columbus right.
But anyone who's ever had a picnic
at the end of the world
and sat as these two
in such utter silence
knows the truth,
the world is flat
and stays flat...
    until...

CAROL: You don't have to decide anything.
See how things turn out?
It might not be so bad.

IDGE: You don't understand.

CAROL: I told you I'm sorry.

IDGE: I know. It's just... (*sound of sea*)

CAROL: What?

I: Listen. (*sound of sea*)

CAROL: It could still work for us.

IDGE: I can't bring up someone else's kid.

CAROL: It was a mistake —

IDGE: I know. But I can't. It's not natural.

CAROL: Natural? What's natural?

IDGE: (*shrugs*) Like this place.

CAROL: This place isn't natural.
It's a bird sanctuary.
It's only here 'cos the rest of the world
is full of crap.

IDGE: It's no good talking to you.

CAROL: You think I should get rid of it?

IDGE: Why not?

CAROL: So we can all go back
          to how it was before
          you with your mates
          and me with mine
          dancin' round handbags on floors.

IDGE: Yeah.

CAROL: I hated it back there.
          I was nowhere — I was nothing.

IDGE: Thanks a lot. (*exit*)

CAROL: Idge!

I: Below the surface of the world
          we found a cave
          and in the cave
          we found some treasure.

          (*A group of 12/13 year-olds (plus I) have found a cave.
          Light shines in from the entrance so that at first the group
          are silhouettes. As they advance the sound of the sea re-
          treats.*)

1:        Hey, come over here.

2:        What is it?

1:        I don't know.

2:        Ugh, it's horrible.

4:        Looks like a big slug.

5:        It's a seal.

3:        Is is dead?

4:        Must be.

3:        Don't...

4:        What?

3:        Go near...

4:        Why?

2:        Ugh, its eyes have been eaten out.

1:        It's horrible.

4:        What's it doing here?

2:        Nothing, it's dead. You don't have to do anything
          when you're dead.

3:	Poor thing.
1:	Must have been washed up.
	(*They gather round the dead seal.*)
DARREN:	I saw me grandad when he died. He was laid out in a coffin.
4:	Bet he had his eyes in though.
3:	What are you doing?
5:	I want to see what it feels like.
3:	What for?
5:	To see what it feels like.
3:	Poor thing.
I:	Fishermen used to hear the cries of seals and they sounded so human they mistook 'em for mermaids.
4:	Who told you that?
I:	A mermaid.
2:	I want to go out.
4:	Why?
2:	I don't like it in here, it smells.
5:	It's just a cave.
4:	And a dead seal.
1:	Why don't we take it out?
3:	Don't! Just leave it.
1:	We could drag it down to the sea.
5:	What for?
1:	(*shrugs*) Bury it. Give it a Christian burial.
4:	Do you think seals are Christians?
DARREN:	Makes you wonder though, doesn't it?
5:	What about?
DARREN:	Well, like, why are we on the planet? (*Everyone turns to look at DARREN.*)
4:	To buy records, Darren, Everyone knows that.
DARREN:	You're a cynic.
4:	You're a twat.

154

SHARON: Don't call my brother a twat.

5:    Yeah, he's a dickhead, not a twat.

2:    I want to go out.

1:    Why?

2:    It's spooky.

EINSTEIN: It's only death.

I: Said Einstein,
and the world
and the waves
at the edge of the world
stopped in their tracks
to listen.

EINSTEIN: It's only death, that's all,
nothing to be scared of,
if you consider the fact
that we live in a universe
that was born and will die
like everything in it
including the sun and the stars
and the seals in the sea.
The Universe is not eternal
anymore than a single cell.

(silence)

2:    Where's Daz?

1:    Don't know.

2:    Maybe we should find him.

4:    Leave him be, he's cracked.

2:    He shouldn't be on his own.

(They all leave except no. 3 and I)

3:    Poor thing.

I: What can you do?

3:    My trouble is, says Mum
I care too much.
I care about everything,
the trees in Brazil,
the spots on the sun.
I know all about whales
who are hunted
and Greenpeace

155

and, "Prisoners of Conscience".
I gave away a pair of shoes
to a girl on the street
who begged me.
I walked home barefoot,
and hid from me Mum.
I don't like to think of myself
as no more than a
grain of sand.

VOICE 2:   Come on you two.

VOICE 5:   The tide's coming in.

(I approaches IDGE. The scene mirrors the previous scene between the two girls, KAREN and CAROL. IDGE is throwing stones into the sea.)

I: Have you seen Daz?

IDGE: Nope.

I: What's up then?

IDGE: Nothing. *(silence)*

I: Something.

IDGE: When do you leave then, for college?

I: October.

IDGE: October?

I: Yeah. I thought I'd go round the world. *(silence)* Do you want to come? You could, if you wanted.

IDGE: Can't — I've got a job.

I: Yeah?

IDGE: Packing biscuits into boxes. *(Silence. He throws a stone aggressively.)*

I: What about you and Carol?

IDGE: History.

I: I hate history. *(they grin)*

IDGE: Hey, look out there.

I: Suddenly, out at sea

IDGE: 'bout half a mile

I: A fishing boat entered the frame
an' its engine could be heard
grumbling beneath the war of rock an' wave.

156

An' as we watched
the boat shuddered
an' shook like a wet dog
an' all went quiet.

IDGE: There's someone coming out.

I: A little man
in an ill-fitting jumper
who waved at us.
I waved back
an' Idge looked at me
like I was mad.
So I put my hand down
an' said nothing but stared
out to sea, as...

IDGE: ...another boat...

I: ...came at speed across the water.

IDGE: There's smoke an' all.

I: It came from the guts
of the fishing boat,
an' the man in the jumper...

IDGE: ...hurls himself
headlong into the sea,
an' he looks like nothing
in the great grey swell.

I: Then the other boat was by him
and someone took his hand
and pulled him up.

IDGE: And he's saved.

I: Then they were off
'an round the headland, gone.
And they never saw what we saw.
We saw the little red boat
we saw it go down.

IDGE: It just went down...

I: ...an' left only...

IDGE: ...a smudge of smoke...

I: ...an' a rainbow glint of diesel...

IDGE: ...on the surface of the sea...

I: ...and the sea was as bare as blackboard,

157

	an' Idge said...
IDGE:	It's just like a film.
I:	An' there was a film crew somewhere...
IDGE:	...hiding in the cliffs.
I:	It was strange standing out there on the edge of a rock an' Idge saying...
IDGE:	It's just like a film.
I:	Without any sound, but the wind.
IDGE:	They won't believe us.
I:	No.
IDGE:	They won't.
I:	I know.
IDGE:	They won't believe he was saved, neither.
I:	I would.
IDGE:	Yeah, you would, 'cos you are.
	(enter CAROL)
CAROL:	Idge! Idge!
IDGE:	What?
CAROL:	It's Daz.
I:	Where is he?
CAROL:	He says he's going to jump. He says he's going to jump.
	(All characters and dancers now involved in an explosive movement section which quickly brings us to an image of DAZ on the edge of a cliff – wind blowing.)
I:	And there he stood at the edge of the world an' that's what it was, this place where the earth had stopped and said enough is enough.
ALL:	Daz. (all stretch arms out to DAZ) An' he said
DAZ:	I can fly. I can fly.
I:	An' Shearwaters an' Gannets came out of their implausible homes

	and circled his cries.
5:	Come on, Daz.
GEOFF:	Come back from the edge.
I:	An' he laughed the crazy laugh of his Dad who's in the T.A.'s an' reads books about Nazis an' knows how to punish a boy without bruising. And he went an inch closer and grinned as if to say that down there two hundred feet below where the sea grinds its jaws...
ALL:	...all day, all day...
I:	...down there where the world no longer exists.
ALL:	He could be kind of his own rock.
I:	And his eyes were dark and full of the gap between heaven and earth and in my head I saw him leap in a great joyous arc into that vital space between rock and sea rock and air.

(This imaginary action of DAZ jumping is then acted out.)

ALL:	And the wind took him up like a sheet of newspaper, and for a moment he flew with the birds whose names he did not know.

(Then DAZ is replaced on the cliff's edge.)

GEOFF:	Daz, you've got to come back.
SHARON:	You've got to.
IDGE:	Come on, Daz.
CAROL:	We need you.
DARREN:	I found yer crisps.

(They silence DARREN.)

DAZ: (*dreamily*)
A sailor went to sea sea sea
to see what he could see see see
but all that he could see see see
was the bottom of the deep blue sea sea sea.

GEOFF: Daz — please. Step back.

ALL: Daz Daz — Daz.

I: And who can tell
if by stepping back
the boy on the cliff would be saved,
but the sky and the sea
spoke convincingly of life
and that was the choice he made.

        (*DAZ steps back.*)

ALL: It's called the Isle of Skomer.
It's a sanctuary for birds.
It's lovely in the spring,
beauty beyond words.

I: We carried Daz down to the boat

ALL: Which most of us thought would never float
with all of us on board.

I: And Idge took Carol's hand
an' made it fit his own.

ALL: And we sat in small rows of three,
under the sky,
over the sea.
And the sky was dull
and the sea grey.
We held out our hands
to catch the spray
from over the gunnel.

I: And for a moment
no-one spoke.
All were diminished
by space and colour...

EDWARD THOMAS
Hiraeth

Award-winning Edward Thomas (b.1961) was born in Ystrad-gynlais and now lives in Cardiff. He has been at the forefront of contemporary theatre in Wales for ten years. Writer and director of plays for the stage, radio and television, his work has been made into an opera and he has his own theatre company, Y Cwmni. Perhaps best known for his play, *House of America*, now a major film, Thomas is obsessed with identity and Wales as an imagined nation that needs to re-invent itself. Originally staged in 1994, *Hiraeth*, a short play for two voices, is a clear example of Thomas' powerful rhetoric. His characters question, investigate and threaten each other in their quest for meaning and purpose.

CHARACTERS
Gwenny
Tyrone

(Two heads appear in a landscape as if being born. They have no bodies. Both are blind.)

GWENNY: All right?

TYRONE: All right.

GWENNY: You been here long?

TYRONE: As long as I can remember, why?

GWENNY: Grim innit.

TYRONE: Terrible.

GWENNY: Hopeless.

TYRONE: Un-bastard bearable.

GWENNY: It's a crime.

TYRONE: An outrage.

GWENNY: Shouldn't be allowed.

TYRONE: Like animals in a zoo.

GWENNY: Who would have said.

TYRONE: What the fuck do they think we are? Exhibits?

GWENNY: Who?

TYRONE: Them out there.

GWENNY: Who out there?

TYRONE: Those bastards watching.

GWENNY: You reckon there's somebody watching?

TYRONE: I'm sure there is.

GWENNY: How come.

TYRONE: I heard a cough.

GWENNY: Just the one?

TYRONE: A cough's a cough.

GWENNY: Could have been a sheep.

TYRONE: This was no sheep.

GWENNY: They can sound very similar.

TYRONE: This was a man.

GWENNY: I was once out in the country late at night on my own when I heard a cough that sounded like a man's cough but it turned out to be a sheep's cough... it made me feel very stupid.

TYRONE: This was definitely a man's cough... like a smoker's cough.

GWENNY: Where did it come from.

TYRONE: Over there.

GWENNY: Left or right?

TYRONE: Right, which way are you looking?

GWENNY: I can't tell. I'm as blind as a bat.

TYRONE: Jesus.

GWENNY: I can't help it, I didn't lose my eyes on purpose, mister.

TYRONE: I wasn't saying.

162

GWENNY: Could have happened to anyone and besides a bit of sensitivity goes a long way.

TYRONE: I'm sorry.

GWENNY: Forget it.

TYRONE: I didn't mean to.

GWENNY: Let's just drop it, shall we.

TYRONE: Yes, I'm sorry.

GWENNY: You're not from Banwen by any chance are you?

TYRONE: Banwen?

GWENNY: A by-passed town in the South that nobody's ever heard of and nobody goes to.

TYRONE: No...

GWENNY: I used to live there once.

TYRONE: Oh...

GWENNY: I had a boyfriend there called Cat... well that's not his real name. His real name's John but he had a dog, he took it everywhere, he called it dog. So we called John, Cat.

TYRONE: Because they fell out.

GWENNY: Who now?

TYRONE: Well... Cat and his dog.

GWENNY: No. The dog was Cat's best friend. He called it Shinc after his father, Jenkin.

TYRONE: Oh...

GWENNY: Jenkins went to Jenk then Shenc then Shinc, you follow?

TYRONE: I follow.

GWENNY: So Cat called his dog Shinc, see.

TYRONE: I see.

GWENNY: He was a mongrel, cross between a sheep-dog and retriever. Lovely dog too. I reckon Cat loved him more than he loved me. It was the only thing we used to argue about. He's in Stoke now.

TYRONE: Who is?

GWENNY: Cat is... he threw a dart on the map with his eyes shut and thud, it landed in Stoke. Do you know

163

Stoke?

TYRONE: No, I've never been there.

GWENNY: Nor me... Cat said it's alright. Cat's a bit of a loner really but he used to write to me regularly, even when I was ill. Mental problems. My head. Thought I was somebody else. I went bananas. You ever gone bananas, mister?

TYRONE: I've come close a couple of times

GWENNY: Everybody goes bananas one time or another. My brother went bananas see, killed my other brother with his own hands. Nobody ever thought he'd do such a thing, but it happened. They gave him fifteen years for that. He's served five. He reads a lot now. I wrote him a letter a couple of years ago. I told him I forgave him. He was thrilled to bits. He never meant to do it, see. He just snapped. Things got on top of him. He could have played international rugby if he hadn't got injured playing an away game in Merthyr. Ligaments they said. He packed it in, started drinking, and got barred from the pub for smashing up the toilets for no reason. Him and Cat were big mates. Cat was no rugby player, mind you. Cat was a hunter. I used to like that about him. Do you like international rugby, mister?

TYRONE: I used to go to every home match.

GWENNY: They say there's a good atmosphere.

TYRONE: There is.

GWENNY: I've never been. I could have gone once but I went to the fairground instead, in a space between the bowling green and a factory, not much more than a car park, really. I could have worked in that factory.

TYRONE: I worked in a factory for a bit.

GWENNY: Making what?

TYRONE: Washers mostly. I collected them.

GWENNY: That's nice.

TYRONE: All different sizes.

GWENNY: It's good to have variety.

TYRONE: It is. That's why I like Bournemouth.

GWENNY: Bournemouth?

164

TYRONE: We used to go on holiday there.

GWENNY: Oh.

TYRONE: I saw Max Bygraves there.

GWENNY: In the street?

TYRONE: In a show. He drove a Rolls Royce. One day my father saw him riding around in it. My father turned to my mother and said "He's made it, that Max has" and she said "Must have". Not long after that we booked two tickets for this Summer Spectacular.

GWENNY: Was it good?

TYRONE: I suppose. I was only small. We were staying in the Durley Dean. A small hotel it is, not very big. It was alright.

GWENNY: Were you an only child?

TYRONE: Yeah...

GWENNY: What's your name?

TYRONE: Tyrone. And you?

GWENNY: Gwenny.

TYRONE: Pleased to meet you, Gwenny.

GWENNY: And you, Tyrone. (*pause*) Tyrone's a funny name, Tyrone.

TYRONE: My father thought I'd be an actor.

GWENNY: Did you get very far?

TYRONE: No, but I went on Blue Peter with my tortoise. Valerie Singleton showed me how to hibernate it. His name was Smudge. He was a good tortoise. They gave me a badge and I took it to school. I made six Dougals out of Fairy Liquid bottles and orange wool. I even gave them out as presents for Christmas.

GWENNY: Who's Dougal?

TYRONE: Everybody knows who Dougal is.

GWENNY: I don't.

TYRONE: From the Magic Roundabout, mun. He was a dog. He didn't get on with Brian the Snail but he was big mates with Florence.

GWENNY: Who's Florence?

TYRONE: Christ, didn't you ever watch television?

GWENNY: Of course I watched television.

TYRONE: In that case, you'll know who Spock is. It was my nick-name in school.

GWENNY: Spock?

TYRONE: Yeah, Spock. Star Trek. Leonard Nimmoy.

GWENNY: Who's he?

TYRONE: A space travel TV show set in the future. He had pointy ears.

GWENNY: Who did?

TYRONE: Spock did. He was a Vulcan...

GWENNY: You were in a TV show?

TYRONE: No, Spock was.

GWENNY: But you're Spock.

TYRONE: Spock is Leonard Nimmoy.

GWENNY: Who the hell's Leonard Nimmoy?

TYRONE: He was a Vulcan with pointy bastard ears, mun. They named me after him.

GWENNY: What's a Vulcan?

TYRONE: A bloke from another planet.

GWENNY: You're not from another planet.

TYRONE: No, I'm from Caerbont for fuck sake. They called me Spock because they thought I had pointy ears like the Vulcan Spock in the TV series played by Leonard Nimmoy, that's all. You get it?

GWENNY: Oh.

TYRONE: Do you understand now?

GWENNY: Yes, but I think I'd rather call you Tyrone if that's alright with you.

TYRONE: You call me what you bastard want, Gwenny.

GWENNY: Thanks.

TYRONE: Don't mention it. (*pause*)

GWENNY: Do you mind if I get something off my chest, Tyrone?

TYRONE: No, you fire away.

GWENNY: Did you know that you snore like a lawn mower?

TYRONE: Jesus Christ. Is it that bad?

GWENNY: You kept the whole park awake last night.

TYRONE: What park?

GWENNY: This park.

TYRONE: This is no park.

GWENNY: Course it's a park. Can't you hear the birds singing?
           (*pause*)

TYRONE: What birds?

GWENNY: They were singing a minute ago.

TYRONE: This is no park.

GWENNY: They must have migrated.

TYRONE: They don't just up and off and migrate just like that.

GWENNY: They do. I've seen them. When the time's right they
           just clear off. Whoosh. Just like that.

TYRONE: Not all of them go, though.

GWENNY: Uh?

TYRONE: Some breeds stay. Like the Robin stays all through
           winter, living off crumbs.

GWENNY: Yeah.

TYRONE: So why can't we hear a Robin, then?

GWENNY: I don't know, do I?

TYRONE: I do. This isn't a park.

GWENNY: Will you stop saying that?

TYRONE: Well, it's obvious innit? No birdsong, no rustle of
           trees, nobody walking, just nothing.

GWENNY: So? Where do you say we are then?

TYRONE: I don't know, but I once heard a radio announce-
           ment.

GWENNY: Where was I?

TYRONE: You must have been asleep.

GWENNY: I never sleep. I get terrible nightmares.

TYRONE: Then you weren't here.

GWENNY: I was here before you.

TYRONE: You weren't.

GWENNY: I was.

TYRONE: Never. I remember Eric.

GWENNY: Who's he?

TYRONE: He was a Rugby player who'd been sacked from his job.

GWENNY: So?

TYRONE: He was here before you, talking. He said he was being overwhelmed. Things started to fall down from the sky for no reason.

GWENNY: What kind of things?

TYRONE: Domestic things: fridge, cooker, bike, electric kettle...

GWENNY: Really?

TYRONE: Really. He came here.

GWENNY: Why doesn't he say anything now, then?

TYRONE: Maybe he's just lost his voice.

GWENNY: Why didn't you mention him sooner?

TYRONE: I didn't want to frighten you.

GWENNY: Don't you think I'm frightened already?

TYRONE: I do, and I was only trying to protect your feelings.

GWENNY: I didn't know you cared.

TYRONE: I'd rather not be here alone, Gwenny.

GWENNY: Nor me...

TYRONE: Can you imagine how it would be?

GWENNY: I can.

TYRONE: More than anyone could bear.

GWENNY: I know... it frightens me, Tyrone.

TYRONE: And me.

GWENNY: I've been trying not to think about it.

TYRONE: I can hardly get it out of my mind.

GWENNY: Nor me. (*pause*) Did you really hear a radio?

TYRONE: I'm sure I did.

GWENNY: What was the programme?

TYRONE: I forget its name, but it was like a phone-in show with a highly regarded vet. They were explaining how Northern European pigs push trotter-activated shower systems in their sties to escape the Southern

Italian heat.

GWENNY: What?

TYRONE: It's the only way to keep them cool, Gwenny. A caller from the South of France phoned in. She owned two long-haired dogs and her vet had advised her that the only way to keep her dogs cool was to shave all their long hair... you follow me?

GWENNY: I suppose, but...

TYRONE: So the phone-in vet suggested she do what the pigs do in the pig styes up Southern Italy.

GWENNY: Get the dogs to shower like the pigs do but in specially set-up paw activated kennel shower systems!

TYRONE: Bingo! No self-respecting long-haired dog would be seen dead without a shower in a hot country. How else to escape the midday sun?

GWENNY: Exactly.

TYRONE: I'm glad we see eye to eye on this, Gwenny.

GWENNY: So am I, Tyrone.

TYRONE: It's a shame we couldn't have met in less perilous circumstances, Gwenny.

GWENNY: I know.

TYRONE: I couldn't handle this situation without you, you know.

GWENNY: You must have felt the same about Eric, surely?

TYRONE: Eric was different, Gwenny. For a start he was a man and I'm strictly heterosexual. Secondly, he was consistently more depressed than you. And thirdly, he started telling me stories I could no longer understand.

GWENNY: He rambled?

TYRONE: Worse than that. He told me stories that were patently untrue.

GWENNY: Like what?

TYRONE: He said he was a soldier injured in a battle carrying the luggage of a ruined Indochina in his damaged head.

GWENNY: And he wasn't.

TYRONE: He was talking about Vietnam, Gwenny. And the only thing he knew about Vietnam was what he saw on his TV screen.

GWENNY: Which was?

TYRONE: I don't know. I stopped watching TV after Sandy died in *Crossroads*.

GWENNY: Sandy?

TYRONE: A soap opera character I very much admired.

GWENNY: Were you in love with her?

TYRONE: No. Sandy was a man, Gwenny, confined to a wheelchair but played by an able-bodied actor.

GWENNY: I see.

TYRONE: I hope that doesn't make a difference to the way you feel about me, Gwenny.

GWENNY: I don't know. How do I feel about you?

TYRONE: I don't know.

GWENNY: I've only just met you.

TYRONE: Haven't you heard of a whirlwind romance?

GWENNY: Romance? In these circumstances?

TYRONE: Crazier things have happened, Gwenny. I once had a deeply spiritual experience while listening to Georgie Fame.

GWENNY: Good God.

TYRONE: Do you think that's weird?

GWENNY: No. Georgie Fame is, in my opinion, a very fine musician.

TYRONE: You reckon?

GWENNY: I reckon, Tyrone. I really reckon.

TYRONE: Thanks, Gwenny. That's really kind of you.

GWENNY: Don't mention it.

TYRONE: It happened when I was in Wyoming, see. My uncle had a farm there. His name was Morgan. He was a good man, but a creature of habit. He used to keep engine washers in his pocket and liked to pass them off as dimes. We used to get up at five and work on the crops. Then around eight, nine o'clock, me, my uncle and all the other farm workers would go to the interstate highway for a huge breakfast. Every day would be the same. My uncle would pass the washers off to the same waitress as a tip with a dime on top so it looked like a big tip. She'd say "Thank you, kindly" and smile and all the guys would laugh. Then they'd wink and walk out of the diner to their pick-ups and drive away. THIS HAPPENED FOR 101 CONSECUTIVE DAYS, Gwenny!

GWENNY: Jesus!

TYRONE: On the hundred and second day, I couldn't take it any more and did a bunk with a man I met in a bar who dealt drugs. We drove all through the night taking lines of coke. When we reached the redwood forests of California, we stopped in a clearing. I was coked out of my head. The stranger turned on the radio and bingo it was Georgie Fame (*fade in music, low level*) I thought I was going to go crazy. The stranger laughed at me. I shut my eyes. I started to dream.

GWENNY: About what?

TYRONE: Home.

GWENNY: Home?

TYRONE: Home.

GWENNY: Oh. Oh.

TYRONE: But it wasn't the home I knew. The rivers and seas had dried up. A howling wind blew through the land and the whole place was grey and frozen. On the seashore was a dead and fallen king amongst dried trout and cod stuck to the stones and rocks. I saw a people with painted blue bodies, large heads and long arms mourning and pointing to the sun and moon alike. I was afraid. They told me the king died of longing. What longing, I asked. A longing for a place he once knew but could no longer see, they said. What place is that, I asked, and is it far? At the far end of your imagination, they replied, is where it can be glimpsed, but be swift if you want to find it for our rivers and seas are drying up and the sky will soon fall down on our heads. That's impossible, I said, the earth is the earth and the sky is the sky and never will they meet. They shook their heads and called me a fool. You will never know what you have lost until you've lost it, they said. And with that they disappeared in front of my eyes as a terrible storm rose up and blew everything before it. All I could do was shut my eyes. (*pause*) When I opened them, I was no longer in the redwood forest and I wasn't coked out of my mind either. I was in the middle of nowhere in a dicky bow, white shirt and smart suit. (*pause as music fades*) Three weeks later I arrived home, but it was no longer the place I'd remembered it to be. They'd found somebody else to do my job and unfamiliar faces passed me on the street. They took no notice of me. I was invisible.

GWENNY: There's nothing worse than invisibility, Tyrone.

TYRONE: So I dreamt of Wyoming and the forest and Georgie Fame. I saved up and went back there hoping to call it my new home. But when I got there, my uncle was dead and the land was overgrown. The waitress in the diner made a necklace of all the washers and engraved a dime on it in memory of Morgan, my uncle. She was having a baby and was quitting the diner. She was going back East. I asked if I could go with her, but she said there wasn't anything there for me. So I went to the forest of redwoods but never found the clearing and I'd forgotten the song. I found myself alone. I came back to this country and found a room in the city and took a job on the factory floor making engine washers. I took the spares to my room and built a miniature of the town I used to call home. I smiled at what I'd achieved and then quit my job. I sat in my room and stopped going out. I looked in through the windows of the miniature town I used to call home and had conversations with the people I remembered from childhood. I remembered when the canal froze over and the summers swimming in the mountain streams. (*pause*) I got thinner and thinner. I stopped eating. I wanted to shrink so small that I could fit into one of the houses. I wanted it to be my home. It was the only thing I had left. (*pause*) But they threw me out for not paying my rent. I watched them smash everything down. I tried to fight back but I was too weak. There was nothing I could do but leave and start a life of wandering.

GWENNY: Where did you go?

TYRONE: Everywhere. I became a fisherman. Bought a second hand ambulance with a bed, stove and fishing rods and hit the road.

GWENNY: Did you know who you were?

TYRONE: I think I did, but I may have been wrong.

GWENNY: Were you happy?

TYRONE: In the beginning I found it rough and hard. I found I couldn't fish all day and every day so I had to slow myself down, take things step by step. I'd arrive at a place to fish and spend perhaps a day looking at the water, examining the water or pacing the beach. And then when I was ready, I'd start to fish.

GWENNY: It sounds good.

TYRONE: It was good. I only knew time by the passing of the fish seasons. I'd travel North to fish the early rivers for salmon and then as the snows melted I'd move to the lakes and brooks for trout. Then with the spring I'd head to the South and West where the beaches were desolate and barren. By the time October winds blew, I'd catch the cod as they started their southward migration.

GWENNY: Where would they go?

TYRONE: The warmer seas of the Mediterranean... who knows?

GWENNY: So why did you stop? (*pause*) Tyrone?

TYRONE: I reeled in my rod one day and at the end of it was a man's head... severed from his body. At first I thought he was dead, but then I saw his face, he was smiling at me and then he spoke.

GWENNY: He was alive?

TYRONE: He was. He told me I was a better story-teller than a fisherman. "Who are you to say that to me," I said, "you don't even know me". "Oh yes I do," he said, "Your name is Tyrone Collomazza and you went to Sunday School as a boy on windy afternoons wearing a velcro fitted waistcoat and elasticated yellow tie".

GWENNY: And did you?

TYRONE: Yes... yes.

GWENNY: Jesus.

TYRONE: I shut my eyes and cried. When I woke up my rod, reel and ambulance was gone and I found myself alone here. In limbo. (*pause*) Gwenny? Gwenny?

GWENNY: I'm still here, Tyrone.

TYRONE: You're the only person I've told my story to.

GWENNY: I'm honoured, Tyrone.

TYRONE: Does it make any sense to you?

GWENNY: No, but it may do to someone... someday...

TYRONE: It helps me explain my desperate predicament, Gwenny.

GWENNY: I understand how you feel.

TYRONE: If it wasn't for my own personal experience of things that are beyond understanding, I'd have gone crazy by now you know.

GWENNY: You reckon you're not crazy then?

TYRONE: No.

GWENNY: So what are you?

TYRONE: In a bit of a tight corner, that's all... a limbo.

GWENNY: Limbo?

TYRONE: Limbo... I don't know where I am or how I came here.

GWENNY: Oh Jesus, Tyrone, that's a big one.

TYRONE: Can you help me?

GWENNY: I'm afraid I can't.

TYRONE: Haven't you thought about it?

GWENNY: 'Course I've thought about it.

TYRONE: And...?

GWENNY: It leads to nothing and gets me all stressed up for days on end. The best thing for you, Tyrone, is to forget it.

TYRONE: How can I forget about it when I can't feel my arms?

GWENNY: You can't feel your arms?

TYRONE: No.

GWENNY: Jesus

TYRONE: Or my legs.

GWENNY: Bloody hell.

TYRONE: In fact, I can't feel a fucking thing.

GWENNY: You'll never believe this but I feel exactly the same.

TYRONE: What?

GWENNY: I'm exactly the same, I said. I can't feel a thing either.

TYRONE: Jesus Christ, I thought it was just me.

GWENNY: No, the only thing I can feel is my head, mun.

TYRONE: Aaaarghhh!!!

GWENNY: There's no need to make a scene.

TYRONE: "Make a scene", she says. "MAKE A FUCKING SCENE."

GWENNY: Yes.

TYRONE: BUT THIS IS ABSOLUTELY BASTARD SERIOUS, WOMAN. I DON'T KNOW WHAT'S HAPPENED TO ME.

GWENNY: Neither do I, but there's no point in panicking, is there? It'll only make things worse and besides, we still have our heads.

TYRONE: Oh great, mun. Two talking heads, talking bullshit in limbo.

GWENNY: It's not much to brag about, I know, but...

TYRONE: Brag about? I AM SHRINKING TO A FUCKING VOICE, WOMAN.

GWENNY: At least you still have a voice. Some people I know can't talk at all. They just sit in the corner in silence. And there's nothing worse than silence when you've got something you want to say, is there?

TYRONE: I'm not...

GWENNY: IS THERE?

TYRONE: No, but...

GWENNY: So there... don't bastard complain.

TYRONE: Don't you talk to me like that.

GWENNY: I'll talk to you as I want. I don't have to be polite to you. I don't even know you.

TYRONE: Five minutes ago I was trying to help you.

GWENNY: And I appreciate it, thanks.

TYRONE: Now all you can do is scream at me and pour scorn on my desperate predicament.

GWENNY: Our desperate predicament, please. We're in this together whether you like it or not.

TYRONE: So don't shout then.

GWENNY: I'm not shouting.

TYRONE: You are.

GWENNY: I'm not.

TYRONE: Listen to you.

GWENNY: Listen to you.

TYRONE: This is ridiculous.

GWENNY: I know.

TYRONE: It's getting us nowhere.

GWENNY: Absolutely.

TYRONE: We should be pulling together, not falling apart.

GWENNY: You took the words right out of my mouth.

TYRONE: Good, at least we can agree on something. (*pause*)

GWENNY: All I was saying was... what I mean is... perhaps we're just a weird phenomenon.

TYRONE: Uh.

GWENNY: That can't be explained rationally.

TYRONE: What about irrationally?

GWENNY: Well, I did think once...

TYRONE: What?

GWENNY: It's only a theory.

TYRONE: What theory?

GWENNY: I read it in a book in the hospital.

TYRONE: What book?

GWENNY: Like Myths.

TYRONE: Like what?

GWENNY: Orpheus.

TYRONE: Who?

GWENNY: He was a Greek.

TYRONE: So?

GWENNY: He got his head chopped off but he carried on talking, they found his head on a beach in Lesbos.

TYRONE: Where's that?

GWENNY: In Greece.

TYRONE: I've never been to Greece.

GWENNY: You don't have to go to Greece, Tyrone.

TYRONE: So what are you saying?

GWENNY: I'm saying that the Greeks reckoned the head carried on living after the body had died. The seed of life was the head, and the head was packed with seed.

TYRONE: Like a pomegranate.

GWENNY: Something like that.

TYRONE: Are you saying the head's like a pomegranate?

GWENNY: No, but...

TYRONE: Sticking out from the earth?

GWENNY: Tyrone!

TYRONE: That is fucking outrageous, Gwenny.

GWENNY: You're not listening to me.

TYRONE: I am no Greek story-teller who's turned into a fruit you eat with cocktail sticks, Gwenny. I'm a warm and sensitive human being.

GWENNY: Will you just shut up and listen?

TYRONE: There's no point in listening. All I'm going to get is bullshit.

GWENNY: "Bullshit," he says, "bullshit". ME?

TYRONE: Yes.

GWENNY: WHO MENTIONED THE TROTTER-ACTIVATED SHOWER SYSTEMS?

TYRONE: That was on the radio.

GWENNY: It was bullshit.

TYRONE: I was making light conversation.

GWENNY: Exactly... what's the point of light conversation when our only hope of survival is that someone out there watching will hear our stories and do something about it.

TYRONE: Your stories are lies.

GWENNY: Bollocks.

TYRONE: I bet your family didn't murder each other.

GWENNY: They did.

TYRONE: Prove it.

GWENNY: It drove me insane!

TYRONE: You're as sane as me.

GWENNY: That doesn't say much. You're the only bloke I've ever met who's caught a mythical Greek hero with a fishing rod.

TYRONE: It wasn't a mythical Greek hero.

GWENNY: Who was it then?

TYRONE: None of your business.

GWENNY: Who was it, Tyrone?

TYRONE: Nobody you know.

GWENNY: WHO THE FUCK WAS IT?

TYRONE: IT WAS A FUCKING ANGEL, ALRIGHT? (*pause*)

GWENNY: I don't believe you.

TYRONE: You believe what you want. It's the truth.

GWENNY: What did it look like?

TYRONE: Like nothing I've ever seen before... something good.

GWENNY: Good?

TYRONE: Yes, good. (*pause*) Do you believe me? (*pause*) Gwenny?

GWENNY: I saw an angel once. I ran away from the hospital. I wanted to go home, but when I got there our house was gone. Strangers and wild dogs roamed the empty streets and a cold wind whirled through the forgotten town. (*pause*) I got on a bus. I was the only passenger, the driver smoked Marlboro and looked straight ahead. I asked him where he was going and he said nothing. He put a new version of an old song into the cassette player and started the engine. (*fade in Frank and Nancy Sinatra's "I love you"*) I looked out of the window and the land was covered in frost. It was a different land than the one I remembered. (*pause*) We passed an upside down horse laying dead on the road. Two foals stood next to it staring at it. They looked cold and alone. I asked the driver to stop but he said that his bus never stopped. I got angry. I pulled at the wheel and he pushed me away. He hit me. My head smashed against the seat. I was bleeding. (*pause*) I remember the drone of the engine. He'd taken off my clothes. He was burning my breasts. I could feel him inside me, tearing me apart. I couldn't move, I felt weak. He was laughing at me. (*pause*) I looked at my pale yellow dress. I remember mam buying it for me to go to a dance in the summer. She said yellow was my colour. (*pause*) He said he was going to kill me. I tried to fight back, he had his knees on my chest, two nicotined fingers moved towards me. I called out, my head rang but the fingers tore into my eyes and plucked them out. I tried to call out, but I had no voice. I felt blood run like tears down my face. He said he was the devil. (*pause*) He blinded me. There was no-one around.

TYRONE: Where the fuck was everyone?

GWENNY: I could have died of shame, Tyrone. (*pause*) He put my eyes in a plastic goldfish bowl for decoration. There were two goldfish. They lived in a castle at the foot of the tank surrounded by rainbow-coloured stones and weeds. They asked my eyes where my body was as they fanned them with their fins. I said I didn't know. They asked me if I remembered what I looked like. I said I was wearing a yellow dress. They said that if they saw a woman in a yellow dress they'd make a tidal wave which would send my eyes cascading out of the tank and into my hands and I would see again. But I never walked by. (*pause*) Five days went by. The tank became dirtier and dirtier. The rainbow stones turned green and on the sixth morning the goldfish lay dead on top of the water, their eyes dulled and glazed. On the seventh day, the tank was in total darkness and I couldn't see. (*pause*) I woke up naked and blind on a shingly beach, the tide at my feet. I heard a voice call out my name. It sounded like mam's voice and then she touched me. (*pause*) She

179

said that I was safe. She said that she was looking after me from above. (*pause*) She said she was happy and that she loved me... and then she said good-bye. (*pause*) She was an angel too, Tyrone... and I still miss her. (*pause*) She's out there somewhere watching over me now. Like she always said she would. But she won't answer when you call, Tyrone. Angels are funny like that. (*pause*)

TYRONE: I'm sorry, Gwenny, I didn't...

GWENNY: She died four years ago in her sleep, but she's still with me, Tyrone, she's still here. (*pause*)

TYRONE: I'm sorry.

GWENNY: Forget it. (*pause*) They say I've got her eyes and my father's forehead.

TYRONE: Yeah?

GWENNY: Yeah.

TYRONE: With me it is the other way around.

GWENNY: That's nice. (*pause*) Have you got any brothers and sisters?

TYRONE: No, it's just me.

GWENNY: Oh... (*pause*)

TYRONE: I'm glad I met you, Gwenny.

GWENNY: That's good.

TYRONE: It could have been under better circumstances I know, but...

GWENNY: I've always had plenty to say, me...

TYRONE: I don't think I could handle this on my own.

GWENNY: Nor me.

TYRONE: I'd go bananas.

GWENNY: Yeah.

TYRONE: Reach the end of my tether.

GWENNY: I know what you're saying. (*pause*)

TYRONE: We should talk again.

GWENNY: We should. (*pause*)

TYRONE: Fancy you not knowing who Spock is.

GWENNY: Fancy you going to Sunday School in an elasticated yellow tie and a velcro-fitted waistcoat.

180

TYRONE: Fancy.
GWENNY: It's a wild and weird world, Tyrone.
TYRONE: You can say that again.
GWENNY: You hungry?
TYRONE: Starving.
GWENNY: Haven't eaten for days.
TYRONE: Weeks.
GWENNY: Can't have eaten even a Kebab.
TYRONE: I could murder a curry.
GWENNY: Sausage and chips.
TYRONE: Lager.
GWENNY: Tea.
TYRONE: Shortbread biscuits dunked into tea till they're soft.
GWENNY: Marvellous.
TYRONE: Lovely.
GWENNY: Heaven, mun...heaven.
TYRONE: Heaven. Huh.
GWENNY: Huh.

TIM RHYS
The Old Petrol Station

Born in Bridgend, Tim Rhys (b.1959) graduated in psychology from University College, Swansea. He worked with adults with learning difficulties and taught English in Italy before becoming a full-time writer. Author of surreal, black comedies such as *Dead Man's Fall*, *The Ghost of Morgan Morris* and *Ted's Creatures* (co-devised with Peter Jones), and the BBC radio series *The Last Visible Dog* (also with Peter Jones), he has also written more sinister, poetic plays such as *Riding With Buffalo Bill* (for radio) and *Stone The Crows*. *The Old Petrol Station*, written in 1994, is set in a deserted heritage centre high above a Welsh valleys ghost town. The two attendants, funny and menacing by turns, "help out" two stranded travellers.

CHARACTERS

Attendant 1
Attendant 2
Lance & Gwen (a young couple)

(*A tiny petrol station on a winding road, half way up a dark mountain. A couple of tall, glowing petrol pumps dominate the stage. It is night. The light comes from the two glowing pumps, and from the window to the small office. An attendant – A1 – is polishing the petrol pumps with a rag. Hearing something, he stops, and looks up, startled. He peers at the audience, anxiously, then returns to his task. Then he stops again abruptly, anxiety all over his face.*)

A1:   Did you hear that?

(*A2 emerges. From the office, offstage, to join in the polishing of the pumps.*)

A2: What?

A1: I thought I heard a harmonica playing. In the distance.

A2: Didn't hear a thing.

A1: A cowboy, passing by. On his way down there, to that tiny little cluster of lights.

A2: What, the town?

A1: Yes, the lights of the town. They look like fallen stars.

(*A2 stops, comes forward, squints into the audience.*)

A2 Do they?

A1: It looks like Heaven fallen to Earth down there.

A2: Not when you get down there, it don't. Boarded-up houses. One little shop, scraping by, selling fags and videos. And one hotel. With no guests and a broken jukebox in the bar. (*sings*) "I was bor-orn under a wanderin... wanderin... wanderin... (*A1 pushes him in the back.*)

A2: ... star."

A1: It's not like that.

A2: Go down there. See for yourself.

A1: No, I couldn't. I've populated that town over the years. With mysterious alleyways and strangers. I don't want to destroy my dreams.

A2: What you doing out here anyway?

A1: I don't know. I feel restless. I feel a strange longing for something. I can sense it, out here in the sweet night air. On this forgotten mountain. A strange, indefinable longing for... something....

A2: Sex. That's what you're longing for.

A1: No. It's more than that.

A2: Sex. That's what it is.

A1: I think something's going to happen tonight. I think someone is going to come riding up over that hill and pay us a visit.

A2: Nobody ever comes here, mun.

A1:   I heard a harmonica playing, out there in the dark.

A2:   It's just an old Western going round in your head.

A1:   Maybe.

A2:   Brrr! It's cold out here.

A1:   Someone just walked over your grave.

A2:   Cobblers. Hasn't been dug yet.

A1:   That's what you think. (*A2 goes back to his polishing. A1 sniffs the air.*) Somethin'll happen tonight. It's a time of reckoning.

A2:   You reckon?

A1:   The God of Iron is angry with us. He hasn't thrown a car down the mountain for weeks.

A2:   We should give him something. A burnt offering, at sunrise.

A1:   I know. But where are we going to find one of them?

      (*Two visitors enter. LANCE & GWEN are a young couple, aged 17 or 18. They have an empty petrol can.*)

GWEN: Excuse me?

      (*The attendants stare at them in amazement.*)

A2:   Why, what have you done?

LANCE: (*stops playing*) Our car's run out of petrol. About a mile down the road.

A1:   Oh aye?

A2:   So?

GWEN: (*showing can*) So we need some petrol.

A1:   Petrol? (*sharp intake of breath*)

A2:   Better go to a garage then.

LANCE: (*looks around*) This is a garage, isn't it?

BOTH: Nope.

GWEN: Well, what are those pumps for?

A2:   To look at.

A1:   They're Heritage pumps.

LANCE: What?

A1:   Part of the Enterprise Zone Experience.

LANCE: What the hell is that?

184

A1:   It's a celebration of our glorious post-industrial heritage, sir.

A2:   On this very spot there was once a working petrol station.

A1:   And a big warehouse over there, selling fridges.

A2:   Another one over there selling microwaves and TVs.

A1:   And there used to be a car showroom next door to this place.

GWEN: What, a kind of market place?

A1:   That's it.

GWEN: Selling goods made by local people.

A2:   Local people? (*They both laugh. A2 stops suddenly.*) Hey, there's no need to take the piss.

GWEN: I'm not. I just...

A1:   And those pumps there, sir, are the very same pumps they used to use in them far-off days.

LANCE: Never?!

A1   Lovingly preserved.

A2:   Makes you want to touch them, doesn't it? Feel the ancient vibrations of Wales.

           (*He wraps his arms around a pump, shuts his eyes and has a mystical experience. He opens an eye to stare at GWEN.*)

A2:   (*to GWEN*) I bet you feel the same, don't you, miss?

LANCE: (*to A1*) So you've got no petrol at all in those pumps?

A1:   Not a drop.

GWEN: Oh, great.

LANCE: Well — couldn't we siphon a bit out of one of your cars? Just enough to get to the nearest all night garage.

GWEN: We'll pay you for it.

A2:   We haven't got any cars here, miss.

LANCE: You must have a car.

A1:   We've got lots of other things. Look at this — a fish. A thousand million years old, dug out of the ground, right here. So old it's turned into stone.

A2:   Like Lot's wife.

A1:	No, salt, she turned into.
A2:	Salt, that's it.
A1:	(*to LANCE and GWEN*) Now then, what were we talking about?
A2:	Salt.
A1:	No, Before that.
A2:	Fish.
A1:	Fish?
A2:	Yes, I like a bit of salt on my fish.
LANCE:	Well how do you get up here without a car?
GWEN:	Don't tell me you catch a bus up here. It's miles off the beaten track.
A1:	The beaten track. There's a lovely phrase, innit?
A2:	An ancient pathway, beaten through the forest. From one clearing to the next.
A1:	In the days before cars.
A2:	Beaten through the brambles, with an old knotty stick. Swish swish.
LANCE:	So how do you get here?
A1:	We don't.
A2:	We live here.
A1:	No time to go anywhere else.
A2:	There's only the two of us here. To look after the whole place.
A1:	Have a look round. We've got some wonderful exhibits. We've got a miner's lung, cut in half so you can see the dust.
LANCE:	Have you?
GWEN:	Urgh! (*to LANCE*) Let's go.
LANCE:	We need petrol.
GWEN:	Well, they haven't got any.
LANCE:	Where's the nearest real petrol station?
A1:	Can't think of one.
A2:	We're miles from anywhere.
A1:	And it's late.
GWEN:	There must be an all night garage here somewhere.

A2:   Well there is one. But it's a long way away.

A1:   Too far to walk.

GWEN: Have you got a phone?

A1:   A phone? We have indeed, sir.

          (*They smile at him inanely.*)

LANCE: Can I use it?

BOTH: Nope.

LANCE: It's an emergency!

A1:   Says you.

A2:   Not everyone would call it an emergency.

GWEN: Stuck halfway up a mountain, miles from anywhere, in the middle of the night with no petrol. 'Course it's an emergency!

A1:   Everything's relative, miss.

A2:   Auntie Maureen, Uncle Ernest, Grandma... (*A1 clips him round the ear.*) Ow!

A1:   You might think it's an emergency, but imagine if there was someone else in here, whose legs had just been chopped off. Eh?

A2:   He'd need the phone more than you, wouldn't he?

LANCE: There isn't anyone here with chopped-off legs!

A1:   All I'm saying is....

A2:   It's not as if someone's just gouged your left eye out with a spoon, is it?

GWEN: What?

A2:   For a laugh.

A1:   Now that would be an emergency.

A2:   That would warrant a phone call.

GWEN: Look! We just want to use your phone to get some-one....

A1:   All I'm saying is — there's no need to get in such a flap about it. All that shouting and bawling.

A2:   Stress! You want to watch that, sir. You'll get an ulcer.

A1:   Now that would be an emergency.

          (*A2 Grasps his stomach, pulls a face and keels over,*

187

hitting the floor.)

GWEN:	(*to LANCE*) What's he doing?
A1:	Dying. From an abdominal complaint.
A2:	(*recovering*) Brought on by too much stress.
A1:	You want to relax.
A2:	Take it easy.
A1:	Roll with the head-butts.
A2:	Punches.
A1:	Have a wander round our heritage centre. That's relaxing.
GWEN:	(*to LANCE*) We haven't got time.
LANCE:	Could we just use your phone?
A2:	No, really? It is relaxing.
A1:	Look, sir! Visitors' book. (*produces a visitors' book*) Here we are. "A thoroughly relaxing day out. I especially enjoyed the Cwmblast Colliery disaster. The roof-collapse was most convincing, and certainly had me reaching for my hard hat." — Mrs Jean Poole of Tonyrefail.
A2:	(*takes the book*) And here's another one — "My husband found it so relaxing he fell asleep in Room Four, with all the Hellfire preachers." — Mrs Beacon of Brecon.
A1:	See? Relaxing.
LANCE:	(*through clenched teeth*) I want to use your phone!
A2:	Can't!
A1:	Staff only!
LANCE:	What?!
A2:	I'll do it for you! The all-night garage, is it?
GWEN:	Yeah, just tell them our car's broken down.
A2:	Broken what?
GWEN:	Down.
A2:	Down where?
LANCE:	Wouldn't it be easier if I did it?
BOTH:	No!
A2:	Staff only!

A1: We'd get sacked on the spot.

A2: Jobs don't come ten a penny round here, see. You got to grab what you can and keep hold of it.

A1: I won mine in a raffle. We all crammed in down the DSS, bought our tickets and...

A2: "This week's lucky winner is ticket nine hundred and sixty one!"

A1: That's me! Aaargh!

A2: "Congratulations. You win this week's job."

A1: What a day that was.

LANCE: (*to A2*) How did you get the job?

A2: I killed the previous incumbent, sir. Stole his uniform, and assumed a new identity.

A1: They don't mind, see. Long as someone's doing it.

A2: Only cannon-fodder we are.

GWEN: (*to LANCE*) Come on, let's go.

A1: He could be lying, of course. To make his life sound more dramatic.

A2: Spice it up a bit.

A1: Make it sound more exciting.

A2: Something to tell my grandchildren.

A1: Can't just say, "Worked all his life in Cwmblast Heritage Centre. Liked maps." I mean, it doesn't convey anything of the man's soul. Does it?

GWEN: No. Quite.

A2: Whereas, if I tell them, "In my day, unemployment was so bad, I had to kill another man to get his job."

A1: They're gonna think, "Oooh, there's exciting."

A2: That's what family history is all about.

A1: Remembering colourful incidents.

A2: Blowing them up a bit.

A1: Lying.

A2: Assuming I am lying, of course.

A1: He might not be.

LANCE: Just phone the garage and get them over here!

A1: Right.

A2:	Certainly. What make is the car?
LANCE:	Ford Millenium.
A1:	Colour?
LANCE:	White.
A1:	You sure, sir?
LANCE:	Yes, white.
A2:	We do a lovely red.
A1:	No, no. The gentleman said white.
A2:	Very well. White it is. Dry or sweet, sir?
LANCE:	What?
A2:	Would you like dry or sweet wine?
A1:	His thoughts often stray to drink. He's an ex-alcoholic, you know.
A2:	I'd kill for a drink.
A1:	So he says.
GWEN:	It's a white car.
A2:	Car! Of course, not wine, car!
LANCE:	Yes.
BOTH:	(*frowning*) Hmmmm....
GWEN:	Now what?
A1:	Well, the thing is, miss, we don't actually sell cars.
V:	Aargh!!
A2:	They used to sell them.
A1:	Back in the old days. You'd have loved it.
A2:	When the dragon fluttered on the flagpole and the daffodils waved in the breeze.
A1:	And the children of Gwalia pinned the giant vegetables to their lapels and sang in an ancient, forgotten tongue.
A2:	Long ago, when this was an Enterprise Zone.
A1:	But not any more.
A2:	No cars at all, I'm afraid.
LANCE:	Are you taking the piss?
A1:	Don't be too hard on him, sir. Poor boy's got trouble with his memory.

LANCE:	Oh aye?
A1:	Big problem these days. Some say it's all that poisoned air — wafting up from the coast. Or it could have been something he ate.
A2:	It was the bad water, plopping out of the tap.
A1:	It was lumpy.
A2:	Water shouldn't be lumpy, should it?
A1:	He never should have drunk it.
A2:	Haven't been able to think straight since.
A1:	If you write your message down, sir, he can read it straight off the card.
GWEN:	He'll forget the number!
A2:	It's alright. I've got his business card. (*produces it with a flourish*) Here we are — "Sammy Snip — Mobile Hairdresser." You want a haircut? At this time of night?
A1:	Wrong pocket.
A2:	Oh. (*produces another*) Ah yes! "A.J. Phillips — The man with the spanner! — Twenty-four hour call-out."
LANCE:	(*to A1*) Couldn't you phone him instead?
A1:	Oh, no. You wouldn't want me to do it, sir.
A2:	He's even worse.
A1:	I get blackouts on the phone. I forget who I am and talk gibberish. It's a form of epilepsy.
A2:	No, it's a form of stupidity.
A1:	Stupidity! That's it.
GWEN:	Couldn't I just make this one little call?
A2:	No bloody chance!
A1:	You'd phone Australia.
A2:	Or one of them 0898 numbers.
A1:	In a sad search for human warmth on a party chat line.
A2:	Pound a minute, them calls. I've made enough of 'em, I should know.
A1:	You'd bankrupt us overnight.
LANCE:	Alright, alright. Just tell him — "Bring some petrol."

191

A2:	Bring petrol.
LANCE:	That's it.
A2:	Fine. Soon have you sorted, sir.
A1:	Back on the road in no time.
	(*A2 exits. A1 Grins insanely at the visitors.*)
GWEN:	(*to LANCE*) Is he alright?
LANCE:	Are you alright?
A1:	It's being up here all alone, sir. It's done our heads in a bit. Come from the coast, have you?
GWEN:	How do you know?
A1:	You've got that salty seaside fish-and-chip shop look.
GWEN:	Oh.
A1:	Wonderful weather we've been having! If you ignore the pollution. Ha ha!
LANCE:	Yes. Ha ha.
GWEN:	Quite.
A1:	Makes for good sunsets.
LANCE:	Yes, I'm sure.
GWEN:	(*nods*) Mmm.
A1:	Have you heard of R.S. Thomas?
LANCE:	No.
A1:	He was a Druid, sir. We've got some of his spells in there.
GWEN:	What about him?
A1:	Well, he said, "To live in Wales is to be aware at the setting sun of the spilled blood that went into the making of the wild sky." Did you know that?
BOTH:	No.
A1:	Nor me? All those blazing red skies. All made of blood from Welsh people who've been killed.
GWEN:	Really?
LANCE:	Fancy that.
A1:	Good job it doesn't clot, isn't it?
LANCE:	Yes.
A1:	Or we'd be stuck with it all day. "Nice red sky

192

today." "Yes, it's the blood. It's clotted." Do you know, I don't think it's blood at all, sir. I think it's pollution. (*winks knowingly*)

LANCE: Could be.

A1: (*thrusts out his hand*) Got any money?

LANCE: What?

A1: For the phone call.

GWEN: Yes, of course. (*hands him a coin*)

A1: Fifty pence! Wow! You want to be more careful, miss, walking up that dark road, with money in your pocket. Lucky you weren't attacked and thrown off the mountain.

GWEN: Really?

A1: Dangerous up here. Coal thieves raiding the private mines, rustlers, the dispossessed taking justice into their own hands — well, you can't blame 'em. (*sudden thought*) Of course! That must be why we get so few visitors! Hah! Well, well.

(*A phone rings.*)

A1: Excuse me, sir. (*A1 reaches behind the counter and produces a phone, to visitors' surprise.*) Hello? Yes? this is the Heritage Centre. Yes... yes... fine... okay. (*he replaces the receiver*) That was my colleague, sir. He's been onto the garage and Mr Phillips will be here in one hour.

GWEN: Can't he come any quicker?

A1: 'Fraid not... Hey! Why not kill time by having a look round. We've got some lovely exhibits.

LANCE: Well that won't take long. There's hardly room to swing a cat in there.

A1: There's an old mine shaft in the office. It goes right down into the bowels of the earth. You see, before this was an Enterprise Zone, it was a coal mine. The tunnels are packed full of living history exhibits to celebrate our glorious past. Come down, have a look. It'll be nice to have the company.

GWEN: No, it's alright.

LANCE: We'll stay here.

GWEN: In case we miss him.

A1:   (*sighs*) Oh well... there we are then.

               (*Lights fade to dim, backlit silhouettes. They freeze. Four
               loud chimes from an old clock tower. Lights fade up. Same
               place, a couple of hours later. The sky is beginning to
               lighten. The Second Attendant is nowhere to be seen.*)

GWEN: Where the hell is this mechanic? You said he'd only
               be an hour.

A1:   He'll get here, don't you worry. Relax.

GWEN: We've got to get somewhere by sunrise.

A1:   Sunrise? That's when the ancient Celts used to
               sacrifice victims to their fierce pagan gods. Imagine
               that, eh? Blood spurting all over the place! Eyeballs
               popping out... (*he notices her look of horror and then
               gives a cheesey smile*) Where you off then, somewhere
               nice?

LANCE: Into the mountains. Further north.

A1:   Oh, lovely!

GWEN: Up through the mists to the highest peak in south
               Wales.

LANCE: We're on a quest.

A1:   Well, well. You've got hidden depths.

LANCE: When we get to the top we must gaze out over the
               land.

A1:   You won't see bugger all this time of night.

LANCE: At sunrise, we'll see a sign.

A1:   "Welcome to Powys — Kilvert's Diary Country."

GWEN: Where the first ray strikes the land, that is where
               King Arthur lies buried.

A1:   King Arthur! You're looking for King Arthur?

LANCE: Merlin contacted us. On her mum's Ouija board.

A1:   Never?

GWEN: He told us to awaken King Arthur, so that he may
               save the Welsh nation.

A1:   Good God.

LANCE: So we must get there by sunrise.

A1:   Well, why didn't you say, mun? We got him here.

LANCE: You what?

A1:   Yes. We dug up the entire grave, tombstone and all. Quite a find, really.

LANCE: (*appalled*) You've got King Arthur's grave, in this dump?

A1:   Stroke of luck for you, eh? Saves you traipsing all the way up there in the dark. Your quest is at an end. You can wake him up, he can save Wales and we'll all have a cup of tea.

       (*A2 enters.*)

A2:   I'll tell you how to save Wales.

A1:   How?

A2:   Stop harpooning them. Bloody disgraceful. Beautiful, mysterious creatures. Brains the size of Land Rovers. Only two left now, in the whole world. And they don't turn each other on.

LANCE: Not whales, Wa...

GWEN: Oh, never mind.

A2:   The largest creatures the world's ever seen. And once they're gone, they'll never come back.

A1:   You'll never guess what — they're looking for King Arthur's grave.

A2:   Oh! There we are.

A1:   I was just telling them. We've got King Arthur's grave here.

A2:   Have we?

A1:   Yes!

A2:   King Arthur?

A1:   Bit of luck, innit?

A2:   Arthur King, you're thinking of, mun. The old miner.

A1:   Oh, I'm sorry. Arthur King, not King Arthur. My mistake.

A2:   You can see his grave if you like.

GWEN: No thanks.

A2:   It's good. It says, "Here lies Arthur King. Lying again."

A1:   He was a famous liar.

A2:   Oh, no-one could lie like my Uncle Arthur.

LANCE:	(*grabs A2 roughly*) What did the garage say?
A2:	Oy!
LANCE:	You did phone the garage?
A2:	(*breaking away*) Yes! A.J. Phillips, crypton tuning, tyres fitted, MOTs.
LANCE:	What did he say?
A2:	Nothing.
LANCE:	Nothing!?
A1:	Well, he wouldn't, sir. He's been dead for twelve years.

(LANCE breathes deeply, restrains himself.)

LANCE:	What!?
A2:	No spanner have turned in that workshop for twelve winters.
A1:	No petrol have spurted from them pumps ever since he clutched his head and keeled over right in front of us.
A2:	That poor old garage. It's falling apart without him.
A1:	No-one to oil the tools. No-one to mend the roof.
A2:	No-one to look after the vintage Ford Escort.
A1:	Shame he never left a child to take over where he left off.
GWEN:	So the garage you just phoned has been empty for twelve years?
A2:	Absolutely.
LANCE:	(*shouts*) Why did you phone it then?!
A1:	Well, you did ask, sir. We try to please.
A2:	I did wonder, "Why does he want me to phone a dead mechanic?" But then I thought, "No, that's no concern of mine".
GWEN:	He didn't tell us he was dead.
A2:	You didn't ask.
A1:	Be fair.
LANCE:	(*to A1*) Hang on! Just a minute.
A1:	Problem, sir?
LANCE:	You told us that he had phoned Mr Phillips and Mr

	Phillips would be coming here.
GWEN:	That's right. You did.
A1:	Ah... Yes. So I did. I was hoping he might have got better.
A2:	But he hadn't.
GWEN:	What are you playing at?
A1:	I just wanted you to forget your troubles and enjoy the Cwmblast Heritage Experience.
A2:	We've got such beautiful things here. But no-one ever comes to see them.
GWEN:	(*to LANCE*) Let's get out of here.
A1:	It breaks my heart, miss. We take such good care of it. The miner's lamps, the coracles, the old Wimpy Burger Bar.
A2:	The women in their tall black hats.
A1:	The police attacking the pickets.
A2:	All lovingly cared for.
A1:	We're preserving it for the next generation.
A2:	So they know who they are. What they came from.
A2:	But nobody cares. They'll forget everything.
LANCE:	We've got to use that phone!
A1:	I don't know. Maybe, just this once.
LANCE:	Yeah, just this once.
A1:	(*to A2*) What do you think?
A2:	Staff only!
A1:	Sorry. Staff only.
GWEN:	Come on. Let's go.
	(*They start to leave. A1 scurries after them.*)
A1:	No, wait! (*whispers to them*) I'm sure we'll persuade him. Give it a few minutes.
LANCE:	(*sighs*) Oh, alright.
A2:	(*suddenly shouts*) Phillips the Spanner, we used to call him!
LANCE:	What?!
A1:	Old Welsh tradition, sir. Nicknames, relating to what people did. Jones the Milk. Evans the bread.

A2: Williams the Fish.

A1: Miss Davies the Stamps.

A2: Ran the post office.

A1: Miss Roberts the Sweetshop.

GWEN: Don't tell me — she ran the sweetshop.

A1: Not quite. She was the sweetshop.

LANCE: Get out of it!

A1: It's a long story.

A2: She was a big woman.

A1: She was killed and turned into a shop. They used her arm for the counter.

A2: Her ribcage for the shelves.

A1: And her skull for the till.

A2: Beautiful till. Got it here, somewhere.

A1: You rang the change on the teeth, and two pound signs jumped out of her eye sockets. Ching! Like cuckoos from a wrist-watch.

A2: Clock.

A1: That's it.

A2: It's alright, miss, we're only pulling your leg off. She did run the sweetshop.

A1: And she died peacefully in her rocking chair.

A2: With a real fire burning in the grate.

A1: And a black and white photo of her late husband smiling down at her.

A2: From the mantelpiece.

A1: And the shelves of her little shop stuffed full with jars of Welsh toffee.

A2: Everton mints.

A1: Licorice allsorts.

A2: Welsh fudge.

A1: All sitting there, unsold.

A2: Nobody ever went there.

A1: Big supermarket, see. Down by the motorway.

A2: Sucked all the life out of the place.

A1:   Used to be bursting with people once.

A2:   Turned the whole place into a ghost-town.

A1:   (*sobs*) It broke her heart. She put another log on the fire, rocked herself off to sleep and never woke up.

              (*Both attendants fall silent and stare into the middle distance, looking incredibly sad and forlorn, almost parodying the emotion. Throughout the following, the sky begins to grow lighter, until dawn breaks.*)

GWEN: (*to LANCE*) Let's get out of here!

A2:   You can't go now, mun!

A1:   Nowhere to go.

GWEN: What about those lights?

LANCE: There must be someone down there with a can of petrol.

GWEN: (*glares at A2*) Or a phone that works.

A1:   I've always wanted to visit that town down there. That cluster of fallen stars, nestling in the dark.

LANCE: Is it far?

A2:   Hell of a way. Take you all night to walk there.

A1:   I sometimes look at that necklace of little jewels through my binoculars.

LANCE: Is that right?

A1:   Do you know what it looks like through binoculars?

LANCE: I've no idea.

A1:   Like a necklace of big jewels.

              (*GWEN groans*)

A2:   Dangerous walking down there now. Gangs in the hills. They'd hear you coming. Jump at you in the dark.

A1:   Wait till the morning.

LANCE: We've got to get there tonight.

A2:   You won't manage it now. Wait till sunrise.

A1:   Trucks go past here in the morning. Stick your thumb out, you'll get a lift easy.

LANCE: There must be somewhere closer.

A1:   No.

A2:   Yes. There's Bethesda Chapel.

A1:   Oh, yes, you could try in there, sir. It's only half a mile away.

GWEN: Would they have a phone?

A2:   Dunno. They might have.

A1:   They've got a nest.

LANCE: A nest?

A1:   A bird's nest. Where the window used to be.

A2:   They haven't got a roof, mind....

A1:   But they have got a ghost.

A2:   Yes, the old vicar.

A1:   Nice feller, sir. Decent.

A2:   Gone a bit moody since he died, mind. Always knocking things over.

A1:   Yes. Do you know — I think he blames us in some way.

A2:   For his death?

A1:   Oh yes.

A2:   Well — that's understandable.

A1:   S'pose so.

A2:   I mean, he's got a point, hasn't he?

A1:   Yeah. Still, he might be able to help.

A2:   Worth a try.

(They beam helpful smiles at him.)

A1:   I'll show you the way. I've got a map.

LANCE: No, it's alright.

GWEN: We'll stay here.

A1:   Yes, relax.

A2:   Do you know, I had such a sad dream last night, it put me in a melancholy mood all day.

A1:   Really?

A2:   I dreamt everything was back how it used to be. I saw it all through a child's eyes. When the world was a simpler place and you could be whatever you wanted.

A1:   Ah yes.

A2:   When the old town was alive and full of people and the sweetshop was the sweetshop and everyone went there — and the corner shop — and your picture in the paper for catching a trout, or playing the trombone, and everyone said hello in the morning and sang in their living room round the piano — (*breaking down*) when I was little — and everyone had a job they were proud of and everyone had somewhere to live, and no-one went hungry, and...

A1:   (*puts an arm around A2*) Don't upset yourself.

A2:   It's just that — I've never known such times.

A1:   (*forlorn*) Nor me.

A2:   Is it only in dreams we can live like that?

GWEN: There's always tomorrow.

A2:   (*suddenly sinister*) For some of us.

        (LANCE *leaps to his feet. Heads for exit, with GWEN.*)

LANCE: We've got to wake Arthur up! He'll save us.

A2:   Arthur King? You won't wake him up.

        (LANCE *shoves A2 across the stage.*)

LANCE: Give me the bloody phone! Now!

A1:   Oh, alright. If you insist.

A2:   (*to A1*) What are you doing?

A1:   Oh, let him use it. He's been going on about it all night.

        (A1 *fetches it for him.*)

GWEN: Oh! Thank God!

LANCE: Civilization! At last.

A2:   I know how you feel, sir. It's very cut-off up here.

        (LANCE *Dials a number, punching three numbers with great urgency. No joy. He shakes the phone, dials again, pressing the buttons even harder.*)

LANCE: It's not working.

        (GWEN *lifts the phone up, looks inside. It's completely empty. The first pink glimmer of sunrise creeps in.*)

GWEN: There's nothing inside it.

A1:   No.

A2:   It's a heritage phone.

A1:   For future generations to come and marvel at.

GWEN: (*puts it down, with a sigh*) Right.

A2:   (*suddenly bellows*) Phillips the Adjustable Spanner! That's what I used to call him!

A1:   We don't call him that now, obviously.

A2:   No. Phillips the Dead, we call him now.

A1:   Buried him with all his tools.

A2:   In his overalls.

A1:   With his tow-rope and his spanners.

A2:   And his jack and his jump-leads.

A1:   And his oily rag.

A2:   For his journey to the other side. 'Cos you never know, sir. Better safe than sorry.

A1:   Our ancestors did it. The ancient Celts.

A2:   Buried their dead with their helmets and shields and swords and daggers.

A1:   Just in case.

A2:   And their lucky charms.

A1:   Buried them all over the place. In secret graves.

A2:   On ley-lines. Where corn circles appear and UFO's are often seen.

A1:   In caves above the swirling sea. By the side of enchanted lakes.

LANCE: So where did you bury Mr Phillips? Up on the mountain?

A2:   No, in the boot of his car.

A1:   Don't look like that. It was a charming funeral.

A2:   It's what he would have wanted.

LANCE: What did he — actually — die of?

A1:   Spanners.

                (*pause*)

LANCE: He died of spanners?

A1:   Lovely funeral. We drove him to the top of the mountain. Got out. Breathed in the fresh mountain air, smashed his head in with a couple of spanners,

	locked him in the boot, set fire to the car and rolled it down the mountain.
LANCE:	You — er — killed him then?
A1:	(*genuinely concerned*) You don't mind, do you, sir?
LANCE:	Mind? No. We don't mind!
GWEN:	What?! I do!
LANCE:	(*nudging her*) I'm sure he deserved it.
A2:	He thought so, sir.
A1:	He saw it as a great honour.
GWEN:	An honour?!
A1:	For goodness sake, we were only having a bit of fun!
A2:	Don't tell me you've never seen a burnt car rolling down a mountain.
GWEN:	Not with a murdered body in the boot.
A2:	Oh well! That makes all the difference! Pardon me!
A1:	We didn't really kill him.
LANCE:	Oh. Ha ha. You had us going there.
GWEN:	So you didn't....
A1:	No. Not really. — No, we sacrificed him.
A2:	To the God of Iron.
A1:	He was proud to be chosen. It was a sacred ceremony.
GWEN:	Right. Fine. We'll be off then.
A2:	You're not going?
LANCE & GWEN:	Yes.
A1:	Oh, I'll come with you.
LANCE:	There's no need. We'll be fine.
A1:	No, I could do with a good walk.
A2:	And me. Where are we going?
A1:	I know. Let's go up the mountain! We can watch that big red ball of rust come up over the ridge.
GWEN:	No, it's alright. You go.
LANCE:	We'll stay here.
A1:	Oh. Gone off the idea?

GWEN: Yes, you carry on.

A2:   No, I think I'll stay here, too.

A1:   And me. Keep you company.

LANCE: (*smiles*) Oh... good.

          (*A2 switches something, and we hear a choir singing "Sospan Fach".*)

LANCE: What's that?

A2:   It's an ancient recording.

A1:   They're chanting an old spell. About saucepans.

A2:   Iron saucepans.

A1:   They're invoking Scrapo, the God of Iron.

          (*The attendants suddenly attack the visitors, putting a rope round each one, tying them to the petrol pumps.*)

GWEN: Get off! What's going on?!

LANCE: You mad bastards!

          (*A2 reaches behind a pump and produces a piece of white scrap metal.*)

A2:   (*calls out to the sky*) Scrapo! God of Iron!

LANCE: Hey! That's come off my car!

A2:   Oh, I dismantled it while you were looking round the museum, sir.

A1:   We recycle it, see. Nothing's wasted up here.

LANCE: My car!

A1:   You don't need it, sir. Cars are no good to the world.

A2:   They're just burning it up.

A1:   Turning the earth into a nightmare desert of grey dusty roads. Killing us with acid rain.

A2:   Punching holes in the atmosphere.

A1:   What we need is a new religion that doesn't place us above the animals and the earth.

A2:   That believes in harmony with nature.

A1:   The goddess of trees.

A2:   The god of rocks.

A1:   The goddess of mountains.

A2:   The God of Iron.

A1:   We've come full circle.

A2:	Back to the old gods.
A1:	But the old gods have to be pleased. In the old ways.
	(*The pink-red light of sunrise has replaced the blue of the dawn.*)
A2:	I found some petrol for you, sir! (*He produces the can. It's full.*) We're gonna pour it over you and light you.
A1:	For Scrapo, the Iron God, to devour your smoke.
A2:	Then he will be pleased and throw more burnt-out cars down the mountain for us.
LANCE:	Throw cars off the mountain?
GWEN:	There's no god up there doing that! That's people.
A1:	(*appalled and terrified*) What are you saying?!
A2:	Blasphemy!
LANCE:	Scrapo! God of Iron!!!
BOTH:	Sssh!
A1:	We'll be struck down!
	(*LANCE makes a rude gesture at the sky, and blows a raspberry.*)
LANCE:	Come and get me!
BOTH:	Sshh!
	(*A1 and A2 back away from him, expecting God's wrath.*)
LANCE:	See? There's nobody there!
GWEN:	Those wrecks aren't thrown off the mountain by a god. People drive them off there. For the insurance!
	(*pause*)
A2:	Insurance?
LANCE:	Yeah. Or for a laugh.
A1:	But why do they bring them to us?
GWEN:	They don't bring them here for you. They come up here 'cos it's steep.
LANCE:	And 'cos no bugger can see them.
	(*The attendants look at each other.*)
BOTH:	Oh.
A1:	Well, I never knew that.
A2:	Nor me.

(A2 switches "Sospan Fach" off. They glance upwards.)

A1: So we're all alone down here?

LANCE: Looks like it.

A2: Oh. No point in sacrificing you then, really.

LANCE: No, I suppose not.

GWEN: Now you mention it.

A2: *(untying LANCE)* Oh well. Lucky escape, sir.

A1: *(untying GWEN)* But what can we believe in? Now you've taken that away, what's left?

GWEN: I don't know. But we're off before you think of something.

LANCE: Yes. All the best.

(LANCE and GWEN exist briskly.)

A2: Goodbye! Call again!

A1: Missing you already!

(They gaze about them.)

A2: Well, I feel like a right dick-head now.

A1: They may have been lying.

A2: Why did I believe you? How could anyone believe that?

A1: Strange beliefs often take hold. It's human nature.

(A2 advances on him, menacingly.)

A2: People drive them off there!

A1: They don't. He was lying. It's a sacred mountain. It's where the gods live.

A2: You've never been there! You don't know a damn thing!

A1: *(gabbling frantically)* I do! I know the population of Aberdare. I know the length of Llanberis Pass, the height of Cader Idris. How many tons of coal got dug out of the Garw Valley in 1962. *(A2 shoves him violently across the forecourt.)* I know exactly where we are on this map! Look! "You are here!" *(A2 tears the map from his hands and knocks A1 to the floor.)*

A2: You've never been anywhere! *(He throws the map on the floor.)* I'm going up that road, all the way. To see for myself. And I'm not coming back!

(A1 crawls over to his map and examines it.)

A1:   You've torn my map.

(A2's temper disappears.)

A2:   I'm sorry.

A1:   It was a hundred years old.

A2:   I'm sorry. I'll mend it. With Sellotape.

A1:   I'll do it. *(He holds the map protectively to his chest.)*

A2:   It'll be alright. It's only a tiny little rip.

A1:   You're not really going. Are you?

A2:   *(looks sadly at A1)* I want to see where the road goes. I want to follow it up over the ridge and see what's up there.

A1:   But I'll never manage on my own. It's too much work.

A2:   You'll be fine. I'll send you a postcard from every town I pass through. For the collection.

A1:   We could do with some more postcards. We've only got four thousand and one.

(A2 offers his hand. They shake hands.)

A2:   I'll be off then.

A1:   Do you need a map?

A2:   No. It's alright. — So long, pardner.

A1:   So long, pardner. *(A2 exits. A1 watches him go, consulting his map.)* Blaenbanog — with the Lady of the Lake shimmering above the water, and the three rocky giants of Cwmgarth. I'd love to see them. Gotta stay here, though — someone's got to look after the place. East, west, home's best. Let's see, now — Blaenbanog, Aberfelin... Cwmgarth...

(He gazes up above the audience, at the distant mountains. The map slips from his fingers. He stands motionless for a few seconds, overwhelmed by the vastness and loneliness around him.)

A1:   You dopey git. It's a dead end!

HELEN GRIFFIN
The Ark

Born and raised in Swansea, Helen Griffin (b.1958), studied psychology and sociology and trained as a psychiatric nurse before starting a successful acting career in 1986. She has recently ventured into writing and has had work appear on the stage, radio and television. *Skin Deep* and *Lady in Red* have been recorded for BBC Radio Wales and *Killjoy*, her play for young people, was produced by Theatre West Glamorgan. She co-wrote and performed *Mental* with Jo Brand for the Sherman Theatre Company in 1996. *The Ark*, written in 1994, deals movingly with a family of women grieving for the death of the father.

CHARACTERS
Cecilia: The Mother
Agnes: Her eldest daughter
Martha: A couple of years younger than Agnes

> (*We are in CECILIA and JIMMY'S bedroom in the family home in Swansea. It is comfortably and solidly furnished. Before the lights come up we hear CECILIA quietly praying.*)

CECILIA: HailMaryfullofgracethelordiswiththeeblessedart thouamongstwomenandblessedisthefruitofthywomb JesusAmen.HailMaryfullofgracetheLordiswiththee blessedartthouamongst...

> (*The lights fade up and there is no-one to be seen. AGNES comes into the room carrying a cup and saucer.*)

AGNES: Mum... cup of... Mum? Mum, where are you?

CECILIA: ...womenandblessedisthefruitofthywomb — alright

love, I'll be there now in a minute. JesusAmenHail MaryfullofgracetheLordiswiththeeblessedartthouam ongstwomenandblessedisthefruitofthywombJesus Amen. There.

(She emerges from under the bed and takes the tea.)

CECILIA: Thank you love. Oh good, you've let it stew a bit.

(MARTHA comes in.)

MARTHA: Morning, Mum. It's a brilliant day for the beach.

AGNES: Mum, what were you doing under the bed?

CECILIA: What time is it?

MARTHA: Under the bed?

AGNES: She was under the bed. When I came in she was under the bed.

CECILIA: Oh, it's alright, it's alright, I haven't gone mental. It's just... I just... woke up this morning and I... you know... I turned over to give your father a cwtch and he wasn't there and then... I know it sounds stupid but I suddenly thought, "He's under the bed, that's where he is. He's been hiding under the bed". So I... I crawled underneath and... well, well, he wasn't there, was he? But it was lovely and warm and dark so I thought I might as well stay down here for a bit and say the rosary. So I did.

AGNES: Oh Mum.

CECILIA: *(sneezes)* I'll tell you something — it's terribly dusty down there. I'll have to see to that.

MARTHA: Muuum, there's more to life than dusting bed-springs.

CECILIA: Is there? I can't think of anything much more at the moment. I daresay you go round your flat like that Mortisha woman putting out the dust but your grandmother used to scrub the attic once a week so at least it's getting watered down over the genera-tions. Did you bring me the *Western Mail*?

AGNES: Mum, I'm not sure it's such a good idea.

CECILIA: Well, it's not up to the standard of *The Guardian* but it's the only English language national newspaper we've got.

AGNES: I just don't think it's good for you to read the death columns.

CECILIA: On the contrary, I think it's very good for me to read the death columns. It brings it home to me how many people are in the same boat.

AGNES: But it's making you obsessed.

CECILIA: It can't make me any more obsessed than I already am and if I wasn't obsessed there'd be something wrong with me in my opinion.

AGNES: But it's so morbid.

MARTHA: Depends on how you look at death. The Mexicans don't think so.

CECILIA: Don't they?

MARTHA: No. Not like us. They have this thing called The Day Of The Dead. It's really amazing. They have all these bright colourful costumes and masks and they celebrate death with all the favourite music and food and the people who've died and...

CECILIA: ...celebrate death? How on earth can you celebrate death?

MARTHA: Because it's all part of the cycle of life. It's all part of accepting the cycle.

CECILIA: Well, I can't even accept it. I can't accept that our father's gone. And now you're suggesting that we ought to celebrate it. You think we ought to have a party do you, Martha? And wear loads of masks like the Mexicans and then we'll all feel better, is that it?

MARTHA: Yeah. Why not? I would anyway. I'd feel a lot better.

AGNES: Martha, leave it.

MARTHA: It's all part of their traditions.

CECILIA: Well, maybe the Mexicans should stick to their traditions and we'll stick to ours. I won't wear a mask and they won't have to eat egg and cress sandwiches, how's that?

MARTHA: I'm just saying that I think we could learn something from their culture.

CECILIA: I'm not interested in anyone's culture at the moment, Martha. Not even a yogurt's.

MARTHA: Oh, never mind.

AGNES: Did you sleep alright, Mum?

CECILIA: Yes, eventually, but I had terrible dreams working on me all night.

MARTHA: What were they?

CECILIA: I don't know where the last one came from. I was in a little bungalow with a sort of corrugated scullery attached — on the edge of Stevenage for God's sake, which is absolutely ridiculous because I wouldn't even go there for a day trip — but there I was, measuring for curtains in the scullery, when this skin head with tattoos all up his arms puts himself through the window and says, "Hello, I'm blind Bob from the chicken shack next door. I'll be popping in from time to time". I thought "Well, might be handy for free range eggs", but I felt a touch uneasy, you know? And I went into the living room and there was this council official with peaked cap and one of those yellow waterproof jackets wheeling these four old men in wheelchairs into the room. Wheezing and dribbling terrible they were, and he puts them spaced out around the room like armchairs and I say, "Excuse me, but what's going on here?" — and he says — "It's all there in the contract, madam, if you read the small print, they're here every day from two 'till ten." And then I started to panic and thought, "Oh, God, I can't cope with this, I really can't. They're probably all incontinent, God love them. I'll be running back and fore all afternoon changing them" — and then I woke up exhausted.

           (*Throughout this speech AGNES has been looking increasingly worried but MARTHA has been struggling not to laugh. She can't contain herself any longer and now bursts out laughing.*)

AGNES: Martha!

CECILIA: What's so funny?

MARTHA: Oh, I'm sorry, Mum, but I think that's hysterical, I really do.

AGNES: What's so funny about it?

MARTHA: I dunno. All the imagery. My therapist would have a field day.

AGNES: Oh, God.

211

MARTHA: Can I borrow it?

CECILIA: What for?

MARTHA: Can I borrow it to tell my therapist? See what he makes of it.

CECILIA: You can tell it to the marines. I don't want it.

MARTHA: Thanks. Was he definitely wearing a yellow jacket?

CECILIA: Yes. Yellow and shiny. Made a noise when he moved.

MARTHA: Fab. What about the old men?

CECILIA: Black and white. Not a spot of colour on them.

MARTHA: Weird. And blind Bob from the chicken shack?

CECILIA: I'm not sure but his tattoos were every colour in the rainbow.

MARTHA: Brilliant. Psychedelic Bob who'd be popping round from time to time with a basket of free-range eggs. (*beat*) You'd have had sex with him if you hadn't woken up.

AGNES: Martha!

CECILIA: Well, thank God I did. What does it all mean?

MARTHA: Well, I'd say...

AGNES: ...it just means that you're worried about your future, mum. It's perfectly natural.

CECILIA: I'm not worried about my future at all. It's the past I'm worried about.

AGNES: You can't change the past. What's done is done.

CECILIA: Exactly! That's what bothers me. (*beat*) I should have let your father build that boat. I should have let him and now it's too late.

AGNES: Oh, Mum. You musn't give yourself such a hard time about it. He didn't mind in the end.

CECILIA: Oh yes he did. He might not have shown it because that's the way he is. He never complained. But he did mind. He minded very much indeed and I stopped him. I stopped him having that little bit of pleasure and I can't forgive myself for that.

AGNES: It certainly doesn't matter to him now.

CECILIA: That's not the point. It mattered to him then. Anyway, how do we know it doesn't matter to him

212

now? Perhaps it matters to him now more than ever. (*pause, more to herself*) Oh come back Jimmy and I'll build the boat with you, hammer and nail. I'll saw the wood and sand it down and varnish it and I'll sew the sails in perfect little stitches so small you won't be able to see them without your glasses. (*beat*) Your glasses! Where's your glasses? Where's your father's glasses? Oh God, they've gone and buried him with his glasses. I told you I didn't trust that undertaker.

AGNES: (*taking the glasses from a drawer in the dressing table and handing them to CECILIA*) Here they are.

CECILIA: (*clutches them*) Oh thank God for that. And to think I tried to persuade him to have contact lenses. Thank god you held your ground on that one, Jimmy. (*beat*) We shouldn't have had that undertaker, you know, we should have gone to Pritchards. I shouldn't have let myself be swayed by Bert.

AGNES: It doesn't matter now, Mum.

CECILIA: That funeral parlour was tatty. Tatty's the only word for it. And leaving us sitting there in the window displaying our grief in full view of all the passers-by. I'll be writing to them.

AGNES: Mum, it really doesn't matter now.

CECILIA: It matters to me, Agnes! I'm talking about basic standards. And I don't care what you say, but that young man with the earring was casual to the point of disrespect.

MARTHA: It's just a job to him, I suppose.

CECILIA: Well, it ought to be more than just a job in matters of life and death.

MARTHA: I thought he was quite sexy.

AGNES: Martha!

MARTHA: What?

AGNES: How could you?

MARTHA: What?

AGNES: How could you at Dad's funeral?

MARTHA: Death and sex are all linked up. They're powerful forces.

AGNES: He bit his nails. Right down to the quick.

MARTHA: You noticed that, then?

AGNES: You can tell a lot from hands.

CECILIA: That young man was too aware of himself to be seriously sexy. Your father was seriously sexy. And Humphrey Bogart.

(*silence*)

MARTHA: Father Geoffrey's got nice hands, hasn't he? I noticed that at the funeral.

AGNES: Yes. He has. Gentle. They almost caress the host.

(*silence*)

MARTHA: I think you can undo the past.

CECILIA: What do you mean?

MARTHA: I think you can change the way you think about it. It's the same thing.

CECILIA: Do you?

MARTHA: Yes. I do.

CECILIA: I don't understand that. I don't understand that at all.

MARTHA: If you change the way you think about it it can't affect you any more.

CECILIA: Oh, I'm sorry but that's beyond me. What's the time?

AGNES: Half past nine.

AGNES &
MARTHA: Hang your knickers on the line!

CECILIA: Oh dear God in heaven and here's me still in my bed. It's shameful.

MARTHA: Let's all go down the beach for a good blow.

CECILIA: What, and have all those boats look at me accusingly? No thank you. Anyway, there's things to be done.

AGNES: Stay there and have a rest. It'd do you good.

CECILIA: Oh no, I'm not letting myself go. I'm not having people say, "Oh look there's that poor widow woman, she's gone to pieces". That's what I am now, isn't it? A widow woman. I'll have to go round in sad, old grey woollens smelling of mothballs,

214

carrying a string bag with a few lonely vegetables in the bottom.

MARTHA: Not necessarily. You could wear a black veil and look distant and enticing.

CECILIA: Oh grow up, Martha. I refuse to buy one of those little tins of beans whatever happens. (*beat*)

AGNES: Another cup of tea, Mum?

CECILIA: Yes, alright, one more cup of tea and then I'm getting up.

(*AGNES moves to go.*)

AGNES: What about just one slice of toast?

CECILIA: Oh alright, just one then. Dry and thinly sliced. And then I'm getting up.

AGNES: Oh good. (*she exits*)

CECILIA: (*calling after her*) You could just show it to the butter knife.

MARTHA: I think I know what your dream was about.

CECILIA: What?

MARTHA: I think it means you don't want to settle for second best. The bungalow symbolizes a man.

CECILIA: Good God, Martha, are you seriously suggesting I'd go for a bungalow of a man with a corrugated attachment?

MARTHA: I hope not.

CECILIA: Well then. I don't want another mansion of a man anyway. I just want your father back.

MARTHA: I know.

(*silence*)

MARTHA: Your hair looks nice, Mum.

CECILIA: Do you think so?

MARTHA: Yes, I like that colour.

CECILIA: Deborah suggested it. You don't think it's too obvious?

MARTHA: No, it looks really natural. I don't know what to do with mine.

CECILIA: Let it grow a bit. It looked lovely when it was shoulder length with you.

215

MARTHA: Hmmmmmm.

CECILIA: Don't go having a tattoo though, love. They've gone terribly common. Deborah's got one on her ankle, I noticed.

MARTHA: What's she got?

CECILIA: A little blue swallow.

MARTHA: Oh yeah, they are common.

CECILIA: Do you know, when Deborah showed me that little blue swallow on her ankle, your father was still alive?

            (*silence*)

CECILIA: I still can't believe it.

MARTHA: I know.

CECILIA: I still can't believe he's not here.

MARTHA: I know.

            (*silence*)

MARTHA: I went to that spiritualist meeting last night, Mum.

CECILIA: You said you were going out for a drink.

MARTHA: I did. After the meeting.

CECILIA: And before I daresay. What happened?

MARTHA: Well, I had a chat with David first and he said I wasn't to expect a message from Dad or anything. He said lots of people came expecting messages when their loved ones had just passed over and they were usually disappointed...

CECILIA: ...were those the words he used, "passed over"?

MARTHA: Yes.

CECILIA: It makes it sound as if you've not been selected to play.

MARTHA: No, passed over to the other side.

CECILIA: That's even worse.

MARTHA: Oh, Mum, it's only semantics.

CECILIA: Is it?

MARTHA: All he was saying was that when people die they don't change, like, their personalities don't intrinsically change. (*AGNES comes in with tea and toast.*) So if they've disapproved of spiritualism in this life

216

then they're not suddenly going to change. So it wasn't very likely that Dad was going to come through with a message.

CECILIA: Well, yes. Your father does disapprove of all that stuff, "Mumbo jumbo" he used to say.

AGNES: He used to say more than that. He used to say it was the devil's work.

MARTHA: Oh for God's sake, Agnes!

AGNES: I'm only saying what he used to say.

CECILIA: She's right, you know. He did. Oh Martha, maybe you shouldn't have gone. I told you to talk to Father Geoffrey about it first.

MARTHA: Look, you've met David. Does he strike you as an evil person?

CECILIA: No, no, I wouldn't say David Frisby has got the devil in him. (*takes tea and toast*) Well, no more than anyone else. Go on.

MARTHA: And he said that when you first pass over you tend to, initially anyway, end up with people who are similar to you. So like Hitler and Mussolini and all the fascist dictators are all stuck in one quarter, scrapping it out until they reach a compromise, if they ever do. Ha! They'll probably have just signed a peace treaty when Maggie Thatcher arrives and then they'll be off again for another aeon.

CECILIA: How bizarre. So who's your father going to be with, I wonder? Eric James the choir, I daresay. That'll be alright. And your Uncle Arthur. Oh and Kitty Williams, they were always real soulmates when they were on the council.

MARTHA: He might not be with them yet. David says there's a sort of waiting period first, kind of a journey there, that can take a while.

AGNES: Purgatory.

CECILIA: Oh, your father's not in purgatory, is he? He's not in some cold grey doctor's waiting room, waiting for his turn to be called? He won't be able to bear it. You know what he's like.

AGNES: I'm sure they have the celestial equivalent of back issues of *Woman's Own* and *Country Life*, Mum. He'll

217

be alright.

MARTHA: No, no, it's not like that. It's just like... like a slow, gentle, peaceful boat trip down the Nile, with the warm breezes caressing the skin.

CECILIA: All those years your father wanted to go sailing and look at the circumstances that he finally gets his wishes. It's like a joke. It's like God playing a cruel, nasty, horrible joke with no punchline!

AGNES: Mum, don't say that.

CECILIA: Why shouldn't I say it? It's what I feel!

AGNES: Dad would hate to hear you say that.

CECILIA: Yes, he would, I know. But why should God have him now, Agnes? What does God want him for now?

AGNES: You musn't take it so personally.

CECILIA: How else am I supposed to take it? He's got millions, billions, trillions, of other souls. Why does he have to be so greedy? (pause) Oh, I seem to have finished the toast.

AGNES: Do you want some more?

CECILIA: Yes, go on then, just a wafer thin slice, and then I'm getting up.

(AGNES leaves. She stops on the landing and "sees" her father at the top of the stairs, then moves on.)

CECILIA: (shouts after her) You might as well finish up that lime marmalade I suppose. (beat) Go on, quickly, tell me what else happened.

MARTHA: Well, not a lot really, that was the funny thing. I mean, I think David was definitely hearing people talking to him.

CECILIA: Oh God, do you think your father is trying to get through to us?

MARTHA: No, don't worry, I've told you, he's on a slow boat trip to heaven.

CECILIA: Slow? What do you mean, slow?

MARTHA: Nothing, Mum. It was just a turn of phrase.

(The phone starts ringing.)

CECILIA: (shouting) Agnes! Use your discretion! If it's Delyth Murphy or anyone from Skewen I'm not receiving visitors! Yes, go on, I'm listening.

MARTHA: So David's listening right, and then he starts to smile and he says, "I've got a gentlemen here with me now. He's quite a character. Says he comes from the Mount Pleasant area of Swansea and he used to have a little black dog and he died of a chest complaint last year."

CECILIA: What, the dog?

MARTHA: No, the man! And this woman says, "Oh, he was my next door neighbour. I never knew him very well." And David bursts out laughing and says, "Well, he says to tell you that at least he doesn't have to listen to you playing Whitney Houston at volume ten every night now." And she says, "Oh, he was always a grumpy old bugger!"

CECILIA: Oh dear, that is quite funny, Martha. (*beat*) Do you think she really plays Whitney Houston at volume ten every night?

(*AGNES comes in with more tea and toast which CECILIA does consume at some point.*)

AGNES: That was Geoffrey. He sends his love and says he'll pop up this afternoon.

MARTHA: Oooo, Geoffrey now, is it, since you're on the parish council?

CECILIA: I hope you didn't tell him I was still in bed.

AGNES: Of course not.

CECILIA: What would he think?

AGNES: He won't think anything. God's not concerned with bedtimes. Stay there and have a rest. It'll do you good.

CECILIA: No, no, there's things to be done.

MARTHA: What things?

CECILIA: There's all the chores.

AGNES: We'll do them.

CECILIA: You can't do them all.

AGNES: Yes we can.

CECILIA: And the ironing. There's a pile of your father's shirts. Oh God, he's never going to need a clean shirt

	anymore. I used to love to do his shirts and see them all hanging up in the wardrobe, clean and fresh.
MARTHA:	No, you didn't. You used to complain sometimes...
AGNES:	I'll sort them out.
CECILIA:	I suppose we ought to sort everything out. I suppose we ought to go through his things. That's what people do, isn't it? And see what we want to keep and put the rest in black rubbish bags and give them to the Salvation Army for some poor old down-and-out to wear while he's drinking his soup.
MARTHA:	And having the Bible thrust down his throat.
AGNES:	There's no need to do it now, Mum. You can wait until you feel like it.
CECILIA:	If I wait until I feel like it, I'll be sitting here like Miss Haversham covered in cobwebs.
MARTHA:	We could burn them!
AGNES:	Martha!
CECILIA:	Burn them?
MARTHA:	Yeah. Have a big bonfire in the back garden. We could do it tonight. It's a full moon.
AGNES:	What's that got to do with it?
MARTHA:	It's symbolic.
AGNES:	Symbolic of what?
MARTHA:	Life, death, the whole cycle. A gift to the Goddess. The Pagans were really into it. And the early Christians.
CECILIA:	Burn them, burn them. There is something appealing in it. They'd have something to say about it next door.
MARTHA:	Oh, sod next door.
CECILIA:	Yes, sod next door. Burn them. What, everything?
MARTHA:	No, only what you don't want to keep.
CECILIA:	It's very final.
MARTHA:	So's giving them to the Salvation Army. You can hardly go and ask some poor old down-and-out for them back.
CECILIA:	That's true, I suppose. Burn them. What do you

	think, Agnes?
AGNES:	I think you should wait.
MARTHA:	Why?
AGNES:	Because I think it's too soon for Mum to decide what she does and doesn't want. She might regret it. Anyway, it's a waste and I don't think Dad would have liked that.
CECILIA:	Yes, you're right. He wouldn't. He hates waste.
AGNES:	Yes, he did.
CECILIA:	There's no need to correct me, Agnes, as if I'm a child! I know your father is dead. I just can't believe it, alright?
	(*silence*)
CECILIA:	Open that wardrobe for me, will you Martha?
	(*She does so to reveal Jimmy's clothes hanging up. They are all quiet for a while looking at them.*)
CECILIA:	Look at them all standing to attention empty.
	(*silence*)
AGNES:	He's had that sports jacket ever since I can re-member.
	(*silence*)
CECILIA:	I don't know how many times I've re-patched those elbows.
	(*silence*)
AGNES:	I keep thinking I can see him.
CECILIA:	Do you? Where?
MARTHA:	Where?
AGNES:	Doorways mainly. Sometimes at the top of the stairs.
CECILIA:	Oh, I wish I could see him. Just for a moment. A precious moment.
MARTHA:	What, do you actually see him?
AGNES:	Well, no. Yes. I don't know. I... I look up and I can suddenly imagine him there. I can picture him. But do you know what I actually see? It's like... do you remember in *Lost in Space* when they used to stand on that thing to travel somewhere and they'd sort of change into a shimmering cylinder of light before

they disappeared? Well, that's what I see. I look up and imagine Dad and that's what I see.

MARTHA: That wasn't *Lost in Space*. It was *Star Trek*.

AGNES: No, it wasn't. It was *Lost in Space*. I remember.

MARTHA: We never used to watch *Lost in Space*. We always used to watch *Dr. Who* with Dad.

CECILIA: Oh, those were the days. You girls with your father shrieking and laughing behind the settee at the Daleks while I stuffed the chicken in the kitchen with the radio. Where did they go those days? Where have they gone?

AGNES: I used to watch *Lost in Space* sometimes. I was allowed to go over to Sian Thomas's house to watch it.

MARTHA: Did you?

AGNES: Yes. You used to want to come with me but you weren't allowed.

MARTHA: That wasn't fair.

AGNES: Life's not fair.

MARTHA: No! It was definitely *Star Trek*! Do you know how I know? (*triumphant*) "Beam me up, Scottie!" That's what they were doing. They were beaming them up.

CECILIA: Is that what's happening to your father, then? Are they beaming him up somewhere?

AGNES: Yes, but not to the planet Zog. To heaven.

CECILIA: Oh God. (*pause*) Do you know what I see all the time? His hands. I can see his hands everywhere: on the kitchen table, on the steering wheel, big and strong and gentle. Whenever I was in a state about something he would put a hand on my shoulder, just here, and he would say, "It'll be alright, Cil, it'll be alright, you just have to trust in God." And I would calm down. Just feeling his hand there I would calm down. He was my protector, your father. I know you think you don't need a man, Martha, but there's need and need and when you get to my age you might feel differently. Oh, I'd give my back teeth to feel his hand on my shoulder now.

MARTHA: It wasn't always like that, Mum. Sometimes he'd tell you to calm down and you'd go bananas.

AGNES: Martha.

CECILIA: Yes, alright, alright, but I'm not talking about those times.

MARTHA: All I'm saying is that there's no point idealising...

AGNES: ...Martha, drop it!

MARTHA: You don't even know what I was going to say.

AGNES: I just don't think it was going to be very helpful.

MARTHA: How do you know?

AGNES: Because I know you and I know Mum.

MARTHA: Oh, so you know best, do you?

AGNES: I'm not saying that. I'm just saying that...

CECILIA: ...Oh my God!

MARTHA: What?

AGNES: What's the matter?

CECILIA: Cake!

AGNES: What?

CECILIA: There's no cake in the house!

MARTHA: What?

CECILIA: Father Geoffrey is coming to visit and there's not a crumb of cake in the house.

AGNES: I'm sure there's some of that madeira left in the Roses tin.

CECILIA: I can't give him that. It's only good for trifle.

AGNES: He won't mind. He's coming to see you. He's not coming for a piece of cake.

CECILIA: That's beside the point.

MARTHA: We'll buy some.

CECILIA: Buy some?! I've never bought a cake in my life and I don't intend to start now.

MARTHA: Why not?

CECILIA: Because it's the thin end of the wedge, Martha, that's why.

MARTHA: The thin end of what wedge?

CECILIA: Of standards. Of letting standards slip. You see! This is exactly what happens when you stay in bed for too long. I'm ashamed. (*CECILIA starts to get out of bed.*)

AGNES:	Oh, Mum.
MARTHA:	Ashamed? Ashamed of what?
CECILIA:	I am ashamed that I can't offer a visitor — and the parish priest at that — who doesn't call as often as he could — a slice of tidy home-made cake.
MARTHA:	Well, I think that's absolutely ludicrous.
AGNES:	Martha.
CECILIA:	I daresay, Martha. I daresay you think I'm ludicrous and silly and a pathetic old woman. No, a pathetic old widow woman now, isn't it?
MARTHA:	I didn't say that.
CECILIA:	No, but that's what you think, isn't it? Well, I think some things about your life are ludicrous, as a matter of fact, but I don't say so.
MARTHA:	Yes, you bloody do. In not so many words, you do. But I didn't say that. I just think you're making life more difficult for yourself, that's all.
CECILIA:	How can I make life any more difficult than it already is? I've lost your father! He's gone and he's not coming back. Don't you understand that? (*She leaves to go to the bathroom.*)
MARTHA:	(*shouting after her*) Of course I understand that. Don't you think I'm missing him too? That's why it doesn't make any difference what sort of bloody cake Father Geoffrey has. (*beat*) He'd rather have a double whisky anyway.
AGNES:	Martha, drop it.
MARTHA:	And will you stop hovering over every bloody word I say!
AGNES:	You're upsetting Mum. Can't you see that?
MARTHA:	No, I'm not. I'm upsetting you because you want everything to be calm and quiet and controlled and life's bloody well not like that!
AGNES:	I just want what's best for Mum, that's all.
MARTHA:	No, you don't. You want what's best for you.
AGNES:	Meaning?
MARTHA:	You keep telling her to stay in bed when she wants

	to get up. It'd do her good to go down the beach for a walk.
AGNES:	She doesn't want to go down the beach for a walk. She said. You're the one that wants to go down the beach for a walk.
MARTHA:	You put the dampers on the bonfire and she was really into that to begin with.
AGNES:	I just didn't want her to do something she might regret.
MARTHA:	Oh, regret, regret. You can live your whole bloody life in regret. Why couldn't you let her do something spontaneous for once?
AGNES:	She's never done anything spontaneous in her life. I hardly think now is the time for her to start.
MARTHA:	She's never been in this situation in her life, either. Drastic situations call for drastic measures.
AGNES:	Oh, for God's sake, Martha, it would have been really embarrassing.
MARTHA:	Embarrassing? Oh, now we're really getting to it. Dad's dead and you're worried about being embarrassed.
AGNES:	He would have been highly embarrassed at you dancing around a bonfire of his clothes chanting some pagan litany.
MARTHA:	The dead don't suffer from embarrassment.
AGNES:	That doesn't mean to say we shouldn't still respect them.
MARTHA:	How do you know I wouldn't have been respectful? The only person who would have been embarrassed would have been you. I'll still do it anyway. I'll take something of Dad's down to Three Cliffs and I'll burn it under the full moon and I'll smoke a spliff and I'll dance around the fire naked and then I'll sacrifice a young virgin boy and drink his blood and I'll have a *South Wales Evening Post* photographer there to prove it.
AGNES:	Oh, do what you want. Why should I care? It's not my responsibility.
MARTHA:	No, it's not. It's not your responsibility.

225

AGNES: You've got it all worked out, haven't you?

MARTHA: No. I don't think anybody's got it worked out. That's why you've got to keep searching. That's what's wrong with you, Agnes. You've stopped searching. You've given in.

AGNES: Do you think so?

MARTHA: Yes, I do.

           (*silence*)

AGNES: He wouldn't rather have a double whisky. Geoffrey never drinks whisky.

MARTHA: What?

AGNES: He got horribly drunk on whisky five Easters ago and he's never touched it since. He likes a bottle of well-chilled, dry white wine. Or two.

MARTHA: What?

AGNES: Chablis, actually, if the collection's been generous. Which it hasn't been for some time.

MARTHA: (*slowly dawning*) That's when you went to Lourdes. Five years ago.

AGNES: That's right.

MARTHA: And had a fling with... bloody hell, Agnes.

AGNES: Yes. Bloody hell.

           (*silence, then CECILIA comes back in.*)

CECILIA: What do you mean he'd rather have a double whisky?

AGNES: What?

MARTHA: What?

CECILIA: You said Father Geoffrey would rather have a double whisky than a slice of my home-made cake.

MARTHA: Ask Agnes.

AGNES: Martha.

MARTHA: What? No... I... I just happen to know that he likes a drink, Mum, that's all.

CECILIA: Do you? Do you indeed? Well, he can have a slice of my home-made cake this afternoon and he can like it or lump it. And he can tell me why God has decided to be so cruel to me while he's at it. Right. I'm getting

226

dressed. I want you girls to do what you want but if anyone wants to check the cupboard I'm going to be making a large fruitcake.

MARTHA: Alright.

AGNES: I'll check the cupboard.

(They go. CECELIA starts looking through the clothes in her wardrobe.)

CECILIA: No, no. That's not right, too summery... umm... no... umm, yes, that's a possibility. What do you think, Jim? Shall I wear that? ...No... maybe not... um, no... no... no... Oh come on, Cecilia, make a decision...

(She starts going back through them again.)

No, no, no, no, no... Oh God, I can't make a decision. Isn't it ridiculous, Jimmy, but I can't make a decision about what to wear to make a cake to feed a priest. *(She sits down on the bed and looks at Jimmy's clothes.)*

Oh Jimmy, love, what am I going to do? How am I ever going to make another decision without you?

(She goes to his wardrobe and starts gently touching his clothes.)

Where are you, Jim? Are you in there? Come out, love, come on, come out... You're not there, are you? You're not here, are you Jimmy?

(She takes out a jacket and sits down again, holding and stroking it.)

Where are you, Jimmy? Where have you gone? What have they done with you, eh? Are you alright, love? Are they looking after you? Don't go making a fuss in that old waiting room now, love. It's not worth it. Don't go bothering the receptionists, they're very busy. You'll just have to wait your turn like everyone else. I shouldn't bother with *Woman's Own*, you won't find anything to interest you there. Have a look in *Country Life*, love, they've got some marvellous interiors. You'll enjoy working out how you could have done them differently.

Oh Jim, I'm scared, I'm really frightened. How am I ever going to manage without you? What am I going to do? I don't know what to do, Jimmy, I don't know what to do for the best. Come back, love, don't go, don't leave me. Come back and we'll build the boat together, eh? Yes, we'll build an ark of a boat, Jimmy, big and strong and gentle like your hands. And we'll polish the wood until we can see our faces in it and I'll sew little curtains to match the sail — red and white and green — oh, a dragon of a sail we'll have for an ark of a boat. Do they have windows in arks, Jimmy? Well, we will in ours, anyway, we will in our ark. And we'll sail out of Swansea bay and past the Mumbles lighthouse and along the coast to Pembroke and we'll wave to St. David's and the wind will find the sail and we'll sail across the sea to the land with no snakes, eh, Jimmy? We'll do that, shall we? You always wanted to do that, didn't you love? (*she stops*) Oh God, oh God I can't bear it, I can't bear it, Oh Jimmy, I can't bear the pain. Come back, love, come back to me please... Oh Jimmy, I love you, you know that, don't you? I love you, Jimmy, I love you. I love you so much, I love you so, so much. I love you, I love you, I love you, I love you, I love you, I love you.... (*etc.*)

(*She stops and gently unfurls herself. She sits up and ever so slowly brings her right hand up to her left shoulder. She can feel Jimmy's hand. She clasps it tightly and smiles.*)

Yes. Yes, I know, Jimmy. I know. Alright. Alright then, love. Yes, I will. I will. Alright. Alright. And you. And you too, love. Yes, yes, I'll see you there.

(*She bows her head and brings her hand down. She takes a deep breath and sits upright. She calls out.*)

Girls! Girls! Put the kettle on and get the thermos out! We're going down to the beach. We'll buy a home-made cake from Nancy's on the way back but you're to be the souls of discretion. Not a word to father Geoffrey.

(*She moves to take some clothes from her wardrobe.*)

It'll be our secret. (*She chooses something to wear.*) We're going down to the beach! We're going down to the beach to look at the boats!

(*blackout*)

LISA HUNT
A Night Under Canvas

Born in Cardiff, Lisa Hunt (b.1967) has a degree in Drama from Hull University. Early aspirations to act have given way to a successful writing career. She has worked for television, radio and the stage. Her plays broadcast on radio include *Baby, Baby; Never The Bride;* and *A Little Myth Trouble.* Her work for television includes *Every Cloud* for the BBC, *Flying Blind* for HTV and *Stupid Cupid* for Children's ITV. She is currently developing work with Scottish Television and LWT. *A Night Under Canvas* features two working-class women accidentally locked inside the National Museum of Wales Art Gallery.

CHARACTERS
Brenda
Valmai

(*BRENDA stands alone, centre stage, surrounded by picture frames. Downstage, a strange, abstract sculpture stands. It is large and odd-looking. She appears uncomfortable and out of place in this hushed, somewhat high-brow setting. Off stage, the voice of the tour guide echoes and Brenda cynically mimics her posh tones while tentatively peeping at the pieces of art that surround her.*)

GUIDE: (*off*) If you could please try and keep up, ladies and gentlemen, we do have an awful lot to cover this afternoon. I would urge you ladies and gentlemen to look to your left... yes, to your left, sir, where you will notice "The Basino di San Marco: Looking North" by Antonio Canaletto. Could you not crowd ladies and gentlemen? Thank you. Moving on... um, yes, moving on... This way, thank you. We really do

229

have an awful lot to cover this afternoon, ladies and gentlemen.... As I am sure you are aware this is the last tour of the day and we really should press on if we are going to squeeze in the Middle Ages through to Enlightenment. Thank you.

(*The voice fades and VALMAI appears on stage, apparently looking for BRENDA.*)

VALMAI: Eh, come on, will you? We're going to lose them.

(*BRENDA ignores her. She pretends to be interested in the art that surrounds her.*)

VALMAI: Brenda.

BRENDA: What?

VALMAI: Come on, we're going to lose them.

BRENDA: Go on, you go. I'll catch up with you later.

VALMAI: Brenda. Come on!

BRENDA: Val, I will not traipse another step after that woman.

VALMAI: But we'll miss the tour. We paid for the tour.

BRENDA: I'm sorry, Val, but we've been following that woman for the last hour and a half. I didn't take a day off work to be herded about like an animal.

VALMAI: Oh, come on, it isn't that bad.

BRENDA: You're not wearing these shoes. (*BRENDA kicks off her shoes. They clack to the floor.*) That's better. Lovely cold floor.

VALMAI: Brenda, put your shoes back on.

BRENDA: Why?

VALMAI: Brenda, please.

BRENDA: All right. Keep your hair on.

VALMAI: We might still catch them now if we hurry.

BRENDA: I knew I shouldn't have worn these heels. I only bought them last week and they're pinching round the back, you know?

VALMAI: You're doing this deliberately, aren't you?

BRENDA: I'd have been better off in a pair of daps. What do you mean, doing what?

VALMAI: I know you didn't want to come, but if you knew the amount of trouble I went to to have Roy's mother look after the kids...

BRENDA: Oh, come on, Val. Five minutes is all I want. It's not too much to ask, is it? We've had a fair crack at it.

(*VALMAI takes a last look off-stage to watch the disappearing party.*)

VALMAI: Well, that's it. We've lost them now. Thanks, Brenda, thanks very much.

BRENDA: I could have been at home with my feet up with *Esther Rantzen* on the telly, you know that, don't you?

VALMAI: Oh, don't start now, Brenda.

BRENDA: I just hope I set the video right for *Neighbours*, that's all. I'll have you to blame if I miss it. Museum she says, let's get on a bus to Cardiff. Get us a bit of culture. Culture, indeed.

VALMAI: Shhh!!

BRENDA: What? What's the matter?

VALMAI: Will you keep your voice down.

BRENDA: Why? There's no one in here, Val.

VALMAI: Just keep it down, will you? (*she looks about her*) People can hear you.

BRENDA: What people?

VALMAI: Just people, all right? The guard in by there. He was looking... at you... talking... shooting your mouth off about... well, I don't know about what.

BRENDA: Oh, for goodness' sake relax, will you? Expressing an opinion is all I was doing, Val. I paid my money, I'll say what I like.

VALMAI: Oh, come on, let's go. This was a bad idea. Come on.

BRENDA: Look, I don't mind staying if that's what you really want to do. Just let me sit down for a minute and let the blood get to my feet.

VALMAI: But we've lost the guide now. She'll wonder where we've got to.

BRENDA: At the rate she was going the only thing on her mind was getting out as fast as she could. Middle Ages and Enlightenment, my eye. Dying to get her handbag she was, have a quick puff.

VALMAI: All right. All right. Just keep your voice down.

BRENDA: Anyone would think it was a funeral parlour, the way you're creeping about. I have got to sit down.

(BRENDA goes to plonk herself down into a large, odd-looking stool, but she is brought up sharply by VALMAI.)

VALMAI: DON'T SIT THERE!

BRENDA: What! Why?

VALMAI: Why?! Because it's an exhibit, that's why!

BRENDA: Is it?

VALMAI: Of course it is, can't you see?

BRENDA: Are you sure?

VALMAI: Of course I'm sure.

BRENDA: How can you tell?

VALMAI: Well, look at it. It's... it's quite obviously... of course it is.

BRENDA: Well, I'll take your word for it. They could have put a rope round it or something, don't you think? Odd-looking thing. You have to admit, it does look like a chair... or a big stool or something.

VALMAI: Beautiful wood. Probably Norwegian, I expect.

BRENDA: Well, will you hark at her?

VALMAI: Is there a plaque? The plaque will say what it is.

BRENDA: Can't see one. Is there one at your end? Perhaps there's one on the wall over here? *(BRENDA searches for a clue.)* Nope, nothing.

(BRENDA looks at the object, studying it closely, and then at VALMAI.)

BRENDA: Are you sure?

VALMAI: Well, I...

(Defiantly, BRENDA goes and sits back on the chair.)

BRENDA: You have got to learn to relax, Val. Just sit down, will you, and take the weight off.

VALMAI: You can't be too careful in these places. Better to be safe than sorry.

(VALMAI takes a quick look about her, then sits.)

BRENDA: Beautiful wood. Probably Norwegian, I expect... *(they both snort a laugh)* What are you like?

(They sit for a while taking in the surroundings.)

232

VALMAI: Listen to that, Brend.

BRENDA: What?

VALMAI: Quiet, isn't it?

BRENDA: Mmmmmmm.

VALMAI: Worth the two pounds fifty just to get a bit of peace.

BRENDA: Aye.

VALMAI: Lovely. Come on, then, let's go.

BRENDA: Eh? We don't have to.

VALMAI: No, I want to.

BRENDA: Well, you've changed your tune.

VALMAI: No, really. It was a silly idea. I don't know what possessed me. They'll be closing up soon anyway. Just a quick visit to the toilet and out, is it?

BRENDA: Blessed relief. Now, which way was it? Down here, I think.

(They move in one direction then change their minds.)

BRENDA: Or was it this way?

(They exit briefly then reappear.)

VALMAI: Come on, Brenda, you must have seen a sign for the ladies somewhere.

(Their voices fade as they finally exit, then reappear again.)

BRENDA: All the rooms look the same. How should I know where the toilets are? It's not as if it's the local pub, is it?

(They exit through the large double doors upstage, which upon their leaving slowly close, finally resting in place with a loud boom. BRENDA and VALMAI enter the space once more.)

VALMAI: We're back where we started.

BRENDA: Are we?

VALMAI: Yes, I'm sure we are.

BRENDA: It's awfully quiet. Are we the only ones here?

(Another door booms shut.)

VALMAI: What was that?

BRENDA: Sounded like a door closing.

VALMAI: I don't like it, Brenda. It's too quiet.

BRENDA: It's a museum, Val. It's supposed to be quiet. Come on, we'll retrace our tracks. This door wasn't shut before, was it?

(*BRENDA attempts to open the large double doors.*)

BRENDA: I think it's locked.

VALMAI: It can't be.

(*VALMAI rattles it desperately. BRENDA runs across the space and attempts to open the opposite door. It remains locked.*)

VALMAI: It can't be. We can't be locked in. Don't be funny, Brenda, come on, stop it! Let me try.

BRENDA: I'm not being funny, Val. We're locked in.

VALMAI: (*pummelling her fists on the door*) Help! Help! You've locked us in. Open the door! Please! Open the door!

BRENDA: For goodness' sake, Val, calm down.

VALMAI: (*is quiet for a split second, then...*) Please! Open the door. We're in here! You've locked us in...

BRENDA: (*shouting about the noise*) Val! Val! Will you please get a grip. For heaven's sake, Valmai, you are making an exhibition of yourself, for goodness' sake!

VALMAI: Help!

(*BRENDA slaps her across the face. VALMAI is left silent apart from the gasps of air that leak from her mouth at intervals.*)

BRENDA: Have you got your tablets?

VALMAI: Mmmm.

BRENDA: Well, get them out and pop one in.

(*She rummages through her bag and gulps one down.*)

VALMAI: Am I bleeding?

BRENDA: Of course, you're not bleeding. Now, come on, get a grip.

VALMAI: You don't understand. I've got a casserole in the oven. It'll be burnt to a crisp.

BRENDA: They'll be back now, don't you worry.

VALMAI: When?

BRENDA: Soon.

234

(The lights suddenly dim.)

VALMAI: The lights! They've turned out the lights!

BRENDA: Keep calm, just keep calm.

VALMAI: They've turned the lights out, Brenda.

BRENDA: Yes, I know.

VALMAI: They don't know we're here.

BRENDA: Now, don't panic. There must be some kind of switch in here somewhere. Just stay there for a minute and I'll see if I can find one.

VALMAI: Don't leave me, Brenda.

BRENDA: Deep breaths, Val, deep breaths. I'm just going to walk over here and see if I can find...

(BRENDA feels her way about the space. She tumbles into the strange, abstract object. It crashes to the floor.)

VALMAI: *(screams)* What was that? *(BRENDA groans.)* You've broken something. Oh my... you've broken something.

BRENDA: No, it's all right, Val, I'm fine. Thanks for the concern, no really, I'm fine. Now there must be... along here somewhere... aha! Val, you can open your eyes now. I found a light switch. *(lights come on)*

VALMAI: *(gasps)* Look what you've done. Look! It's all over the floor. The... thing... it's all over the floor.

BRENDA: Damn, I broke a nail.

VALMAI: Aww, did you?

BRENDA: Yeah. It's all right, I'll stick another one on tomorrow.

VALMAI: What are we going to do about this?

(They both give the mess around them a worried stare.)

BRENDA: Now let's keep a cool head and think for a minute now.

VALMAI: Do you think it was worth a lot of money.

BRENDA: Bound to have been.

VALMAI: Will they make us pay?

BRENDA: They better not. Anyway, it's not going to come to that.

VALMAI: How do you mean?

BRENDA: What do you think it was, Val? Can you remember what it was?

VALMAI: I can't remember. It was some kind of abstract thing, I think.

BRENDA: Well, there we are then. We're going to be all right. The pieces aren't damaged. We'll just put them back together somehow. No-one will notice.

VALMAI: But they will!

BRENDA: Can you remember what it looked like?

VALMAI: No.

BRENDA: Well, chances are, no-one else will. Come on, let's get cracking.

VALMAI: Brenda, we can't.

BRENDA: Have you got any other ideas?

VALMAI: Well...

BRENDA: No, I didn't think so. Give us a hand. Today please, Val! We haven't got all night. At least, I hope we haven't.

(*VALMAI collects the wooden pieces and hands them to BRENDA.*)

BRENDA: Now, let's have a look. What do you think? This bit there. Where do you reckon, just for starters?

VALMAI: I don't think it was like that.

BRENDA: But does it look all right?

VALMAI: Yes, I suppose so.

BRENDA: Right then, that's where it's staying.

VALMAI: You're very calm about this, Brenda. I suppose the best thing is to keep calm.

BRENDA: Well, it's not our fault, is it? They are the ones who didn't check the property before closing the place.

VALMAI: On top, definitely. Yes, yes, that's all right.

BRENDA: I could get into this, you know.

VALMAI: Eh, that's not bad, Brend. It looks... nice. Yes, very nice. You never know, Brend, abstract could be your thing.

BRENDA: (*laughs*) Do you think so? Well, I've always said, Val, this art thing, it's all a big con, isn't it? I'm sure if I

236

hung my dirty pants in a gallery some stupid bugger would come and look at them.

VALMAI: Aye. It's probably been done, Brend. It wouldn't surprise me. Now, you see that over there? Now John, my youngest, he could have painted that.

BRENDA: I'm sure he could, Val, I'm sure he could.

VALMAI: It seems all you've got to do is splash a bit of paint here and there, and you're laughing.

BRENDA: Still life, it is. Now that's a different thing, isn't it? That's where the skill is, isn't it?

VALMAI: Now me, I was always one for still life. I was told, you know, at school, that I showed a lot of promise.

BRENDA: Were you? You never told me that. Pass me that bit there.

VALMAI: Oh yes. Still life. I was very good at still life. Not people. I wasn't very good at people, and the other stuff like pottery and weaving. Well, I never really got into that at all. But still life, yes, that was my thing. There was something very satisfying about reproducing the order of things on a page. Fruit was nice, furniture and fruit.

BRENDA: You should take it up again, Val.

VALMAI: (*laughing gently*) I tried to draw my mother once, but like I say, I wasn't very good at people and she wouldn't sit still long enough, so I don't know why I bothered, really. Anyway, she wasn't too pleased when she saw the results. Faces, you see, I could never do faces. She said I had made her look like a monster. Threw it in the bin. Can't say I can blame her, mind. I had made a bit of a dog's dinner of it. Furniture was much easier, furniture and fruit.

BRENDA: Oh, yes, fruit. Can't go wrong with fruit. What do you think?

(*They step back to admire BRENDA'S handiwork.*)

VALMAI: Do you know, that's not half bad, Brend....

BRENDA: (*pleased with herself*) Yes, I think it will pass.

VALMAI: No bad, not bad at all.

(*They stand admiring the piece, unsure of what to do next.*)

VALMAI: They haven't come yet, then?

BRENDA: Won't be long now.

VALMAI: They will come, won't they, Brenda?

BRENDA: 'Course they will.

VALMAI: 'Course they will, yes.

BRENDA: Hundreds, thousands of pounds just lying about. 'Course they'll come.

(*They are silent once more. Hanging around.*)

VALMAI: When will they come, Brenda?

BRENDA: Oh, for goodness' sake, I don't know.

(*VALMAI smiles with a look of mischief and reaches a hand into her bag. She produces a small parcel of fruit and biscuits wrapped in clingfilm. VALMAI hands out the provisions from her bag. They sit chewing for a while.*)

BRENDA: You know, I never liked art at school.

VALMAI: No?

BRENDA: No. Shoes. We were always drawing shoes, over and over again. And not interesting shoes either, not even other people's shoes. Our own shoes. Now, where's the interest in that, eh? I got so bored in the end I asked if I could paint some shoes, you know, instead of drawing them.

VALMAI: Oh yeah...

BRENDA: Mmm. I found a couple of tins of emulsion paint in the cupboard under the stairs, lined the shoes up all nice, you know, artistic like, and tipped the whole lot over them.

VALMAI: You never.

BRENDA: Oh aye. Looked good, too, all the colours running into one another. Different, you know.

VALMAI: Must have made an awful mess.

BRENDA: Well aye, yes. But it was very satisfying. One in the eye for the art department, anyway. Mr Haines, the art teacher, said that as an act of rebellion it was very effective but I would never cut it in an exam. So, it was back to the drawing board. (*VALMAI gets up from her seat, still munching, and browses.*) No, never liked art.

VALMAI: Look at this...

BRENDA: What?

VALMAI: This painting here.

BRENDA: What about it?

VALMAI: I knew I'd seen it somewhere before. We've got this painting in our bathroom at home.

BRENDA: What is it?

VALMAI: (reads) "Claude Monet 'Waterlilies', 1905". Roy's Aunt gave us one of these as a wedding present. It came in a lovely frame. Roy doesn't like it.

BRENDA: Good old Roy.

VALMAI: He never says why. Just sneers at it while he's shaving. He says if we wanted cheap tat then we could go out and buy it ourselves, we didn't need other people to burden us with it. I never really took much notice of it. I never realised it was hanging in the art gallery.

BRENDA: Typical of Roy, that, isn't it?

VALMAI: What?

BRENDA: I said that's typical of Roy.

VALMAI: How would you know?

BRENDA: When you live next door to someone as long as I've been next to you and Roy, believe me, you know what's typical and what's not.

VALMAI: Oh yes, I was forgetting, your little hero Roy is, isn't he? Forever popping over to lend you the lawn mower or sort out your wiring or whatever else it is you find for him to do. Comes in very handy then, doesn't he, cultured or not?

BRENDA: Oh yes, he's very handy, just not very good at spotting art.

VALMAI: Roy is very fond of art, actually.

BRENDA: Oh yes, I'm sure he is, when it's shaped like Samantha Fox and smiling at him from his newspaper.

VALMAI: That's not art, Brenda.

BRENDA: Isn't it? Well, you try telling that to David Bailey. I've got his book on my coffee table and as far as he's concerned, women with their clothes off, that's art.

VALMAI: He's probably at home now, worried sick about where I am.

BRENDA: Who? David Bailey?

VALMAI: No! Roy.

BRENDA: I bet he is. Home from work and no dinner on the table. He must be frantic.

VALMAI: Just stop, will you?

BRENDA: What?

VALMAI: I don't know what makes you so you think you know Roy so well. Just stop going on.

BRENDA: You started it.

VALMAI: I know my own husband, Brenda. Roy tries his best.

BRENDA: I'm sure he does, Val. All I'm saying is, it doesn't surprise me that he can't tell a work of art when he sees one, that's all. I'm not going on about him.

VALMAI: Come on, then. Tell me about this picture. Tell me something about this picture that Roy couldn't tell me.

BRENDA: Well, I don't know. I've never seen it before. Roy lives with it, he sees it every day. He's more familiar with it than I am. (*she laughs, embarrassed*) I don't know.

VALMAI: Try.

BRENDA: Val.

VALMAI: You can't, can you?

BRENDA: O.K. Ummmm... The colour. I like the colour.

VALMAI: Why?

BRENDA: I don't know. I've got some sheets that colour. Bought them cheap down Clydach market, oh, must be years ago now. They wash lovely. Kept their colour too, which is incredible considering some of the rubbish you can buy down there...

VALMAI: The painting, Brenda.

BRENDA: O.K. ...Ummm... it's a pond...

VALMAI: Yes.

BRENDA: A purple pond... with lilies... on it.

VALMAI: Yes.

BRENDA: They're my favourites, you know, those sheets. Lovely in the winter, brushed they are. You know, cosy.

VALMAI: Brend....

BRENDA: No listen. It looks familiar, you know, comfortable, warm like the sheets, like I could just slip my clothes off and slide in. Warm. It looks like the kind of place you begged your mother to let you swim in when you were a kid and she never would. Do you know what I mean?

VALMAI: Perhaps.

BRENDA: I can see me now bracing myself for a dive. And in I'd go, just touching my foot on the bottom and then I would burst to the surface with one of those lilies resting on my head, like that woman, you know, in all those old films. What's her name? You know... the swimmer?

VALMAI: Esther Williams.

BRENDA: Yes, that's it. Esther Williams. Yes, I can see me now, rising from the water on a huge platform covered in sparklers surrounded by scores of chorus girls in floral swimsuits smiling broadly, with their hands on their hips. Like this. (*she mimics their actions*) And then... and then four tanned men in grass skirts would carry me over to a fruit-filled bank where an orchestra in full evening dress would strike up something... I don't know, a Latin American number, I expect. And then Carmen Miranda would appear... (*VALMAI stops her before she gets too carried away.*)

VALMAI: Yes, yes, yes, all right. I think I get the picture.

BRENDA: Well, that's what I think. What would Roy make of it, then?

VALMAI: I don't know. I suppose I should, shouldn't I?

BRENDA: I thought that was the point.

VALMAI: He would say it looked cold. I think. (*BRENDA looks back to the picture, reassessing her thoughts.*) I think it looks cold. You can't see the edge. I wouldn't like to swim in anything where you couldn't see the edge. That's how accidents happen.

BRENDA: Does Roy know that you've come here today?

VALMAI: No.

(*BRENDA appears embarrassed.*)

BRENDA: Where are they? Someone should have come by now.

VALMAI: At least the kids will be all right. You know sometimes I think they prefer other peoples' company to mine. When I told them they would be going to their Nan's after school they looked almost relieved.

(*VALMAI makes her way back to the reconstructed abstract piece.*)

BRENDA: Don't talk such rubbish.

VALMAI: No, it's true. I think I bore them.

(*She kneels down by the piece and touches it hesitantly. Then with one swipe sends it tumbling to the floor.*)

BRENDA: Val! What are you doing?

(*BRENDA rushes to retrieve the pieces.*)

VALMAI: I didn't like it.

BRENDA: Well, I did. What are we going to say if they come back now?

VALMAI: We'll build it again. Come on, it won't take long. What shall we do. I mean, where do you think is the best place to start?

BRENDA: Well, I don't know.

VALMAI: Start from the bottom and work up, you reckon?

BRENDA: Well, yes, I suppose, but....

VALMAI: Just forget what was there before, and start again. Close your mouth, Brenda, and pass me the pieces.

(*VALMAI begins to reconstruct the piece.*)

BRENDA: Are you all right?

VALMAI: I'm fine.

BRENDA: Are you sure?

VALMAI: Yes, I'm sure. Come on or we'll never get this done. What artists do you know, Brenda?

BRENDA: Oh, I don't know. None really.

VALMAI: Come on, there must be some. Picasso, there's one to start you off.

BRENDA: Oh, yes, I like him... I think. Rolf Harris!

242

VALMAI: Rolf Harris!

BRENDA: Yeah.

VALMAI: He doesn't count.

BRENDA: Why not?

VALMAI: He plays the accordion.

BRENDA: I used to love him on the telly. Mesmerised I was, the way he used those huge brushes to paint all that detail. I thought he was so clever.

VALMAI: I suppose so.

BRENDA: Yeah, he was great.

           (*they both laugh*)

VALMAI: Give that to me.

BRENDA: Oh, I don't know, Val. It's another world, isn't it? I think I prefer it when there's no-one else here. Just me and you, you know. It's calming, isn't it? Looks good, Val, an interesting start there. (*BRENDA leaves VALMAI to her building and wanders the space, looking at paintings.*) Yes, it's another world. Van Gogh. He's just a name really, isn't he? I mean, I don't think I'd recognise one of his paintings if I saw one, would you?

VALMAI: No, I shouldn't think so. Oh no, wait a minute. There's the one with a chair, isn't there? I think that was Van Gogh.

           (*BRENDA approaches a frame and peers quizzically at it.*)

BRENDA: Do you know who this one is by?

VALMAI: Look at the plaque thing. The plaque will say.

BRENDA: (*reads*) "'Study for Self-Portrait', Francis Bacon, 1909-92" Weird. It says he was a surrealist "largely indifferent to the representational values of portraiture". Fancy having that hanging in your living room. It would give me the willies, that would.

VALMAI: He looks like I feel.

BRENDA: Aye, I know what you mean. I think he was like you, Val, not very good at faces.

VALMAI: Or hands, by the look of it.

           (*VALMAI shivers as she looks at it.*)

BRENDA: You'd think though, wouldn't you, that painting

yourself, you'd do something a bit tidy really. Colours are nice, though. Like a cartoon. What do you think?

VALMAI: I think it's horrible.

BRENDA: Well, he wouldn't be the first choice to do my portrait, but it's not bad... if you like that sort of thing. How would you like to be done, Val, in a portrait?

VALMAI: I wouldn't want one, Brend. It's bad enough looking at old photos.

BRENDA: I know what you mean. Hairdos. They come back to haunt you, don't they?

VALMAI: Exactly. So I wouldn't want a portrait of myself hanging in the house. Oh no, I couldn't cope with that.

BRENDA: I quite fancy it myself. I think I'd like to be done on a chaise longue in a flowing white dress, you know, like those old fashioned ones. Just lying there gazing mysteriously out into the distance. What do you think? I see a bowl of fruit in it somewhere. Eh, you could do that. You're good at fruit. What do you think?

VALMAI: Well, it's nice, but it's not really you, is it?

BRENDA: Isn't it?

VALMAI: (*laughing*) Not really, no bowl of fruit!

BRENDA: How do you see me, then?

VALMAI: I don't know. Not in a white dress, that's for sure.

BRENDA: Well, how then?

VALMAI: In a pub, perhaps, propping up the bar.

BRENDA: Oh, cheers.

VALMAI: Or outside the gents toilet wearing a pair of boxing gloves... or maybe....

BRENDA: Now, hold on a minute.

VALMAI: Well, you did ask.

BRENDA: You don't see me like that, do you?

VALMAI: Oh, come off it, Brenda.

BRENDA: I always saw myself as a bit of a Scarlett O'Hara type.

VALMAI: (*cannot contain herself*) Good grief, Brenda! She's the last person I would have thought of.

(*BRENDA is silent for a while. VALMAI'S words sting her.*)

BRENDA: I must be giving off all the wrong signals then, musn't I? Boxing gloves, is it? Well, at least it wasn't oven gloves.

VALMAI: What's that supposed to mean?

BRENDA: How do you see yourself then, Val?

VALMAI: I don't see myself as anything, really.

BRENDA: You must do.

VALMAI: I don't.

BRENDA: I see you as...

VALMAI: I don't want to know how you see me.

BRENDA: You told me. Now I'm going to have my two penn'orth.

VALMAI: No.

BRENDA: I see you outside a....

VALMAI: Brenda.

BRENDA: Oh, go on.

VALMAI: I don't care, O.K.? I don't care how you see me. So just drop it, O.K.?

BRENDA: O.K.

(*They are silent for awhile.*)

VALMAI: When I was younger I used to imagine myself living on my own. No kids, nothing like that. Just me. I could see it so clearly, you know, the type of house I would have, the sort of clothes I would wear. I was always looking forward into the future then. But now, well this is the future, isn't it, and all I seem to think about is what other people want. Never seem to think about me. I'd like to see myself on my own, just me on a blank page. That's how I would like to see myself.

BRENDA: You'd get bored with it after a while.

VALMAI: Would I?

BRENDA: Yes, I think so. (*she pauses for a while, pondering her own position*) I know so. You've finished.

(*VALMAI looks down at the piece that she has been absent-mindedly constructing during the conversation.*)

VALMAI: Oh yes, what do you think?

BRENDA: I think it's brilliant. Where are they? I'm getting a bit anxious now...

VALMAI: They'll be here.

(*BRENDA turns and walks towards the large double doors upstage. She stops and looks at Rodin's 'The Kiss'.*)

BRENDA: Now, I would see myself with him. Oh yes, definitely.

VALMAI: What?

BRENDA: Look at that, Val, just take a look at that.

VALMAI: Yeah, that is nice.

BRENDA: Look at the shoulders on that, Val. I bet he's a swimmer. Now that is fabulous!

VALMAI: Yes, very nice.

BRENDA: I bet he's a real bundle of fun.

VALMAI: I think I've seen it before somewhere. In a book or something. (*she fishes out a guide book from her bag*) I think it's famous.

BRENDA: Who is it by?

VALMAI: Hang on now... now where did I see it? Yes, this is it. Yes, it's famous. I recognise the name.

BRENDA: Well, go on then, what is it?

VALMAI: "'The Kiss' by August Rodin. Bronze."

BRENDA: Does it say who they are?

VALMAI: "'The Kiss' derives from a group representing the embracing lovers Paolo and Francesca in Dante's 'Inferno'."

BRENDA: Lucky old Francesca.

VALMAI: Well, not really. It says here they were doomed.

BRENDA: To what?

VALMAI: I don't know. It doesn't say. Hell, I suppose.

BRENDA: What a way to go though, eh?

VALMAI: It's big, isn't it?

BRENDA: Do you know I don't think I've ever seen such a huge man. Not even when I went to see the Chippendales that time.

VALMAI: You never went and saw the Chippendales!

BRENDA: 'Course I did. Didn't I tell you? You should have come with us. Honestly, laugh? Well, scream really. You remember Kath Price?

VALMAI: No, I don't think so.

BRENDA: Yes, you do. Stuck up piece. Drives that flash car. Works for the Water Board.

VALMAI: Oh yeah. She never went with you?

BRENDA: Oh yes. I wrestled her for them but she's got an iron grip.

VALMAI: All that flesh, see. It does things to people.

BRENDA: You're telling me.

VALMAI: Did they all look like him?

BRENDA: I think that's what they were aiming for but I don't remember any of them as half as big as him. And they were big! You know what I mean, Val, all oiled and brown.

VALMAI: I can imagine.

BRENDA: I don't think this guy is your Chippendale type, though. He looks more your sensitive type, doesn't he?

VALMAI: Yes, definitely. You don't kiss like that unless you're sensitive.

BRENDA: Or gagging for it.

VALMAI: Yes.

BRENDA: Mind you, she's not being coy about it, is she?

VALMAI: Who's kissing who then, do you reckon?

BRENDA: Hard to tell, isn't it?

VALMAI: I think she's kissing him.

BRENDA: Do you think we're allowed to touch it? Shall we? Go on.

VALMAI: Go on yourself.

(BRENDA also hesitates.)

BRENDA: No, I might get to like it. What you don't know, you don't miss really, isn't it?

VALMAI: I like to just look. Do you think she's beautiful?

BRENDA: I don't know... umm... yes, yes she's not bad. Could do with a bit of uplift in the chest department but yes, I suppose so.

VALMAI: Do you see yourself when you look at her?

BRENDA: How do you mean?

VALMAI: Well, could you see yourself doing that. Sitting like that, completely naked, without thinking... about anything else.

BRENDA: I don't think I'd have too much trouble, Val, no.

VALMAI: Do you think most women feel like that?

BRENDA: I don't know. I expect so. Why, don't you?

VALMAI: I'd like to, but I don't know. Don't you ever feel that sort of thing is what other women... I don't think I could keep my mind off my thighs, and whether... well, you know... whether everything was up together. Not hanging there, you know. She looks, well, so unconcerned. Like she's never even heard about cellulite. I couldn't be like that.

BRENDA: Oh come on, Val, you must forget about it some-times.

VALMAI: I don't, well... no, I don't.

BRENDA: What about in your wildest fantasies? You must let it all hang out then.

VALMAI: But I don't. It goes even that far.

BRENDA: Do you and Roy still... you know?

VALMAI: Oh yes. It wouldn't be Saturday nights without the usual clumsy tumble.

BRENDA: With the lights out.

VALMAI: And his pyjamas on.

BRENDA: Oh dear.

VALMAI: Yes, oh dear. Oh, it's not Roy's fault. After a while you just... stop making the effort, I suppose. There's too many other things going on to worry about ingenuity. Do you think I'm odd?

BRENDA: Odd? Why odd?

VALMAI: Odd, that I don't mind. That I really don't. I worry sometimes, you know, whether he minds. He was so... energetic once. He's never said anything to you, has he?

BRENDA: To me? Now why would he say something to me?

VALMAI: You would have been his type you see, years ago. He's never...

BRENDA: (*shocked for a moment*) No, Val, he has never.

VALMAI: Have you ever been kissed like that, Brend?

BRENDA: (*laughs*) No, I don't think so. No, wait a minute, yes. Yes, I have. Yes! By Gary Shilling, when the "Swans" got through to the semi-finals.

VALMAI: I don't remember you going out with any Gary.

BRENDA: Oh, I wasn't seeing him or anything. I just happened to be standing next to him when the final whistle went. He came over all unnecessary and kissed me. I don't know who was more terrified, him or me. It wasn't real, I suppose, just a flash in the pan.

VALMAI: A kiss is a kiss.

BRENDA: No, not this one. For a moment, just a moment, I thought he meant it, that it was real. But before I could say anything he had apologised and was heading towards the exit sign. I think he was embarrassed. It's a shame.

VALMAI: The best ones always get away.

BRENDA: Or run in my case. I'm not very good at hanging on. It's funny, isn't it, the ones you don't want, you can't get rid of and the ones you do are impossible to pin down. I should have gone the whole nine yards for him, Val. I would, honest. Still.... (*she looks towards 'The Kiss'*)

(*They are both silent for a while, reflecting.*)

BRENDA: Why did we come here, Val?

VALMAI: Eh?

BRENDA: Why did we come here?

VALMAI: Oh, I don't know, Brend.

BRENDA: There must have been something made you suggest it. I thought you were joking.

VALMAI: So did I... at first.

BRENDA: Why then?

VALMAI: Do you really want to know?

BRENDA: Of course I do.

VALMAI: I feel silly.

BRENDA: Oh, go on. Who am I going to tell? It wasn't just for all this, was it?

VALMAI: No.

BRENDA: Why then?

VALMAI: Because Rebecca Davies' mother always takes in a gallery at least once a month. And Amy Farthing's mother doesn't go a week without a visit to the theatre. And David Brown's whole family have taken up furniture restoration in their spare time, and it seems the whole world and their families are far more interesting than I am.

BRENDA: You can't be serious.

VALMAI: Stupid, isn't it? It was for the kids, really. They come home with stories of their friend's parents and they all seem so... I don't know, exotic. I thought it would give them something to tell people. What would they say? Oh yes, my Mum, she's great. She gets up, takes a valium, watches a load of morning television. And then if she's feeling really adventurous, makes the dreaded trip to the butcher's for a bit of dinner. It must be very demoralising.

BRENDA: You silly old cow!

VALMAI: I know. It's ridiculous, isn't it? And for Roy. I suppose I did it for Roy. Just to surprise him, really. Show him that there is still a bit of mystery tucked away somewhere. That I still have something of my own.

BRENDA: Give us your tablets.

VALMAI: Why?

BRENDA: Just give us your tablets.

(*BRENDA snatches her bag and rummages around. She pulls out Val's bottle of pills. She goes over to the abstract piece and empties a small pile of pills onto one of its surfaces.*)

VALMAI: We can't do that.

BRENDA: 'Course we can.

VALMAI: What about you? We'll have to leave something of yours as well. Those will do.

(*She reaches up and takes hold of BRENDA'S extravagant earrings.*)

BRENDA: But they're my favourites.

VALMAI: Come on, give them here. (*She places them onto the piece.*) There.

BRENDA: Eh, that's not bad. That's not bad at all. (*They both laugh, tickled at their mischief.*) You know, I never quite realised that... well....

VALMAI: Things weren't altogether rosy?

BRENDA: Yes.

VALMAI: They aren't exactly blooming from where I'm standing either.

BRENDA: No, I suppose not.

VALMAI: I suppose what we see and what we would like to be seen as... well, it doesn't always....

BRENDA: No. (*They are silent for a moment. BRENDA becomes embarrassed. She moves towards the large double doors.*) Where are they? We could have stuffed half this stuff up our jumpers by now and been gone. Except this door won't budge. (*She rattles the handle and gently it opens with a creak.*) Val.

VALMAI: What?

BRENDA: I think we should go now.

VALMAI: How did you do that?

BRENDA: It just opened. Come on, quick.

VALMAI: But what about this? (*she gestures towards the abstract piece*) Are we going to leave it like that?

BRENDA: Yes, why not?

VALMAI: Do you think people will notice?

BRENDA: Well, they might do. Come on, will you? There's a bus in ten minutes. If we get a move on I can still catch *Emmerdale*.

VALMAI: But what if they don't like it?

BRENDA: Well, that's it see, isn't it, Val? I don't really think it matters. Art is such a personal thing.

(*VALMAI backs away slowly towards the door, unsure of leaving the piece. Blackout.*)

IAN ROWLANDS
The Ogpu Men

Ian Rowlands (b.1964) is strongly influenced by life in his native Pontypridd. He has a particular fascination with the texture of language and the legacy Welsh has left upon the contemporary Anglo-Welsh dialect. He writes in Welsh and English for the BBC and HTV and is Artistic Director of the company *Theatr Y Byd*. Credits include *Solomon's Glory, Glissando on an Empty Harp, Love in Plastic, Marriage of Convenience* and *The Sin Eaters* (nominated Best Regional Theatre Play for 1992 by the Writers Guild of Great Britain). *The Ogpu Men* eavesdrops on two unemployed men waiting for their appointments in a D.S.S. office.

CHARACTERS
Man
Alex

> (*The action of the play takes place in a D.S.S. office between 9.04 and 9.30 on a wintry Monday morning in the Rhondda. The office is empty. A young man enters, walks round, picks a ticket, then sits down. He pulls out a cigarette packet. It is empty. He crushes and throws it. He pulls out a notebook and pencil and reads...*)

ALEX: (*half to himself*) Damn!

> (*He reads and writes. A MAN enters wearing Woolworth's clothes — no class, no quality, no coat and very wet. It is raining outside. Together they are "The Old Man and the Sea".*)

MAN: Thank God I'm here at last! I've been round the bend and up the ruddy garden path looking for this place. When did they move office?

ALEX: About a month ago.

MAN: They never told me. I 'ad an elluva job getting 'ere...
           couldn't find the place.... It's probably their new
           policy for cutting down on the dole queues. They've
           tried cooking now they're cloaking. (*He dries his
           glasses and puts them back on his nose.*) Wassa time 'en?

ALEX: Six and a half minutes past nine.

MAN: That's precise, innit? Been waiting long?

ALEX: Five minutes.

MAN: Precisely or thereabouts?

ALEX: Thereabouts.

MAN: I've waited longer. I've grown beards before now....
           At least it's as dry as cocum in 'ere.

ALEX: Raining now, is it?

MAN: Cats and dogs, mun...

ALEX: Oh... (*disgruntled*)

MAN: No wonder there's so much pwp on the pavements
           with all those pets dripping down from 'eaven.
           (*ALEX gives a small laugh.*) I hate Rhondda rain, do
           you?

           (*MAN dries himself... ineffectively.*)

ALEX: Yes.

MAN: ...snorkel stuff, innit?

ALEX: Predictable...

MAN: ...in the fact that it falls, yeah. But, mind you, it's not
           the same rain that falls everywhere you know.

ALEX: No?

MAN: No, Rhondda rain falls in dialects.

ALEX: Does it?

MAN: Take Little Moscow, for instance.

ALEX: Maerdy.

MAN: Aye. The cul de sac with a conscience. Maerdy rain's
           got a brain, d'you know that. (*ALEX laughs in friendly
           disbelief.*) On the level crossing heart, mun. Maerdy
           clouds have passed their eleven plus.

ALEX: Really?

MAN: Passed by in monotone, boy, "they're indoors now," think the strato sadists. "So we'll lay off for a bit, give the impression that it's all sand and Sahara." So Muscovites think "It's nice now, we'll go for a stroll." Off with their slippers, on with their sandals, and they step out into the badger blinking world; sun shining with additives and false teeth from a surfeit of squash and chips. For a moment, one brief moment, they believe in employment, and it's this moment that the rain's been waiting for. It melts like candy floss, cellophaning their optimism, shaking hope like killer whales shake sailors in the tattooed seas. "Sucker" it screams to their socialist core, rat-tat-tatting, like death at the door.

ALEX: And Treorchy rain?

MAN: Too posh to fall uninvited, sends a calling card first.

ALEX: Penrhys rain?

MAN: Falls every other Thursday, green as paper.

ALEX: And Porth rain?

MAN: Thick as shit.... (*ALEX gives a small laugh.*) I should've brought an umbrella, mind you, I should've and shouldn't've done a lot of things in this life, but I never learn. Dodged the shower, did you?

ALEX: I did.

MAN: You'll get wet on the way home then. Porth's law... like sod's... 'cept wetter. So, we're all here to see the buggers, are we?

ALEX: There are only two of us.

MAN: I was using the social we, mun. We are the scream-ers defiling the darkness, the Castrati pissing on chips, the bemused abused searching for trip switches in the dark.

ALEX: We're unemployed, you mean.

MAN: That's rather down to earth, innit? I prefer soap boxed metaphor myself.

ALEX: I haven't got a soap box.

MAN: No soap box! What are you? Happy?

ALEX: No.

MAN: Improvise, then. What have you got?

ALEX: This. (*brings out a tissue*) It's nearly clean.

MAN: It will have to do. (*He puts the wrapper down on the seat and stands on it. [C.F. St David]*) St David was a short bloke, see, like his people, so he had a trick up his sleeve. He passed this trick down to me, one night in a drunken dream I 'ad in the Resurrection. Just call me Dull, Patron saint of the Trehafod by-pass. (*declamatory*) In the name of Giggs, God and The Great Escape. Rise, you bugger, rise! (*nothing happens*) Whatever happened to mysticism?

ALEX: Privatised, probably.

MAN: Ay, they'd privatise dust if they could. Those damn Valley Vampires! (*He looks up.*) Can you see them gather, boy!

ALEX: (*not wanting to offend*) Who?

MAN: The Carrion Clouds.

ALEX: No....

MAN: But they've arrived, mun!

ALEX: Where?

MAN: There, mun! Playing fruit machines in the Con club. Waiting to criticise the bones of my thesis. Damn Welsh crows... worse than tea leaves in teeth. They'd criticise the circle for being round, given half a sixpence.

ALEX: What would they do for a penny?

MAN: Introduce you to Dai Lips from Ystrad, Gummy Bugger, there he is putting pennies on poor men's lids; they say he can suck sick through a straw. He once sucked Australia right through the centre of the world, till it popped up in Pentre.

ALEX: No....

    (*half pause*)

MAN: You're right... it was actually Treorchy. The Sydney opera house rose up under the "Parc and Dare", Ayre's Rock made the rugby field unplayable and sharks ate the remnants of Welsh speakers surfing on their own spit down the oceanic high street. The World turned sixes into sevens and the *Rhondda Leader* tucked one paragraph away under the obituaries. Main story that week: Mrs Evans' cat from Ton caught whooping cough whilst on holiday in Corfu.

ALEX: Corfu?

MAN: She couldn't afford Tunisia.

ALEX: Why not?

MAN: Her husband forgot to sign a form. (*Without pausing for breath he gives a speech.*) Carrion at the feast. My paper today is entitled, the fecundity of anger in nine and a half lines. I present it here not for your pecked pity, but for your reflection; to be mulled over in your bird baths of blood. I gave my life to the automobile industry. Though I was hardly a Henry Ford, I was a vital spark in the combustion of global transport, for I was a filter man at Fram; I slaved statically so that you might speed blur by, silk scarves akimbo. And how did I score for a score; twenty years of scarred commitment, twenty years of life and know how?... Twenty minutes they took to sack me, twenty months she took to divorce me, and ahead of me — a decommissioned eternity. A human Trawsfynydd, sealed with indignity in social security... (*to ALEX*) But I shouldn't moan, cause no-one wants me to, for valleys' rhetoric is too dark, they say, and Welsh moaning is the blackest bile of Taffy.

ALEX: Why shouldn't you?

MAN: Well heckled, boy! Why shouldn't I spread my dour seeds of discontent if I'm a walking cliché? All clichés are clichés because they're true and if I make you feel guilty, then bugger you! (*The MAN slumps and sits down. Pause.*) Do you think that shooed the crows away from the marriage bier?

ALEX: Right off.

MAN: You've got to show the buggers, see 'cause we are not sparrows blinded by black beaks on the corrugated roof of the CWM. No, no, no. We are wrens, boy, and we have soared higher than Icarus and the Hapsburgs. Up, up where the Bwlch is an atom and God keeps dogs.

ALEX: Wrens?

MAN: Aye, but at the moment I'm having a bit of a breather, perched on the dole, in a bedsit in Britannia

ALEX: Nice place?

MAN: Nice place! Have you ever lived in a bedsit?

ALEX: Yeah.

MAN: You've lived in a bedsit!

ALEX: Yeah.

MAN: But you can't live in a bedsit, mun, you exist in one.

ALEX: Well, I've existed in a few for a while.

MAN: A few?

ALEX: Yeah, if I didn't like the place, then I moved on.

MAN: Yes, well, I s'pose that it's "have bedsit, will travel" when you're twenty. But by the time you get to my age you become downwardly immobile... Weighed down like a barnacled tortoise.... I don't mean with coloured tellys, videos, washing machines.... I mean with all your hopes, thwarted ambition and inherited dreams squashed into an 'ouse. Everything that you earned the right to hate crammed into a three up, two down 'casa mia' as old man Brachi used to say. Then one day, you get kicked, by your seat, out into the eye-burning road. Neighbours vulturing the self-appointed king deposed and ill-disposed to clearing wardrobes from the street. And so you black bag your life and in time, stitches past nine, you empty yourself into a box. Everything that is, and was you, stuffed into a rented ten by ten and you fell like a fat man's jeans.... Angry, that's how you feel, angry as burst seams. You work for years building up your castle and in a flash it crumbles like Jericho..... Shazamm! And it's gone, and you're in the shit hole, sharing a toilet with ten other people and none of them have heard of Domestos! (*reflection*) I don't understand how some people can be so dirty. Do you?

ALEX: No.

MAN: Not that I'm a fussy kinda bloke, but I can't stand filth, especially other peoples', you know what I mean?

ALEX: Yeah, yeah. A pit, your place, is it?

MAN: Disgusting; more of a dog pound than a domicile; I woke up one morning and there were three fleas sucking breakfast from my ankles.

ALEX: Yeah.

MAN: It was like being rubbed up by a friend's dog, you know.

ALEX: Yeah, obscene.

MAN: That's a good word... obscene, I like that word. Can you be obscened?

ALEX: I don't know.

MAN: 'Cause if you can, I have been obscened. I feel dirty twenty four hours a day; Taff dirty like dustman's nails. I can't stand it, mun. I'd love to have a bath, but that needs a blowtorch to disinfect it.

ALEX: Have you got a shower?

MAN: No.

ALEX: How do you manage?

MAN: I go 'round to a friend's 'ouse once a week, 'cause "Cleanliness is next to Godliness" as my old man used to say. Did your old man use to say that to you?

ALEX: He still does.

MAN: So does mine, probably, up there somewhere chattering amongst the long dead liars of oblivion.

ALEX: Died?

MAN: Of disinfectant.

ALEX: I'm sorry.

MAN: Don't be. He was spotless in heaven. Do you think angels smell?

ALEX: I don't know.

MAN: I wouldn't have thought God cared if they did, and I don't ruddy care, I tell you. It's the stink on earth that counts, innit? Like people on buses smelling the whole deck out, so you have to get off two stops before just to breathe... you know?

ALEX: Yes.

MAN: Never let the stench mark you, boy, I've never let it mark me.

ALEX: I wash regularly.

MAN: Good. See.... Even though you're as poor as Woolworth's jeans, take pride in yourself, 'cause your pride and your shoes are your passports to life, mun. If you lose your pride what the hell 'ave you got? Eh?

ALEX: Your shoes?

MAN: Apart from those, what? (*ALEX shrugs.*) Bugger all bar forty quid a week

ALEX: It's not a lot, is it? (*puts cigarette in mouth, pulls it back out*)

MAN: It's one ellofan insult, though, innit!

ALEX: I don't think they think that.

MAN: Who don't think what?

ALEX: They don't think that.

MAN: Who are they?

ALEX: Them.

MAN: The buggers, you mean? They don't think, full stop, mun. If they did, how the hell would they expect anybody to make ends meet on forty quid a week? You can't even feed guppies on forty quid a week, can you? You can't live on forty quid a week — you survive, like squirrels on Flatholm.

ALEX: Are there squirrels on Flatholm?

MAN: Not since they stopped their dole. They're all re-training to become telephone engineers.

ALEX: The squirrels?

MAN: Well, ay, they got inborn 'ead for 'ights 'aven' 'ey? Made for the job.

ALEX: What about us humans?

MAN: We're not cost effective, mun. The squirrels are taking over and they're developing drugs to make us hibernate apart from three days out of every fourteen. So we can sign on, cash our giros, get pissed, then go back to sleep till our next signing on day.

ALEX: Really?

MAN: Worse than that, boy, honest. I've heard, on the q.t. that they've got plans to donate Maerdy to the Russian food crisis. I can see the headline in the *Rhondda Leader* now. "Two birds with one stone!

Russian food queues and Rhondda unemployed shrink as Little Moscow feeds itself to Big Brother!" (*ALEX laughs*) Ay, you've gotta laugh 'aven' you? 'Cause if you didn't laugh, you'd become a security guard. (*ALEX laughs*)

ALEX: In a dole office.

MAN: Sideways career move. Sick as Sundays, innit? (*ALEX laughs.*) Life's too funny to be real, innit? I'll tell you what, I'll tell you why I'm 'ere, right.... (*he draws on his cigarette*) Yesterday, I received an official manila; an invitation to whine, not dine, in the cubicles of bureaucracy, "come down and see us sometime 'cause we've stopped your money" it said, black tie unnecessary, very considerate and informal. No RSVP gilting the etiquette, giving the option to attend, just an order and no choice. So here I am....

ALEX: What for?

MAN: 'Old your 'orses, boy, I was coming to that.... I am expected to pay maintenance out of my forty odd quid a week. Fair enough normally. But my eldest boy moved in with me week before last 'cause he can't stand living at home; wife's got a new boyfriend and they don't get on, you know. So it's father and son smoking and smelling in a kippered bedsit; it's not a bed of roses, I can tell you. Anyway, I gotta keep him and me out of my dole money and pay a bit of rent so I can't afford the maintenance now, can I? So they've gone and stopped my money. The buggers have stopped all my money 'cause I can't afford to give a measly couple of quid a week to my ex-wife who's got a job and doesn't need it anyway.

ALEX: (*stutters the following out*) That's an unfortunate situation...

MAN: "Situation", it's a ruddy tragedy, that's what it is. I know it's the law, but fair's fair, innit? Chase the buggers that can pay and won't pay is what I say. But she's got money and I got nothing; she lives in an 'ouse and I scrape by in an 'ole — that's a "situation" for you. What's fair about that?

ALEX: Well, nothing really, but....

MAN: But what? Look, you don't have to tell me that life's not all Barry rock and buckets, boy, 'cause I've shovelled it. But the system's all arse backwards, mun, the bureaucracy stinks like dead cats in Dinas.

ALEX: But the law's there to help single mothers.

MAN: 'Course it is. I know exactly what you mean, 'cause I've seen it on *Week In, Week Out*, it just gets my goat, that's all. 'Cause the really funny thing is, I want to pay, but can't. That's hilarious, innit? I wannw, but they haven't asked me that, they've just assumed that I don't, 'cause they're too stupid to ask. It's a silly bugger system, boy, that's what it is. Someone needs to tell 'em, I tell ew.... They're just playing silly buggers.... what's the time now?

ALEX: Seventeen minutes past.

MAN: A bugger for precision, inniw boy? Ever thought of being a traffic warden?

ALEX: No. (*beat*)

MAN: Why are you sentenced to unemployment, then?

ALEX: I'm an out of work boomerang baby....

MAN: So, you had ambition, did you?

ALEX: I've still got it.

MAN: I thought you had a funny accent.

ALEX: My mother's from Wattstown.

MAN: What's her name?

ALEX: Beryl.

MAN: Beryl what?

ALEX: Beryl Tunnicliffe.

MAN: Bit crachach for Wattstown, innit?

ALEX: My grampa kept a shop.

MAN: There's posh. If I'd known that I was going to hob nob this morning I would've worn pants. Has your mam ever mentioned a man on a bike?

ALEX: No.

MAN: Thank God, I couldn't cope with a son with a "voice"... you sound as if you've been away.

ALEX: Now I've come back.

MAN: I wouldn't have bothered if I were you. There's bugger all to come back here for... apart from arthritis.

ALEX: I'm not planning to stay.

MAN: And to what coal truck do you hitch your hope?

ALEX: To the purity of Poetry.

MAN: God! Spare us, please! We've had too many poets jumping off the bridge of alliteration.

ALEX: I'm finding my own voice....

MAN: Quick, lose it again then.

ALEX: But I think that I've got something to say.

MAN: About what?

ALEX: Life.

MAN: So!! You're going to enlighten us in verse, are you? Compare us to Pentre on a summer's day. Have sense, mun? Look around you. Can't you taste the anger. Smell the rot... touch the decay... hear the cracked choir voices bleeding *Myfanwy* from their gums? People don't want poetry, they want dignity. Let them eat sausage not sonnets.

ALEX: I'm not a butcher.

MAN: Shame, there was a job going in Leo's, last week.

ALEX: I mean....

MAN: I know what you mean, boy, but let me give you a bit of advice. We don't want poets in Wales anymore, especially precise ones. We've had enough of them over the years, coal trucks full of them bulging bardically at the seams. Poems and pints are things of the past. These days we just want the pints 'cause the poems are too painful. Drive a fork lift truck or something, spare us all the bother. (*pause*) Sorry, I didn't mean to....

ALEX: It's O.K., it's O.K. My dad says the same: "'Ave a job, bugger vocation!"

MAN: Well, you can't feed stomachs on dreams, can you, boy?

ALEX: No....

MAN: There's no pork in poetry. Get a proper job.

ALEX: Now you're being objective.

MAN: Ay, s'pose I am, it's one of my failings, see — 'cause I'm alley blind when it comes to me. You're right. Be a poet! I s'pose an unpaid calling, beats not working...

ALEX: It's my only hope.

MAN: You think that?

ALEX: My ticket to ride.

MAN: You believe that?

ALEX: Yeah.

MAN: Then it must be true, then... you know, when I was your age I could hop down the Rhondda, the whole length, leaping from job to job like a demented squirrel, drunk as summer. Leave one job on Friday, get another by Monday. You could pick and choose work then, the only thing you can pick now is pimples. Leave a job on Friday these days and the only thing you'll get by Monday is ruddy cancer. That's a fact, mun. Maxie Boy knew, he knew 'cause he was there and I was there and I'm still bloody here, feeling like a ruddy squirrel with no tree. Trapped!

ALEX: I got away.

MAN: You said.

ALEX: I went to university!

MAN: Did you? That's where you got your hoity toity from, was it? And what did you do in university then?

ALEX: Philosophy.

MAN: What!

ALEX: Philosophy.

MAN: I heard what you said, I just couldn't believe it... Phil-o-so-phy! What the hell did you do that for? The last thing you wanna be in this day and age is a thinker, mun. Go off your ruddy rocker if you think too much. Don't think is my Philosophy. Stay thick as Barry rock, it's the only way to be 'appy. (*he laughs and taps his head with his finger*) Good thinking that, innit?

ALEX: It's a thought.

MAN: It's more than a thought, boy. It's dead true.

ALEX: What's true about death?

MAN: Whoa, whoa. Hey, don't come over all university of life with me, boy. Death is like divorce, ruddy inconvenient.

ALEX: It doesn't have to be....

         (*pause*)

MAN: Try saying that to the bloke I saw die on the way here today. He was crossing the road on Cymmer hill, just up from Porth square where the toilets used to be... before the rats put in for a council house. Anyway, this bloke, he wasn't looking where he was going, right, so he tripped the light fandango under a bus and was decapitated. His body clung to the hill by sheer will, his head exited slope left pursued by blood. "Follow that head" I heard the blood shout, but too late. Mrs Evans tried to crochet it back on with pointy needles but it didn't work. He died under no anaesthetic and with half a blanket over his body, half over his head and the road blanketed in dead red. Would you have the heart to ask him what's true about death?

ALEX: No... I saw a tramp once, caught my attention with his flying shoe which arched through the air and landed in front of me. Whilst his head remained stationery, under a tyre, splayed like melon wedges under rubber.

MAN: Was he dead?

ALEX: I didn't hang 'round to ask.

MAN: You left him there?

ALEX: There was nothing that I could do for him.

MAN: He died shoeless and alone?

ALEX: I gave him his shoe back.

MAN: Then you left.

ALEX: There were others around.

MAN: A wise move, never ask directions of the embarrassingly dying, especially when they're shoeless, it's a question of pride.

         (*half pause*)

265

ALEX: My grandfather died shoeless.

MAN: Was he a mason?

ALEX: He played the Jew's harp.

MAN: Was he shaved?

ALEX: Hairy.

MAN: Was he a big man?

ALEX: Fairly.

MAN: Big as bubbles?

ALEX: Maybe.

MAN: How did he die?

ALEX: Um... painfully.

MAN: Common or garden, was it?

ALEX: I guess.

MAN: What happened, then?

ALEX: He just lay there.

MAN: Where?

ALEX: In an hospital bed.

MAN: In a ward?

ALEX: A private room.

MAN: Was there sun?

ALEX: Ribbons of it.

MAN: Was there smell?

ALEX: You could've bottled it!

MAN: How did he sound?

ALEX: Thinly.

MAN: How did he die?

ALEX: Invisibly.

MAN: Like a yellow heron stalking the sunset?

ALEX: Possibly.

          (*pause*)

ALEX: Above his head, he had a mini trapeze, it hung there,
          suspended... He clung to it with one claw, gripping
          and slipping... slipping and gripping. Gripping and
          slipping until he could grip no more.... Then his
          hand slipped off and he slipped away.

MAN: What a way to go!

ALEX: There was no applause.

MAN: Was there a dry eye in the house?

ALEX: Just silence.

(pause)

MAN: Where there pints pulled in the pub?

ALEX: I think that he would have hoped so.

MAN: A nice way to die, toasted posthumously in the odour of bar room belchers. How could he top that!

ALEX: In the crematorium his coffin was caught up in something, it could have been the curtain, but I had my suspicions.

MAN: I would've as well, boy.

ALEX: Anyway, at that moment, in between his life and his scattering, my nose started bleeding uncontrollably bleeding like...

MAN: Brake fluid?

ALEX::   It bled. Shamelessly.

MAN: Like radiators in Summer...

ALEX: Maybe.

MAN: ...or the D.S.S. in winter; where the good, the bad and the living dead confront the desperately ugly in the crematoria of dignity.

ALEX: Something like that.

MAN: That's a sad story.

ALEX: Almost a eulogy... crazy.

MAN: It's nothing compared with ignominy, boy. The living death of poverty is the bitterest breath of all.

ALEX: Is it?

(He takes another cigarette. ALEX obviously desperately wants a cigarette.)

MAN: 'Ard as 'ard an' 'arder. Separation is a soul scissors, boy, cuts ew to the quick... Wass the time now?

ALEX: Twenty-four minutes past. I thought they opened at nine o'clock.

MAN: So did I.

ALEX: Both thought wrong then, didn't we? (*pause*) Why did you get divorced, then?

MAN: I didn't get divorced, it happened to me.

ALEX: After your redundancy.

MAN: And subsequent poverty. She couldn't cope with it... my wife. She could cope with a lot, but she couldn't cope with her skin-tight smile, that framed the pain, as she cooked chips again. Egg and chips, beans and chips, all the chipped clichés plugged with doorsteps to fill the gaps. (*he lights up*) We couldn't afford multivitamins, so my wife took the body of Christ to supplement her diet and I took off to the pub for a liquid lunch. At that point I would've liked to have become alcoholic, 'cept my money ran out before I had a chance to be one. As far as I could see, it was the only way forward for an ex-filter man at Fram, filtered out of industry. But my wife had a different opinion, she didn't want to spiral down to the dole-stormed seas, so she kicked me out one night, after I came home particularly shipwrecked, demanded my dock for the night, and promptly pissed my pants in front of the kids. (*he drags on his cigarette*) If a father's curse is to outlive his son, then a son's curse is to watch his pant-pissing father oblivious of the puddle at his feet; it's hardly an example when you're trying to get your kid to stop flicking bwgies at babies, is it?

ALEX: No.

MAN: We are the bemused abused, you see, boy; strip us of our dignity and we leave stains on the carpet.

ALEX: You sound bitter.

MAN: As bitter as barley sugar.

ALEX: Not bitter?

MAN: Just twisted.

ALEX: To be expected....

MAN: Don't get me wrong, I can see why she kicked me....
(*long pause*)

ALEX: 'Scuse me...

MAN: What?

ALEX: I don't like to ask but... could I buy a fag off you, please?

(*MAN is thrown off guard*)

MAN: Oh, I'm sorry... Ay, God, I should have offered earlier, sorry, son. I didn't think that you smoked.

ALEX: Yeah, I just ran out.

MAN: That's a bugger, innit?

ALEX: I can give you ten p. for one.

MAN: I don't want your money, mun. Don't insult me with charity, boy. I give because I can. If I couldn't give, I wouldn't ruddy offer, would I? (*he pulls one out*) Here we are.

ALEX: Thanks.

MAN: Here, have two, keep one for later.

ALEX: I couldn't.

MAN: Shut it, mun, what the hell's a fag or two between friends?

ALEX: Thanks.

MAN: No problem. Here, I've got a light by 'ere... (*he lights him*) Got it?

ALEX: Thanks.

MAN: You are obviously a man with a need — a desperado, daring the carcinogenic guilt of public opinion. You know, I reckon that most people who get cancer from smoking fags, get cancer 'cause they're told they should get it. It's just another way the buggers control you... suggestive murder through documentary, there should be a law passed, mun. Enjoying that, are you?

ALEX: My first one.

MAN: First one, nothing like it, is there? First fag of the day, first marriage, first kid, first home. After the first, the rest is all imitation all down hill and second best. (*pause*) We were first loves, you see. We met in school, settled down, had a few kids, had a good life... all black pudding, pear drops and Ponty market, 'till my job went down the pan. One day the crows just came down and picked us clean, Dai Lips put pennies on my eyes and the house was sold for half a sixpence. It works like that sometimes, don't it? (*pause for smoking*) I saw my friend wring a crow's neck once, he said it

269

had a broken wing and to be honest, I wouldn't have cared if it hadn't. He just picked it up and calmly wrung its neck 'till the bugger was dead, serves it right I thought, damn Valley Vampire. Forty quid a week they've stopped me... the buggers... forty measly quid... what's the time now?

ALEX: Half past.

MAN: Is that exact or just about? (*He laughs. A voice comes over the tannoy.*)

VOICE: First please.

MAN: Exact. Go on, boy. Wring some neck. You were here before me.

ALEX: No, no please. You go first.

MAN: Don't be daft, mun.

ALEX: No, I insist.

MAN: Are you sure?

ALEX: Ay, I'm in no rush.

MAN: That's kind of you, kid. Thanks then... see you 'round....

(*He walks up to the cubicle. ALEX picks out his book and begins to write. We see the MAN talking but we do not see with whom he is talking. His attitude totally changes. Every bugger is replaced with a please, a pleading please – apologetic of his own existence.*)

MAN: Hello, 'morning. Please could... sorry? ... thanks (*he sits*) No, sorry, I 'aven't got an appoint... Yeah, I've brought it with me, here it is... Sorry? Yes, I keep it in my pocket and it was raining... Yes, please... yeah, I've come here for help, please, because you've stopped... Yes, that's my name... Thomas, yes... No, no, no, it is Dylan... Dylan Thomas... yes (*polite laugh*) no, everybody says that... Yes, it does get a bit...

(*ALEX has been listening to the conversation. At this point he is jolted by disbelief. He looks at his poetry, scribbles on it, tears it up, throws it into the bin and goes to look through the window. Lights fade.*)

MAN: ...Yes, please... please... Oh, thank you, thanks... thank-you very much, it's very kind of you, please, I would be grateful, yes... Thank you... Please.

(*Blackout*)

Acknowledgements

We thank the authors, agents and/or estates for permission to reprint the plays in this volume. Copyright belongs to the authors or their estates. For performance rights, contact the addresses below. In the absence of an agent, contact Seren for futher information.

DYLAN THOMAS: *Return Journey:* Contact agents David Higham Associates Limited, 5-8 Lower John Street, Golden Square, London W1R 4HA.

GWYN THOMAS: *Gazooka*: Contact agents Felix de Wolfe, 1 Southampton Street, London WC2.

DANNIE ABSE: *The Eccentric*: Contact Peters, Fraser and Dunlop, 503/4 The Chambers, Chelsea Harbour, London SW10 OXF.

DUNCAN BUSH: *Sailing to America*: Contact St. John Donald, Peters, Fraser and Dunlop, 503/4 The Chambers, Chelsea Harbour, London SW10 OXF.

ALAN OSBORNE: *Redemption Song:* This play also appears in the *Merthyr Trilogy* (Parthian Books, 1997).

FRANK VICKERY: *The Drag Factor*: Contact agents Bill McLean, 23b Deodar Road, Putney, London SW15. Samuel French Ltd. have amateur and professional repertory rights in this play and also states that *The Drag Factor* is part of a full-length play entitled *Roots and Wings* which is published by Samuel French Ltd.

EDWARD THOMAS: *Hiraeth*: Contact agents Rod Hall at A.P. Watt, 20 John Street, London.

HELEN GRIFFIN: *The Ark*: Contact agents Craig Sills, George Heathcote Management, 10 St. Martin's Court, London, WC2N 4AJ.

LISA HUNT: *A Night Under Canvas*: Contact agents Rochelle Stevens & Co., 2 Terrets Place, Upper Street, London N1 1QZ.

IAN ROWLANDS: *The Ogpu Men*: Contact agents Bill McLean, 23b Deodar Road, Putney, London SW15.

My thanks to all the playwrights in Wales, the Drama Association of Wales, Amy Wack and Brian Mitchell of Seren Books, Patti Wallis, Siân Elin Lloyd, Alison Hindell and Siân Phillips.